CLASSIC TAILORING TECHNIQUES FOR MENSWEAR

CLASSIC TAILORING TECHNIQUES FOR MENSWEAR

A Construction Guide

Second Edition

Roberto Cabrera
Denis Antoine

FAIRCHILD BOOKS
NEW YORK · LONDON · OXFORD · NEW DELHI · SYDNEY

FAIRCHILD BOOKS
Bloomsbury Publishing Inc
1385 Broadway, New York, NY 10018, USA

BLOOMSBURY, FAIRCHILD BOOKS and the Fairchild Books logo are trademarks of Bloomsbury
Publishing Plc

First published 1983
This edition first published 2015
Reprinted 2015, 2016, 2017 (twice), 2018 (three times)

Cover design: Sam Clark at Under the Sky

Library of Congress Cataloging-in-Publication Data
Cabrera, Roberto.
[Classic tailoring techniques]
Classic tailoring techniques for menswear: a construction guide/Roberto Cabrera,
Denis Antoine. – Second edition.
pages cm
Revision of: Classic tailoring techniques. (c)1983.
Includes bibliographical references and index.
ISBN 978-1-62892-170-0 (paperback)
1. Tailoring. 2. Men's clothing. I. Antoine, Denis. II. Title.
TT580.C3 2015
646.4'33–dc23
20140391333

ISBN: PB: 978-1-6289-2170-0
ePDF: 978-1-6289-2172-4

Typeset by Saxon Graphics Ltd, Derby
Printed and bound in India

To find out more about our authors and books visit www.fairchildbooks.com and sign up for our newsletter.

TABLE OF CONTENTS

EXTENDED TABLE OF CONTENTS

ACKNOWLEDGEMENTS

This work could not have existed without the incredible talent of Roberto Cabrera, to whom this second edition is dedicated.

Thanks also go to those teachers and mentors who guided me in my early years to develop a deep appreciation and passion for tailored menswear, Alan Cannon Jones, Chris Stevens and Tibor Rohaly. Finally, deepest gratitude to friends and family for their unwavering support and patience.

D. A.

The Publisher wishes to gratefully acknowledge and thank the reviewers of the first edition whose feedback was invaluable in planning this edition: Vincent Quevedo, Kent State University, US; Casey Stannard, Oregon State University, US; Carla Summers, Utah Valley University, US; Heather Milam, University of Alabama, US; Lori Gann-Smith, Brenau University, US; Amy Bond, Intercontinental University, US; Bill Brandt, Parsons School of Design, US; Dean Brough, Queensland University of Technology, AUS. We also wish to thank Francisco Gonzalez, Johnathan Hayden and Bo Zhao for their diligent contributions to the visuals in this edition. We are proud to bring this work to a new generation of readers.

PREFACE

Generations of young tailors have relied on the first edition of *Classic Tailoring Techniques* in order to gain essential knowledge about the fundamentals of traditional tailoring methods. Since its first publication in 1983, this text has become the key reference used by students, tailoring apprentices and home sewers looking to hone their craft.

While the instructions formulated by Mr Cabrera and Ms Flaherty have remained valid, this revised edition brings new life to the tailoring process, by employing updated artwork throughout. In response to commentary from the custom-tailoring industry, the second edition also includes a discussion of ironwork, the technique used by tailors for shaping and molding fabric prior to the construction of garments.

Also new to this edition are sections presenting regional tailoring styles, as well as the discussion of how traditional tailoring has influenced and been employed by menswear designers in the luxury ready-to-wear market. These conversations are fundamental to remind all readers that experimentation is just as important as tradition to the world of custom tailoring. The techniques discussed in this book should serve therefore as a springboard for the development of personal practices and methods.

1 TAILORING

The art of tailoring can be traced back at least to the fourteenth century, when it became fashionable in Europe to add an underlayer of padding in the **chest** area of men's jackets. Rather than taking its form from the contours of the wearer's body, the garment fabric was cut and carefully shaped to fit over the padded form. Through the ages the padding was extended, according to fashion, to the sleeves, the shoulders, and even the stomach area. The padded understructure provided what was considered to be improvements over the contours of the body. It also enabled the garment fabric to lie neatly, relatively unaffected by the body's wrinkling movement.

The construction techniques developed to create these structured garments were quite different from those used to produce shirts and dresses. By the sixteenth century the makers of men's jackets had formed a separate branch of the clothing makers' guilds, complete with precise specifications for the quality and color of padding materials and lining for gentlemen's silk brocade jackets.

Not until the early nineteenth century did careful fit become a criterion of well-tailored garments. The understructure remained, but the shaping became more subtle, its purpose now being to compliment rather than to distort the natural lines of the body. Great attention was also given to the flawless lay of the garment fabric over the canvas form. The **lapel** was to roll gracefully open at the **chest**, without pulling the garment forward, away from the body. All edges of the jacket disguised the existence of the several layers of fabric beneath, by being flat and sharp, without noticeable bulk. The collar, and all curved edges of the garment, tilted ever so slightly inward toward the body, a graceful avoidance of the awkward, upward curl of collar tips and pocket flaps. Pockets were never to gape open when not in use, and vents were expected to lie flat and firm. The result was a clear definition of design lines, a controlled yet graceful presentation of the garment fabric, impeccable fit, form and detail.

The construction techniques presented in this book and practiced today, with minor variations, by the finest tailors all over the world, have changed very little in the past 100 years. Although new machines and new methods of fusing layers of fabric together offer today's tailor speedy alternatives to time-consuming hand work, relatively few of these faster methods have been adopted by custom tailors. The sewing machine is used for almost all seams and darts, but almost 75 percent of all stitches in a custom-tailored suit are still done by hand, to ensure the most accurate shaping of the fabric. Fusible interfacings are sometimes used by custom tailors to reinforce certain small areas, such as dart tips or the inside of some pockets; however, they are not considered acceptable substitutes for the multi-layered, hand-stitched canvas interfacing which gives body to the entire front of the jacket.

Today's tailors continue to practice their art almost exactly as it was practiced 150 years ago, not because slower is necessarily better, but because these methods produce body and form, detail and durability which faster methods of construction are simply unable to equal.

We encourage you to enjoy the tailoring process as much as its beautiful product, and to afford yourself the necessary time and patience to become proficient in these time-honored skills.

REGIONAL VARIATIONS

Through the years, a few regional styles of tailoring have evolved, influenced by differences in use, fashionable appearance as well as climate. Each school has developed a unique heritage in its approach to the tailoring process. The following, presenting a brief synopsis of the various geographical schools of tailoring, should serve as a reminder of the fact that the techniques presented in this book remain very much only guidelines, open for experimentation by the practiced tailor.

British Tailoring

The most influential geographical region in the development of modern tailoring has been Great Britain. Around the middle of the nineteenth century, social changes led to the establishment of new forms of dress, namely the widespread adoption of the sack jacket. This style, which originated in the casual clothes worn for hunting and manual labor, combined with Britain's military heritage, gave birth to the modern jacket. It is in its humble origins that the jacket finds its purpose. This is after all a garment that was meant for practicality and functionality, concerns that expressed themselves through the pursuit of very precise fit. Great Britain, and particularly Savile Row in London, have since become the primary destination for any gentleman serious about tailoring.

Another factor which contributed to the establishment of Great Britain as the birthplace of fine tailoring is its long and storied heritage of cloth manufacturing. Many of the finer woolens and worsted fabrics used for the production of custom work are still woven in England today.

British tailoring is generally associated with a handful of characteristic traits. The body lines are elegantly contoured, with generous **chest** and hip areas, and a defined nipped-in **waist**. The shoulder and **chest** are strong, supported by multiple layers of canvas. The sleeve head is often roped to further define the shoulder area.

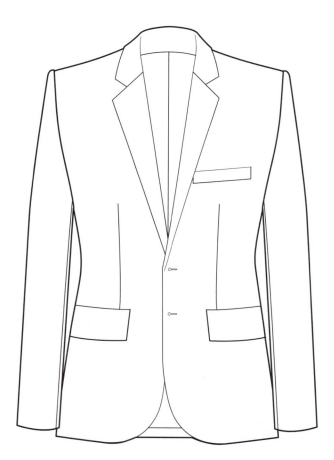

English Tailoring

English Tailoring

Neapolitan Tailoring

The Italian city of Naples evolved its influential lexicon of tailoring from necessity as well as overall southern Italian social attitude. Starting from thorough observation of the methods presented by the classic British school, Neapolitan tailors developed lighter, softer garments. This is what Naples is now known for, a style of make that requires a precise understanding of construction in order to reach the perfect balance between structure and lightness. Maybe this was due to the weather being substantially warmer than in London or maybe it was due to the Italian gentlemen taking a decidedly more casual approach to their style, and life in general.

This certain nonchalance, known in Italian as 'sprezzatura', has become intrinsically associated

Italian Tailoring

Italian Tailoring

with Neapolitan style, and valued greatly around the world. Neapolitan tailoring has played an influential role in the aesthetic development of other schools of tailoring, particularly the French school, which is still to date dominated by tailors borrowing heavily from Italian traditions.

Neapolitan jackets are easily recognizable by a series of details, most visible of which is the shoulder, softly gathered into the armhole, and built without unnecessary padding. This deconstructed style of sleeve, known as 'spalla a camicia' (shirt-style sleeve), is greatly preferred for the summer months. For cooler winter days, Neapolitan tailors still offer the option of a padded sleeve head, although this remains traditionally softer than its British counterpart. Neapolitan jackets tend to be gently structured, without unnecessary canvassing or padding in the **chest**, and are often only partially lined, to allow the garment better breathability.

As a final note on this school, it is important to clarify that soft construction does not mean the garment lacks proper fit, and many Italian tailors pride themselves in making perfectly shaped and exquisitely flattering jackets.

American Tailoring

American tailoring came into its own only around the mid-twentieth century. Until then, tailoring traditions in the United States borrowed heavily from Italian tailors who immigrated to the new continent. The silhouette associated most with American tailoring remains that of the Ivy League jacket, a style first introduced around the 1920s and greatly popularized in the 50s. As the preferred style for young men attending certain reputed colleges, this tailored garment transformed into a boxy, casual shape that renounced its tight-laced business parentage.

The widespread embracing of the concept of 'American sportswear', promoting casually active lifestyle pursuits, pushed this style of jacket also known as a sports coat to common acceptance. While predominantly limited in its popularity to the United States, this silhouette proved greatly

American Tailoring

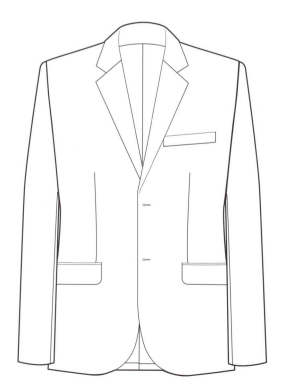

American Tailoring

influential on the aesthetic of Giorgio Armani, who in turn played a pivotal role in defining the fashionable silhouette in the west through the 1980s.

Core characteristics of the American style are a loose torso, not heavily shaped at the seams and darts, a lightly padded natural shoulder extending somewhat wider than on European jackets and a lower **gorge** line.

TAILORING AND FASHION

Just as we have observed in the discussion of the key schools of tailoring, it is also essential to contextualize the techniques discussed in this book as part of a wider movement towards the embracing of quality hand methods of garment construction outside of the traditional custom-tailoring arena. Several fashion houses have built strong reputations on the quality of their garments which, while not traditionally proportioned or detailed, are in fact often built using very similar methods to the ones discussed in this book.

Alexander McQueen

Alexander McQueen built his design reputation in womenswear on his mastery of tailoring and drape, often together. Trained at Anderson and Sheppard, a reputed bespoke house on Savile Row, McQueen introduced elements of hand construction throughout his work, and particularly in the development of finely crafted business and evening tailoring for men. McQueen's menswear displays a certain aggressiveness in shape, structure and detail, which has become the house trademark.

Berluti

Originally a bespoke men's shoemaker, Berluti was expanded to offer luxury ready-to-wear as

Alexander McQueen, Spring 2014

Berluti, Spring 2015

well as custom tailoring services. Building from the finest British and Italian cloths, Berluti has developed an aesthetic steeped in tradition, and sometimes veering to historical referentialism. Berluti's use of color reflects its cultural affiliations with the Italian traditions of tailoring.

Thom Browne

Extensively playing with the silhouette and questioning construction, Thom Browne has established a reputation for his work grounded in the traditions of bespoke processes. This designer's runway shows display fantastic and improbable visions, bending the application of hand tailoring methods to innovative and exciting ends. Interestingly, this designer's radical vision has translated effectively to a thriving commercial business, selling narrow, undersized suits to businessmen across Europe, America and the Far East.

Thom Browne, Fall 2014

Haider Ackermann

Somewhat antithetically to Thom Browne, Belgian designer Haider Ackermann explores the qualities of cloth, color and drape through his work. His tailored silhouettes offer generous swaths of luminescent tones, realized in shimmering blends of luxurious wools, silks, cottons and linens.

Haider Ackermann, Spring 2014

While this is just a snapshot of the many approaches that menswear designers have taken in their re-interpretation of tailoring, it is important to remember that craft, and particularly hand construction methods, remain at the very center of the definition of luxury. Whether your goal is to become a traditional tailor, outfitting bankers and lawyers, or to explore the realm of innovative menswear design, you will find techniques in this book that will, through practice and experimentation, help you raise your work to this coveted market level.

GENERAL TAILORING SUPPLIES

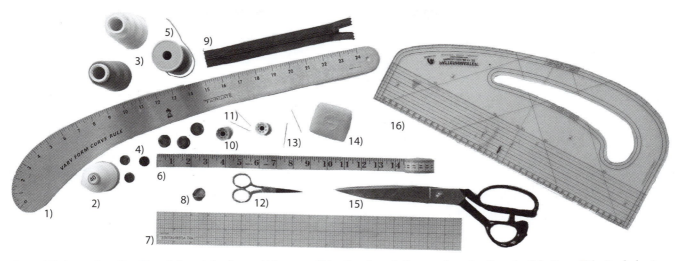

General Tailoring Supplies. From left to right: 1) metal hip curve, 2) basting thread, 3) general sewing threads, 4) buttons, 5) buttonhole gimp, 6) tape measure, 7) transparent ruler, 8) thimble, 9) zipper, 10) silk finishing thread, 11) pins, 12) snips, 13) hand sewing needles, 14) tailor's chalk, 15) shears, 16) transparent pattern curve

Bent Handle Shears

These shears are designed for the most convenient and careful cutting of fabric. In use, the handle bends up and away from the cutting surface while the blade is allowed to slide along the surface without disturbing the lay of the fabric. A ten-inch to twelve-inch (25.4 to 30.5 centimeters) pair will handle most tailoring needs. Fine shears will give best service if they are oiled and sharpened when necessary, and if they are not used to cut materials other than fabric.

Thread Snips

Small, sharp, pointed scissors. Used for easy access to small areas, and for cutting threads.

Clay Tailor's Chalk

White clay chalk. Used for marking pattern information onto the garment fabric. The outer edge of the chalk should be sharpened before use, for a clean, fine line. Clay chalk can be brushed away easily when no longer needed; however, avoid pressing on top of the chalk marks, as this will make removal more difficult. Darker colored chalks are used for markings on interfacings.

Tape Measure

Necessary for taking body measurements. Available with inches printed on one side and centimeters on the other. Special tape measures are also available for taking the inseam measurement for trousers. These have cardboard or metal stiffening at one end. The reinforced end, and not the tailor's hand, can then be placed at the top of the inseam for measuring. Plastic, rather than cloth tape measures should be used, since those made of cloth are inclined to shrink.

Ruler

Flexible, plastic see-through rulers are very convenient for measuring curved areas on patterns and fabric, as well as for flat surfaces. Do keep them away from the iron though!

Hip Curve Ruler

A gracefully curved ruler essential for making and adjusting pattern lines.

Straight Pins

Either dressmaker pins, which are of medium thickness, or silk pins, which are somewhat thinner, are appropriate for tailoring needs.

Basting Thread

White cotton thread #40–#50, easy to break for removal when necessary.

General Sewing Thread

Mercerized cotton thread, #0–#00, or size A silk thread, are suitable for both hand and machine stitching.

Buttonhole Twist

Silk tailor's twist #8 is best for making hand-worked buttonholes. It is also used for sewing on buttons. The twist comes on large pools, six strands of silk loosely intertwined. The strands are separated and used singly. If tailor's twist is unavailable, size D buttonhole twist will do.

Gimp

Stiff cord, in color close to that of the garment fabric. Used to reinforce the edges of hand-worked buttonholes.

Beeswax

Used by tailors to coat thread for hand sewing, to prevent the thread from knotting and gnarling. For hand topstitching, the thread is also pressed between sheets of paper after having been drawn through the beeswax. This process keeps the several strands, which constitute the thread, flat and uniform.

Tailor's Thimble

Worn as a protection for the middle finger, the area which covers the fingernail is used to push the needle through the fabric. Tailor's thimbles are open at the top for comfort. Adjustable thimbles which cover half of the tailor's fingertip and wrap around the other side can provide very good control and comfort.

Needles

Hand sewing needles for tailoring come in a variety of lengths and widths, in categories called sharps and betweens. Betweens are shorter stronger needles. Sharps are medium to long. Within each category, the needle sizes are numbered. The higher the number, the shorter and thinner the needle. A #7 sharp needle might easily take you from beginning to end of your tailoring project.

Buttons

The button size is measured across the diameter in lines. There are 40 lines to one inch. 30-line buttons are used on the jacket front, 24-line buttons can be used for the sleeves, the lining pocket, the vest front, and the trouser fly and back pocket. Dull bone or horn buttons are most attractive on the classic suit. Plastic or resin buttons break easily, and sharp edges in the hole of the button often tear the thread.

Pant Hook-and-Bar Closures

When choosing a hook-and-bar closure for pants, it is preferable to opt for those made of metal attached by clamping instead of sewing, for greater strength.

Zipper

Use a strong zipper with metal teeth for the pants fly. It should be at least one inch (2.5 cm) longer than the fly measurement.

Muslin

A lightweight cotton fabric, from which tailors can make a prototype of the suit, used to check fitting details.

UNDERSTRUCTURE SUPPLIES

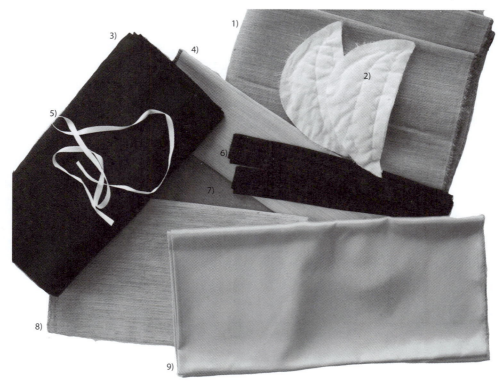

Understructure Supplies. From top: 1) mid-weight canvas interfacing, 2) muslin-covered shoulder pads, 3) flannel cover cloth, 4) haircloth, 5) edge tape, 6) sleeve head roll, 7) French linen undercollar interfacing, 8) light weight canvas interfacing, 9) lining.

Wool Canvas Interfacing

Woven from wool and hair fibers, used as a supporting fabric for the jacket front. The **interfacing** adds shape and body to the garment fabric, and reduces wrinkling. It should be soaked in cool water, allowed to drip dry and pressed before use, to prevent shrinking in the finished garment.

Haircloth

A stiff **interfacing** fabric woven from cotton and hair fibers. Used to add body to the canvas in the **chest** and shoulder area of the jacket front.

Flannel Cover Cloth

A soft cotton flannel fabric, usually in white or grey, which is placed on top of the haircloth to prevent the stiff hair fibers from scratching the wearer.

Pocketing Fabric

Soft, strong cotton fabric, tightly woven and without sizing. Used to form the insides of pockets, and as a stay, or reinforcement for several areas on the jacket and pants.

Lining

A lightweight, smooth fabric of rayon, silk or polyester. Used to cover the understructure of the jacket and to help in sliding the jacket on and off comfortably. Despite being lightweight and soft, the lining must be strong enough to endure constant, long-term wear. Be aware of the fact that silk fibers will deteriorate more quickly than others when exposed to regular wear.

Undercollar Melton

A strong wool fabric in a color that coordinates with the garment fabric. Used to give crisp body and sharp edges to the jacket collar.

French Canvas

A stiff linen **interfacing**. Used both in the undercollar and as added support for the canvas in the shoulder area at the front of the jacket.

Waistband Interfacing

Two layers of stiff **interfacing** sewn together across the top. Used to provide support to the garment fabric at the waistband.

Shoulder Pads

Gracefully shaped layers of cotton wadding covered with muslin. Used to define shoulder area.

Sleeve Head

A strip of cotton wadding or lamb's wool, reinforced with a bias-cut strip of wool canvas **interfacing**, sewn into the cap of the sleeve. The head fills out the sleeve cap and helps create the graceful fall of the sleeve fabric.

Cotton Twill Tape

⅜″ (1 cm) wide, used to define the outer edges of the **lapel** and jacket front, and to control the **lapel** roll line. The tape should be soaked in cool water and pressed before use, to prevent shrinkage in the finished garment.

PRESSING SUPPLIES

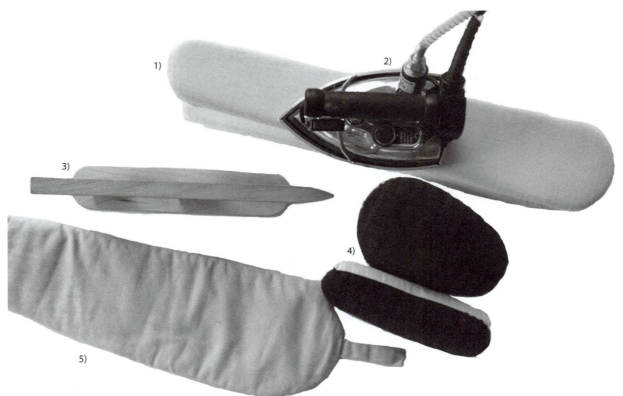

Pressing Supplies. From top: 1) pressing arm, 2) steam iron, 3) wooden seam pressing support/clapper, 4) pressing hams, 5) sleeve pressing pad.

Heavy, Dry Iron

About 12 pounds or more in weight. Heavy irons are preferred by most tailors because of the added pressure the weight affords, especially in the job of flattening and reducing bulk by pressing.

Steam Iron

Professional models offer a powerful surge of steam. Preferred by those who find heavier weight irons difficult to manipulate.

Sleeve Board

A small ironing board convenient for pressing the sleeve and other difficult to reach areas.

Tailor's Ham

A tightly packed curved pressing surface, preferably stuffed with sawdust. Hams come in various shapes and sizes.

Pleater

A wooden block, curved on one side and flat on the other. Used as a pressing surface or as a pounding block for flattening bulky edges.

Brush

Used for brushing the fabric, and for pounding delicate areas.

Presscloth

Soft cotton fabric which is free of sizing. Used to protect the garment fabric from direct contact with the hot iron. With a dry iron, the presscloth is dampened to produce steam.

Press Mitt

A padded mitt worn over the hand. Used to assist in pressing areas that do not lie comfortably on a tailor's ham or ironing board, especially the sleeve cap and shoulder area.

PRESSING TECHNIQUES

Pressing is an integral part of the tailoring process. Besides ridding the fabric of wrinkles, and producing neat, flat darts and seamlines, the iron is used in tailoring to gently shape the fabric. Using heat, moisture and pressure, fabric which is suitable for tailoring can be shrunk in some areas and stretched in others, so that it will hang most gracefully as a finished garment.

The amount of heat, moisture and pressure necessary to accomplish your jobs depends upon the weight and quality of your fabric. Therefore, before using the iron on your fabric, it is essential that you pretest, using a fabric scrap. If your heat setting is too high, the fabric fibers will flatten out and produce an unattractive shine. If your presscloth is too wet, the fabric will shrink and matt.

Wool fabric is very vulnerable when damp. Therefore, rather than pulling the iron back and forth over the fabric, and stretching the fabric off grain, the iron should be placed and lifted, placed and lifted etc. A presscloth is always needed between the iron and the garment fabric to prevent damage to the fabric.

Flat seams can be safely pressed on flat surfaces. However, if a curved area of a garment is placed on a flat surface for steam pressing, and restricted by the flat surface of the hot iron, the fullness in the fabric will shrink as much as it can, in order to fit into this limited space. For this reason, curved areas of the garment are laid over a tailor's ham so that the ham might fill out the shape of the garment. Steam pressing a curved area in this manner will not result in shrinkage, since the fabric is pressed in conformity with its own shape.

Using a dry iron, the best procedure for pressing is to cover the fabric with a uniformly damp (not dripping) presscloth, and then to lay the hot iron on the presscloth until steam is produced. Pressure is added while the fabric is being steamed. Remove the iron and the presscloth while the steam is still being produced. If you are pressing a curved area of a garment, allow the fabric to lay over the ham for a few minutes while it dries. If the ham is stuffed with sawdust the wood particles will absorb the moisture fairly quickly. After pressing flat areas of the garment, the fabric can simply be hung up to dry. Drying the fabric completely before lifting the iron will flatten out the wool fibers and rob the fabric of its life.

Some worsteds or heavier woolens will require more than the normal amount of pressure to create sharp, flat edges. Pressing on a wooden surface, the area to be flattened can be struck sharply with a pounding block while the fabric is still steaming. This extreme pressure, coupled with the instant drying produced by the blow and the wooden surface, usually produces the desired flat, crisp edge.

If a shine appears on the surface of your fabric as a result of excessive heat or pressure, you will probably be able to eliminate it by lightly steaming the shiny area, and then using a soft brush to coax the wool fibers back to life.

Beginners usually err in excess; dampening, pressing and pounding the fabric limp. Remember that the surface life of the fabric is quite vulnerable, as are the many bias and semi-bias raw edges which can all too easily be stretched out of shape. If each of the several pieces of your garment are handled carefully during the tailoring process, and laid out carefully aside when not in use, the amount of pressing needed will be greatly reduced.

HAND STITCHING

If you are not used to hand sewing, we can almost guarantee that you will begin by:

- cutting your thread much too long;
- pulling your stitches much too tight; and
- resisting the use of a thimble until your fingers bleed.

If you can manage to pass through this beginning stage quickly, you will save yourself a great deal of aggravation.

Using a very long thread does not necessarily mean that you will be threading your needle less often. On the contrary, it usually means that your thread will gnarl and tangle, and that you will have to break off the tangled area repeatedly, losing all satisfaction in your work. Use a comfortable length of thread, one which does not require you to stretch your arm with each stitch. If you still have trouble with tangles, draw the thread through a piece of beeswax.

Tightly pulled stitches are usually placed with great care and concentration, and unfortunately, their intensity is usually clearly visible on the front of the garment. There is just no need to nail the layers of fabric this tightly together. Any stitch which goes through to the right side of the garment should pick up only one thread of the garment fabric, and should be drawn softly enough to leave the fabric thread's appearance unchanged on the right side of the fabric.

A thimble is more necessary in tailoring than in other hand sewing, because of the added pressure needed to drive the needle through several layers of fabric. The tailor's thimble is open at the top for comfort. The fingernail area of the thimble, instead of the top, is pressed against the needle. Simply place the thimble on the middle finger of the hand you sew with, and your finger will figure out how best to use it.

Innumerable rows of basting are required in producing a tailored garment. Basting is more accurately done if the two layers of fabric to be joined are laid flat on the table to avoid shifting. With one hand holding the fabric in place, and the other hand placing the stitch, your work will progress quickly and accurately.

Basting stitches, like other hand stitches, should be placed without tension. Since these are temporary stitches, more attentions should be given to their location than to their appearance. Each row of basting begins with a backstitch to secure the thread. Basting thread is never knotted at the end, since knots would make eventual removal of the basting more difficult and more hazardous to the fabric.

The most common hand stitches are illustrated here. Others will be presented throughout the text as their need arises.

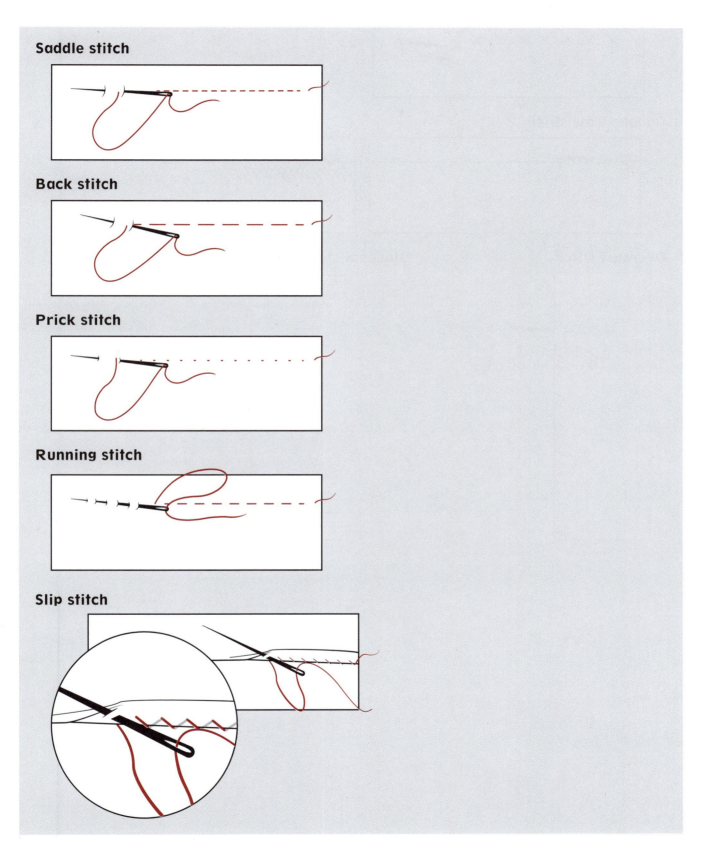

Saddle stitch

Back stitch

Prick stitch

Running stitch

Slip stitch

Cross stitch

Double cross stitch

Overcast stitch

Diagonal stitch

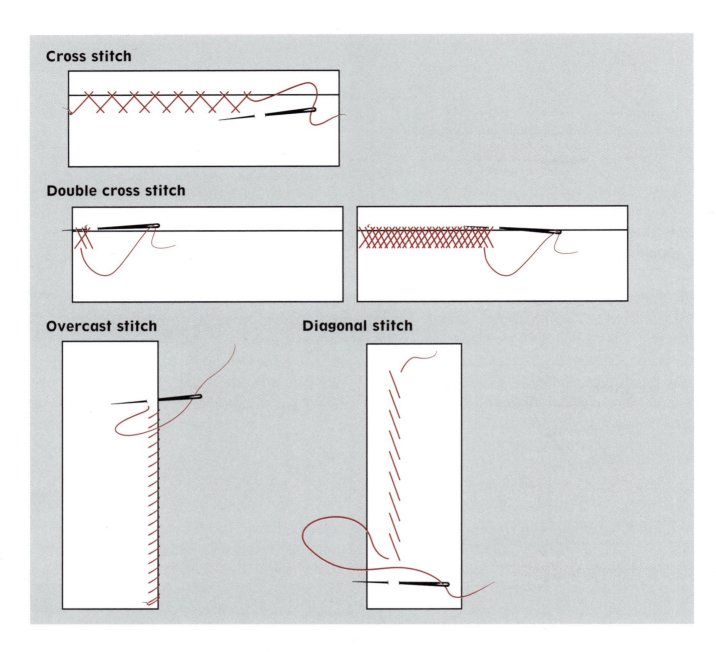

Blanket stitch

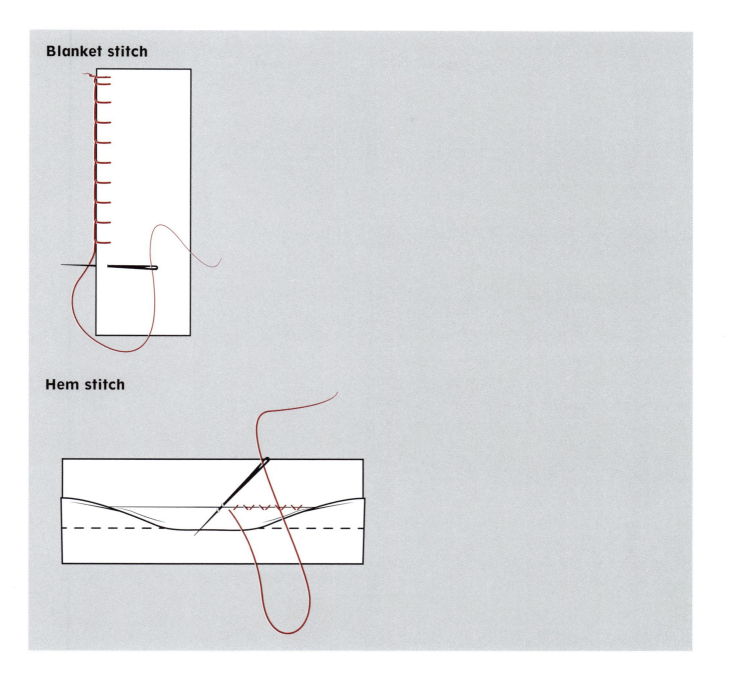

Hem stitch

2 THE PATTERN

MEASUREMENTS

The following are standard measurements taken by tailors, and used by them to draft patterns which will fit their clients as closely and as comfortably as possible. In conjunction with the measurements, the tailor also notes important information about the client's body: whether his posture is stooped or overly erect; whether his shoulders are square or sloped; whether his buttocks are full or flat, whether his stomach protrudes; whether one hip or one shoulder is higher than the other, etc.

In order to get an uncensored picture, the tailor keeps the client away from the mirror during these observations. The temptation to suck in the stomach and stand up straight for the mirror is too strong. If the tailor were to note that version of the body, the suit would fit only in front of a mirror. While making the pattern, the tailor applies his craft to build into the pattern whichever characteristics are needed.

If you are not a skilled patternmaker, and are, therefore, using a commercial pattern, certain fitting and style adjustments will undoubtedly be necessary. Your pattern will have to be customized after the fact, by means of a muslin fitting.

The standard tailors' measurements taken in this chapter will, therefore, most likely be used by you only to choose a commercial pattern closest to your client's fit, and to adjust the length of the pattern. All other adjustments of the pattern will best be diagnosed and made during the muslin fitting.

HOW TO TAKE MEASUREMENTS

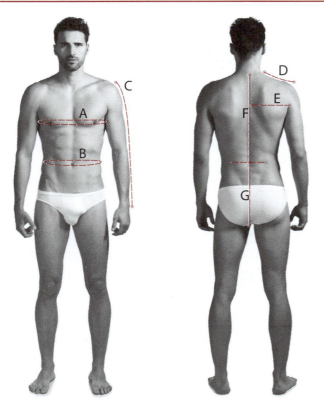

The measurements C, D, E, F and G are taken over the best fitting jacket the client has available. Don't be concerned if the jacket is not a perfect fit. We will have an opportunity to improve the fit during the pattern adjustment and the muslin fitting. All other measurements are taken without the jacket on. A vest should be worn under the jacket if you are measuring for a three-piece suit.

Jacket Measurements

A. Chest

Measure around the body just under the arms. Check that the tape measure is over the fullest part of the **chest** and centered over the shoulder blades in the back. Place two fingers under the tape measure to afford **ease**, and take a comfortable measurement, neither too loose nor too tight.

B. Waist

The **waist** measurement is taken over the vest, but without the belt. This measurement, while comfortable, should have no additional **ease**. The position of the **natural waist** is at the narrowest part of the torso, at the belly button. Keep in mind this is not the **pant waist** (J), which can sit lower on the hip bone.

C. Sleeve Length

Measure the sleeve from the shoulder seam to the hem fold, taking into consideration the slight rise of the sleeve over the shoulder pad.

D. Shoulder

Measure the shoulder seam from collar seam to armhole seam.

E. Half-Back

At about center armhole level, measure across the back from the armhole seam to the center back seam.

F. Center Back/Neck to Waist

With the jacket collar up, measure from the collar seam to the **natural waist** at center back.

G. Center Back/Neck to Hip

With the tape measure touching the body at the **waist**, measure from the collar seam to the bottom of the jacket. The jacket should extend to just below the hip level. If the client's jacket is a flattering length for him, ignore the hip level and use the length of the jacket.

Vest Measurements

Pants Measurements

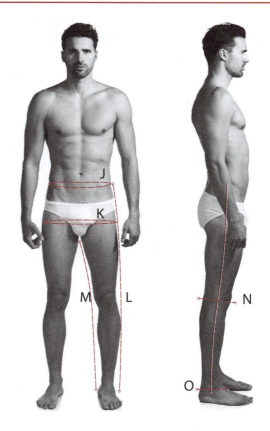

H. Vest Opening

Measure from the neck at center back, over the shoulder and down to the point at which you would like the top vest button.

I. Vest Length

With the tape measure held at the position of the top vest button, continue to measure down to the longest point on the vest front. Keep in mind that the bottom of the vest should cover the customer's belt buckle.

J. Pants Waist

Modern trousers rarely reach as far up as the **natural waist**. This means that the **pants waist** will be somewhat larger than the body **waist**. Make note of the vertical distance between **pant waist** and **natural waist**, for future reference.

K. Hips

The hip measurement is taken with the customer's back pockets empty and his feet together. With two fingers under the tape for **ease**, measure around the fullest part of the hip.

L. Pants Outseam

With the pants **waistline** at a comfortable level for the client, measure down the outseam from the top of the waistband to the middle of the shoe.

M. Pants Inseam

With the pants **waistline** at a comfortable level for the client, measure the pants inseam from the **crotch** to the middle of the shoe. Be sure to check that your client's pants are in fact at the correct level before taking this measurement. The top of the inseam should sit about 1" (2.5 cm) below the customer's **crotch**. There should be no unnecessary pulling, tugging or sagging of fabric in the groin area. As a courtesy to the client, there are special tape measures for taking this measurement. The top few inches of the tape measure have a piece of cardboard attached, so that the cardboard, and not the tailor's hand reaches to the top of the inseam.

N. Knee Width

Measure across the knee of the pants from crease to crease. This measurement is in fact half of the pants circumference at the knee.

O. Width of Pants at Hem

Measure across the bottom edge of the pants leg from crease to crease. As with the knee width, this measurement is half of the hem circumference.

The Fly

Measure the fly from what should be the top of the waistband down to the beginning of the curve of the **crotch**. Do not forget that the pants being worn by the client at the time measurements are being taken may not fit him properly. To accommodate for this, you can either ask your client to raise his pants until the top of the inseam barely touches the customer's **crotch**, or adjust/shorten the fly measurement by eye, which may require a bit more practice.

Crotch Adjustment

Men who wear loose-fitting undershorts and close-fitting pants will need extra fabric at one side of the **crotch** as room for the genitals. Ask the client which side he "dresses" on, so that an adjustment can be made on that side of the pants.

PATTERN SELECTION

Unless you are skilled enough to create your own pattern, your job now is to carefully choose and adjust a commercial pattern in order to produce a personally flattering style and fit. Beautifully detailed construction is wasted on a garment which does not fit, or on a style which does not suit the wearer.

Choose the jacket and vest pattern size according to the **chest** measurement, and the pants pattern size according to the **waist** measurement.

The Jacket Pattern

In selecting the jacket style of the pattern, look to the broad style lines. For the moment, ignore such things as styles of pockets, or whether there is a back vent, or if the jacket pattern includes a lining. Fortified with the techniques outlined in this book, all you will use from the pattern envelope are the basic pattern pieces: the jacket front, side panel and back, the sleeve, and the undercollar.

You will be able to create the rest of the jacket on your own.

Choose the jacket pattern according to your preference for either the close European lines, or the more relaxed, looser shape of the American fit. Decide on a single- or double-breasted jacket, and whether a long or short **lapel** would be most flattering. These decisions are crucial to the

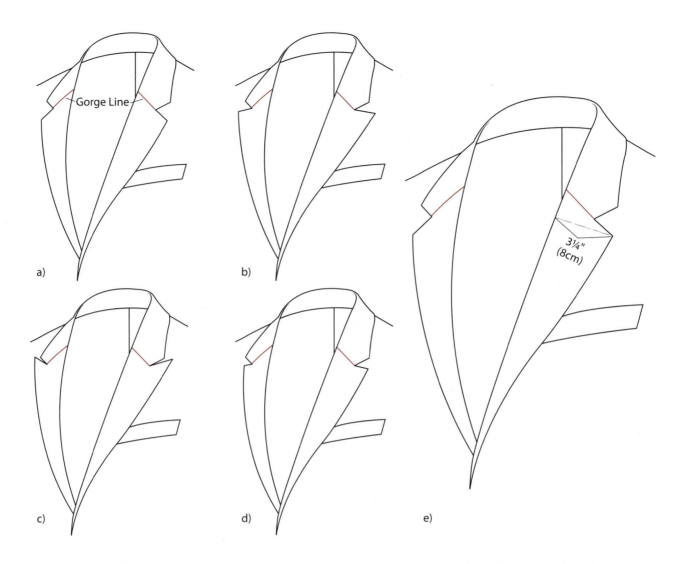

a)

b)

c)

d)

e)

Gorge Line

3¼"
(8cm)

success of the finished jacket, and must be made on a purely individual basis.

Look to the shape of the collar and **lapel** as they meet at the **gorge** line, and choose your jacket pattern. The **lapel** width is a matter of taste and current trend. A safe width for lapels, which will allow the jacket to remain wearable for many years, would be about 3¼″ (8 cm), or between two fifths and a half of the measurement taken from the **lapel** roll line to the armhole seam. Remember that out of style, wide lapels may always be tapered (page 253), but lapels which are too narrow can only hang in the closet until fashion welcomes them back again.

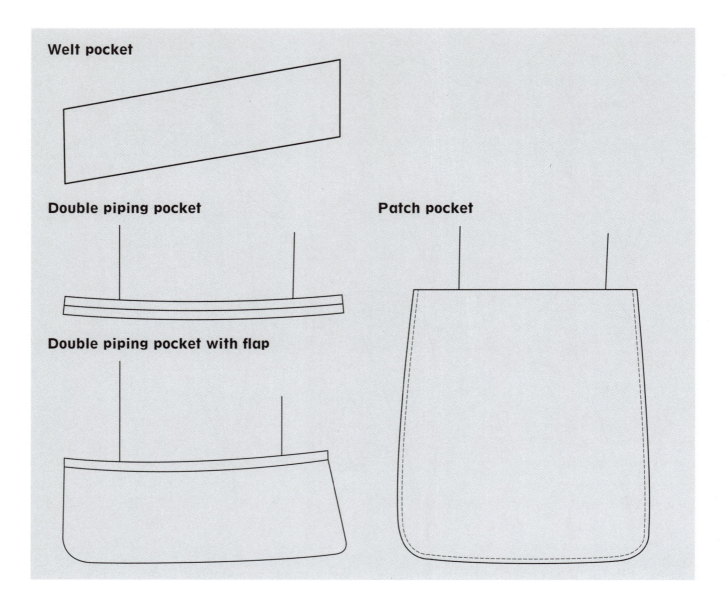

Welt pocket

Double piping pocket

Double piping pocket with flap

Patch pocket

You will be able to interchange patch pockets with double **piping** pockets, or to add a **welt** breast pocket if there is none. You will not need your pattern envelope to help you with making these changes.

If you will be working with a plaid fabric, choose a pattern that eliminates the seam below the pocket by using a dart instead of a separate side panel. The plaid below the pocket is then undisturbed by seamlines, and matching the plaid during the construction of the pockets is not difficult.

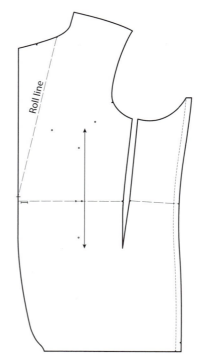

The Pants Pattern

Side pocket

Slant pocket

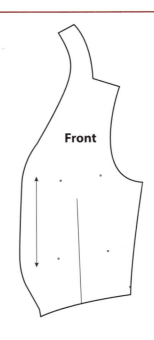

In selecting a pants pattern, select a high or low **rise**, whichever your client has found to be more comfortable, and decide for or against pleats.

No matter what style pockets you would like, the best pants pattern to buy is one that has side pockets rather than any other pocket style. This will give you a pattern with side and **waistline** seams intact – a pattern that can be modified to create all three pockets using the patterns included in this book. (If you choose a pattern with front pleats, of course, you forfeit your option for any pocket style which extends across the pleat position, such as frogmouth or Western pockets.)

The width of the pants leg should not be a determining factor in choosing the pattern, since this is a minor pattern alteration (page 262). Cuffs also can be added or subtracted without difficulty (page 28).

The Vest Pattern

The classic tailored vest is single-breasted, with two or four **welt** pockets. Check the pattern to see that the front of the vest has an extension that continues to the center back of the neck.

Front

PRELIMINARY PATTERN ADJUSTMENTS

1. Jacket Roll Line

Draw the **lapel** roll line on your pattern if it is not already indicated. The roll line begins about ⅝" (1.6 cm) above the top button, and is drawn at an angle which would bring it ⅜" (1 cm) out from the neck cutting edge at the shoulder. Notch the top and bottom of the roll line.

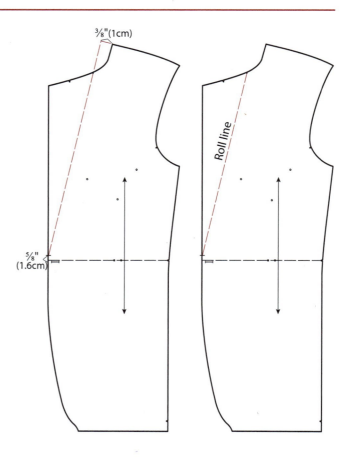

2. Shoulder Seams

The jacket back shoulder seam should be at least ½" (1.3 cm) longer than the front shoulder seam, to allow for ease of movement. Measure your pattern shoulder seams. Add ½" (1.3 cm) to the back shoulder seam if it has not been included.

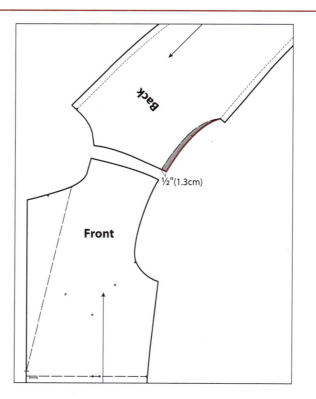

3. Vents

If you would like to add a center back vent to a jacket which does not have a back vent, extend your pattern out 2″ (5 cm) from the stitchline at the top of the vent, and 3″ (7.6 cm) at the bottom. The top of the center back vent is about 1″ (2.5 cm) below the **waistline**, although this measurement is a matter of style preference.

Side vents are more inclined to open than center back vents. The under vent (the side panel) must, therefore, be cut wider to allow for this. Beginning about 1½″ (3.8 cm) below the **waistline** at the back of the side panel, extend your pattern 2½″ (6.4 cm) from the stitchline at the top of the vent, and 4″ (10.2 cm) at the bottom.

The top vent is created by extending the side seam of the jacket back pattern 1½″ (3.8 cm) from the original stitchline, from 1½″ (3.8 cm) below the **waistline**, to the bottom of the jacket.

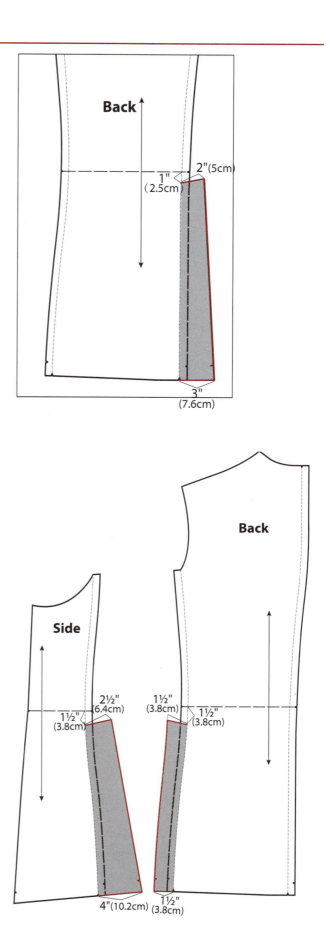

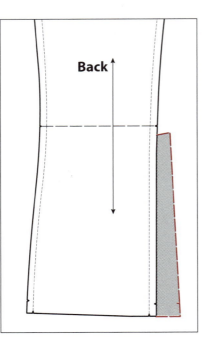

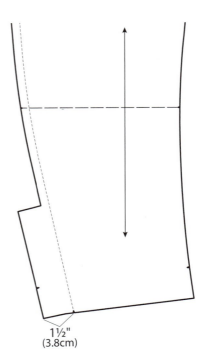

If your pattern includes either a back or side vent and you wish to eliminate it, simply treat the vent foldline as a stitchline, and trim away the pattern beyond the seam allowance.

If the vent is not at least 1½" (3.8 cm) from the foldline on both the topsleeve and the undersleeve patterns, extend it to that amount.

4. Revised Facing Pattern

If the outer edge of the facing pattern is curved to match the shape of the outer edge of the jacket **lapel**, the facing pattern must be redrawn. This procedure is an inconvenience, but one which will produce a far more professional product.

We are redrawing the facing pattern in order to create a pattern that will enable us to place the straight of the grain on the **facing** at the outer edge of the **lapel**. This is essential for a controlled, graceful lay of the fabric. We will also add **ease** to the **facing** to assist in the roll of the **lapel**.

This adjustment, although detailed here, should only be made after the muslin fitting, when the jacket front pattern corrections have been completed.

Use the jacket front pattern as a guide, and draw a new facing pattern on oaktag or brown paper. Trace around the jacket front pattern leaving ½" (1.3 cm) margin at the shoulder, neck and top of the **lapel**. The front of the facing pattern is a straight line, which is drawn ½" (1.3 cm) away

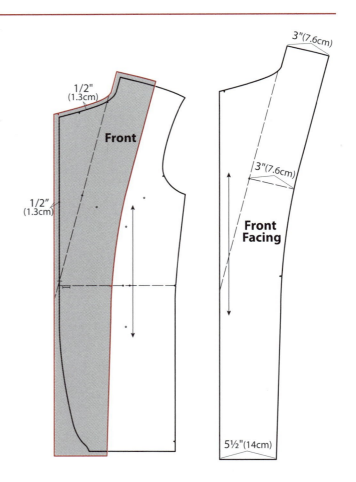

from the center of the **lapel** and continues to ½″ (1.3 cm) below the bottom of the jacket.

The front edge of the **facing** does not yet take the shape of the front of the jacket. This shaping will be accomplished later with the help of the steam iron.

Indicate the bottom of the **lapel** and the **waistline** notch on the facing pattern, and remove the jacket front pattern.

The **facing** extends 3″ (7.6 cm) past the center of the roll line, and should be 3″ (7.6 cm) wide at the shoulder. The **facing** should be cut 5½″ (14 cm) wide at the bottom for a jacket that curves in at the center front hem. For a straight front jacket the bottom of the **facing** is 4″ (10.2 cm) wide.

Add a seam allowance notch at the top of the **lapel**, ½″ (1.3 cm) in from the edge. Your revised facing pattern is complete.

5. The Fly

The fly extension *should not* be included on the pants front pattern. If the extension is attached to the front of the pants pattern, trim it away leaving seam allowance beyond the foldline. Notch the **waistline** to indicate the fly seam allowance.

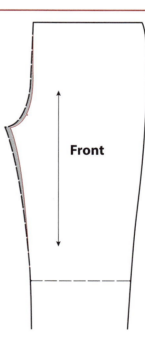

6. The Crotch

Men who wear loose-fitting undershorts and close-fitting pants will need extra fabric at one side of the **crotch** as room for the genitals. When the measurements are taken, the client is asked which side he "dresses" on. Both pants fronts are cut with an additional ¼″ (6 mm) to ½″ (1.3 cm) fabric in the **crotch**. The excess fabric is then trimmed away from the side that does not need the **ease**.

7. Inseams

Tailors often leave extra fabric at the back inseam of each pants leg to allow for alterations. This means that when the pants inseams are sewn, the back inseam is about ⅜" (1 cm) wider than the front. Commercial patterns avoid confusion by allowing the same amount for both seam allowances. If you would like the security of being able to let the pants out in this area (a common alteration), adjust the inseam of the back pants pattern piece by adding ⅜" (1 cm) from the **crotch** to hem to existing seam allowance.

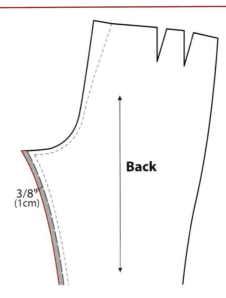

8. Cuffs

If your pattern does not include cuffs and you would like them, extend the bottom of your pants pattern below to what will be the bottom edge of the finished pants. Your pattern should be lengthened by an amount equal to at least three times the cuff width. The average cuff width is 1½" (3.8 cm). If you have the fabric, it would be wise to leave slightly more fabric, since the final determination of the pants length is made only after the pants are completed.

9. Vest

The side seam allowance at the back of the vest should be ½" (1.3 cm) larger than the side seam allowance at the front, to allow for alterations. All alterations of the width of the vest, after its original construction, take place by adjusting the back seam allowance on the side seam, in order not to draw the pockets out of line.

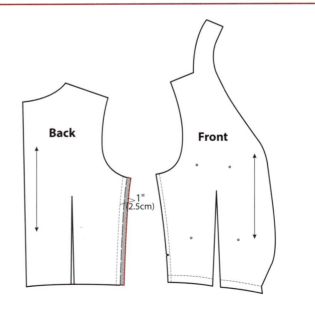

LENGTHENING OR SHORTENING PATTERNS

With the preliminary pattern check completed, lengthen or shorten your jacket, pants and vest patterns as indicated by your measurements. Follow the instructions for length adjustments given on your pattern. As a general guide for length, the jacket should be long enough to extend just below the buttocks. The vest should be long enough to cover the pants waistband. This becomes a challenge, with low rise pants. The pants should be long enough to reach to the middle of the back of the shoe. Leave yourself a generous hem at the bottom of the pants for now.

If you have had successful experience with flat pattern alterations, you may wish to make further adjustments to your pattern at this point. If you have no experience, or only painful memories regarding pattern alterations, leave the adjustments for the moment. The needed pattern alterations will become very obvious in the toile fitting.

3 THE FIT

THE TOILE FITTING

The next step is to cut the basic pattern pieces from a good quality prototyping fabric and to check the fit. Tailors do not always use muslin (also known as calico) for this process. Instead, we recommend using a cheaper wool cloth, which will behave more similarly to your chosen final fabric. The **chest** and shoulder area of your toile should be reinforced with **interfacing**, either fusible or quickly hand-basted in place.

Unless you are a tailor with years of cutting experience, a toile fitting must be made. The toile will serve as an inexpensive prototype of your suit, through which you can become aware of (and then avoid) creases and wrinkles caused by the fact that your client's body is unique, and the pattern is an "average" size. These creases literally "point at" and advertise the peculiarities of your customer's body, such as knock-knees or protruding **seat**.

If you become aware of these creases for the first time in the finished suit, it may be too late to eliminate them; but the prototype offers an early warning system. The knock-knees and protruding **seat** will not disappear, but the wrinkles which note their presence will.

The pattern corrections given here are for some of the most common fitting problems. The procedure is to diagnose the problem, determine the amount needed to correct the fit, and then to apply the corrected amount at certain points on the pattern.

You will have to attach paper to the areas of the pattern that need expanding, so that new lines can be drawn, blending the corrected amounts gracefully into the original lines.

A hip curve ruler is an essential tool for this procedure. The contours of the hip curve coincide with the contours of the body. Use the curve of the original line as a general guide for the contour of the new line. Be sure to blend your new lines into old ones elegantly, as the shape of your pattern will ultimately become the shape of your garment.

If the pattern correction has been at all significant, it would be wise to verify the corrections by changing the toile accordingly, and fitting it a second time on the client. Only then can the cutting of your suit fabric be done with full confidence.

Now that you have decided to make the toile, be aware that it is not an entire suit. For the jacket, cut only the front, back and side panel from prototyping fabric, and the undercollar from French canvas (for body). Eliminate the **facing** and the topcollar. Chalkmark on the cloth lines that indicate the placement of the pockets, the buttons, and the center front.

A muslin sleeve will not be cut at this point. When the jacket is almost finished, the armhole will be measured and a muslin sleeve will be cut to fit (page 185). Forget the sleeve for now. You will need shoulder pads for the jacket fitting. Use a pair of commercial pads. (On page 165 there are instructions for making your own shoulder pads; however, you may wish to make them only after the fitting, when you will have determined the amount of padding best for you.)

The pants prototype should include a zipper and a waistband, so that you get a sense of the actual hang of the pants. The pockets can simply be chalkmarked. The vest muslin needs no **facing**, and only chalkmarks indicating pockets and buttons.

Cut the toile fabric with full attention to the grain. If the fabric is off grain, wrinkles may be quite misleading: they may be indicating bias draping, rather than fitting problems.

Machine stitch the seam allowances and darts accurately, and press the seams open.

The jacket toile should be fit over a well-fitting shirt. We will be using the shirt collar as a guide for the height of the jacket collar. A sweater should not be worn under the toile, unless one will be worn regularly under the finished suit jacket. Attention should be given to the height of the shoe heel, since variation here may significantly alter the length of the pants.

The first view of the prototype suit provides important information about the overall impression. The jacket and pants should be in balance. Although the average jacket length is just below the hip, a man with long legs and a short torso may require a jacket that comes well below his hips in order to create an attractive balance between top and bottom.

Wide lapels and pleated trousers may combine to create too heavy an impression for a shorter, slightly built man. A long **lapel** may be better than a short one on a tall, broad man.

None of this is true all the time. Use your eye and trust your judgment. If necessary, lengthen or shorten the jacket according to your pattern instructions, and then make whatever style adjustments you think best, using the guidelines on the following pages.

THE JACKET

Lapels – Too Wide/Too Narrow

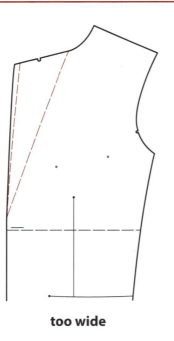

too wide

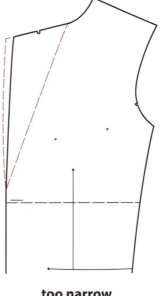

too narrow

If you wish to widen or narrow the **lapel**, add to or subtract from the top of the outer edge of the **lapel**, and taper a line to the bottom of the roll line.

Adjusting the shape of the **lapel** will not prove a problem with the **facing** since we will eventually redraw the facing pattern using the new line of the **lapel** as a guide.

Lapels – Too Long/Too Short

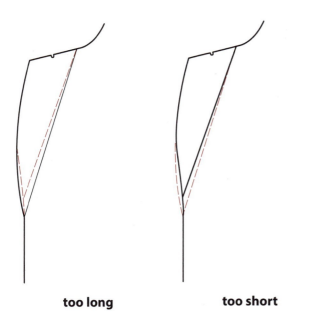

too long   **too short**

If you would prefer to raise or lower the **lapel**, draw a line from the top of the existing roll line to the desired height of the **lapel** roll. Below the roll line, the jacket front tapers to a straight line.

Keep in mind that, if the change required here is substantial, you should change the roll line from the point where the original roll line meets the continuation of the shoulder stitchline. This will help to avoid unnecessary distortion to the collar height.

If you wish, the design of the collar can be completely changed during the construction of the collar (page 169).

Jacket Balance

With the preceding style problems out of the way, we will move on to the problems of fit. The procedure will be to correct the most obvious problems first, and to work our way down to the finer details. The major corrections often eliminate the minor ones before we get to them.

The most obvious fitting problems are those caused by posture and body imbalance. If the client's posture is stooped or overly erect, or if one shoulder is higher than the other, the jacket will not hang correctly.

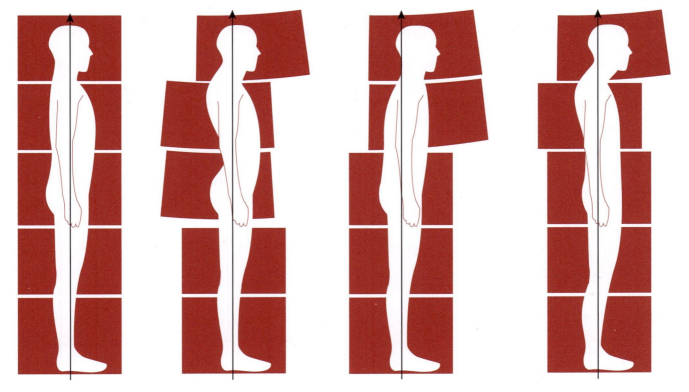

From left to right: Correct, Overly erect, Stooped, Low shoulder

Stooped Posture

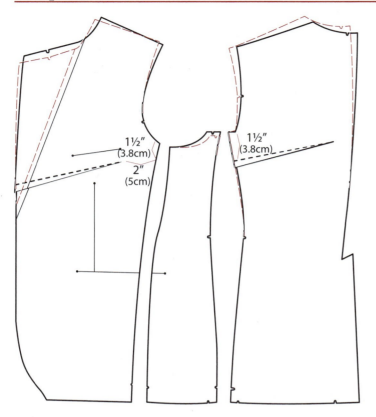

1½″ (3.8cm)

2″ (5cm)

1½″ (3.8cm)

A jacket on a man with stooped posture will pull towards the back and upwards. To prevent the jacket from pulling, fold the pattern at the back side seam about 1½″ (3.8 cm) below the armhole. Approximately ½″ (1.3 cm) to ¾″ (1.9 cm) is folded out of the pattern at the seam, and tapered across the pattern back.

On the pattern front, about 1½″ (3.8 cm) below the armhole, and about 2″ (5 cm) in from the cutting edge of the side seam, draw a line across the pattern to the **lapel** edge, at a level just below the top of the dart. About ½″ (1.3 cm) to ¾″ (1.9 cm) fabric is folded out of the pattern at the **lapel**, tapering to the end of the line.

The top of the side panel is lowered so that the side panel back seam from waist notch to armhole is equal in length with the newly adjusted side seam on the jacket back pattern.

Overly Erect Posture

A jacket on a man with overly erect posture will pull towards the front and upwards. To prevent the jacket from pulling, slash the pattern beginning on the back side seam, about 1½″ (3.8 cm) below the armhole. The slash continues across the back of the pattern to about 2″ (5.1 cm) from the center back seam. The pattern is spread apart at the side seam ½″ (1.3 cm) to ¾″ (1.9 cm).

A slash is cut into the pattern front from the **lapel** edge to about 2″ (5.1 cm) from the side seam. The pattern is spread apart at the slash ½″ (1.3 cm) to ¾″ (1.9 cm).

The top of the side panel is raised so that the side panel back seam from waist notch to armhole is equal in length with the newly adjusted side seam on the jacket back pattern.

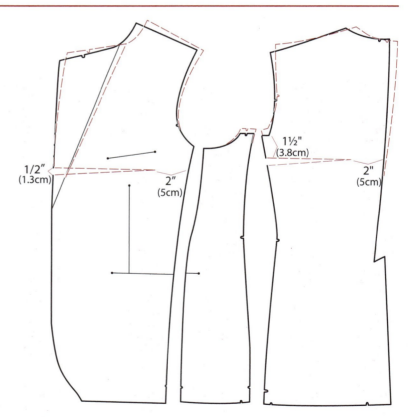

½″ (1.3cm)

2″ (5cm)

1½″ (3.8cm)

2″ (5cm)

Many people have one shoulder lower than the other, usually as a result of their work, or some other regular activity which places the body in an unbalanced position. A clear indication of this peculiarity of the body is visible in the sagging diagonal creases along one side of the jacket only.

Pin the fabric up at the shoulder (as illustrated) until the creases disappear, and measure the amount of the needed adjustment.

It would appear that the logical pattern correction would be a deeper, slanting seam at the shoulder. Doing this would make the armhole smaller, which, in turn, would necessitate making the sleeve smaller. Alternatively, you might be tempted to add extra padding on the lower side, which would also result in a tightening of the armhole and an uncomfortable end result.

The fact is that the correction has nothing to do with the armhole. It has to do with the rib cage area. The shoulder is low because the body is contracting itself somewhere between the armhole and the **waist**, on one side. The adjustment required is somewhat complicated – however, it works. The adjustment requires either a new muslin, or your confidence in being able to make the correction directly on the garment fabric. You decide.

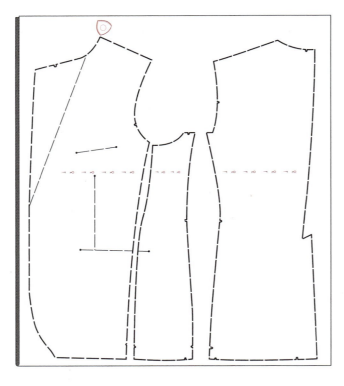

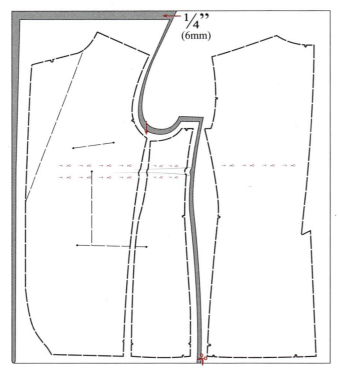

Place the three main jacket pattern pieces on your fabric so that the side of the jacket which does not need correction will be traced on the top layer of the fabric.

In the illustration, the fabric is folded with right sides together and the right side of the jacket is being traced on the top layer of fabric. This is to illustrate the first step in correcting a left low shoulder.

Arrange the pattern pieces so that all seams which will eventually be joined are closest to each other.

Using tailor's chalk, trace the pattern pieces onto the fabric and remove the pattern.

Place a row of the pins horizontally across the fabric at approximately the level of the top of the dart. The pins should go through both layers of fabric.

Cut through only the top layer of fabric (as illustrated) about ½" (1.3 cm) away from the cutting edge of the armhole and the side panel. The fabric layers are still anchored together by the row of pins.

Now, at the top of the **lapel**, move the top layer of fabric in ¼" (6 mm). At the shoulder of the jacket front, move the top layer of fabric down an amount equal to one half the needed correction.

With one hand, hold the top layer of fabric flat, in its new position. With the other hand, smooth the fabric downward toward the pins, and outward towards the side seam. An excess of fabric will appear just above the row of pins.

A second row of pins is now placed through both layers of fabric, confining the ripple of fabric to this area. The two rows of pins should be about 1" (2.5 cm) apart at the side panel.

With the fabric pinned in this manner, cut through both layers of the jacket front and side panel. Be attentive as you cut the rippled area. Follow the chalk guideline.

When both layers of the front and side panel are placed together on the table it will be obvious that the underlayer is shorter between the underarm and **waist**, yet both armholes are equal.

The back of the jacket is adjusted in the same manner. The top layer of fabric is moved in ¼″ (6 mm) at the center back neck, and down at the shoulder an amount equal to one half the needed correction. The fabric is smoothed downward and outward towards the side. The excess of fabric which appears above the pins is pinned in place, and both layers of the jacket back are cut together.

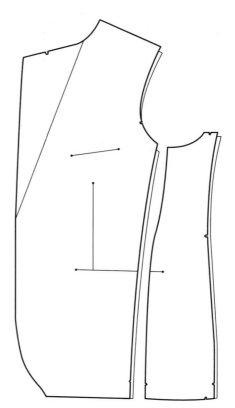

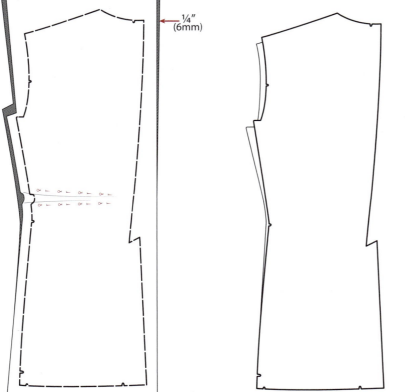

¼″
(6mm)

Too Loose/Too Tight Above Waist

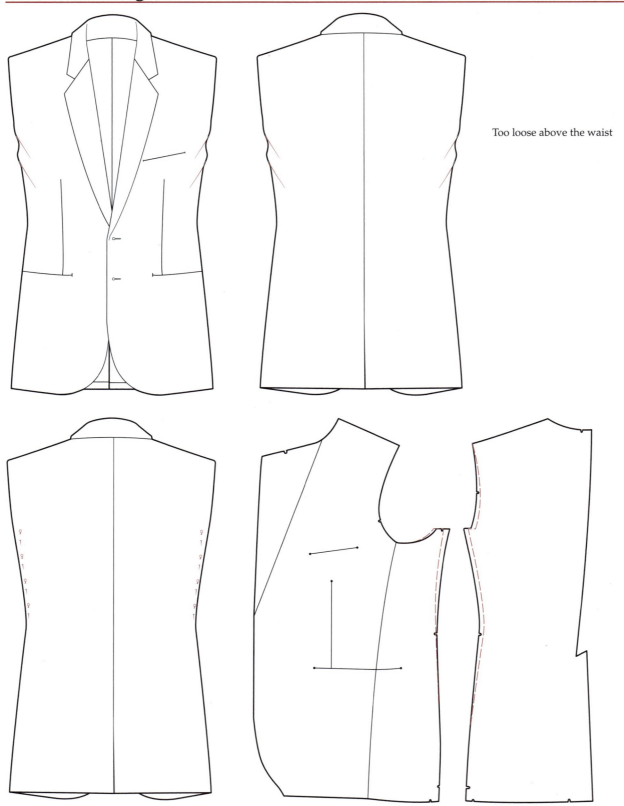

Too loose above the waist

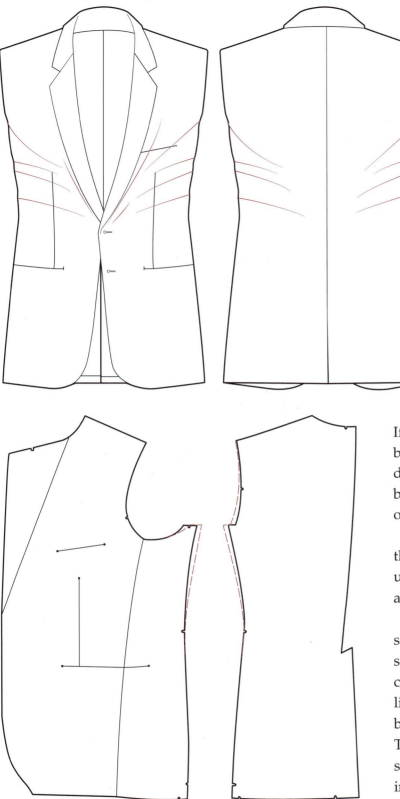

Too tight above the waist

If the jacket is wrinkling above the **waist** because of too much or too little fabric, determine the amount of the correction by pinning (too much fabric), or by opening the side seams (too little fabric).

On the pattern, add or subtract the corrected amount not only from the underarm to the hip, but also at the armhole.

The horizontal line at the top of the side seams, back and front, is equal to the side seam allowance. When your pattern correction is complete, that horizontal line must measure the same as it did before you began to correct the pattern. Therefore, whatever amount is added or subtracted from the side seam must inversely be subtracted or added at the armhole. Failure to do this will result in a gap at the back of the armhole which will destroy the armhole contour.

Too loose below the waist

Too tight below the waist

There should be no wrinkling on the jacket below the **waist**, on front or back, and the vent should lie closed, without pulling to one side or to the other.

On the pattern, add or subtract the corrected amount at the bottom of the side seam, and taper gradually to the **waist**.

Shoulder too wide

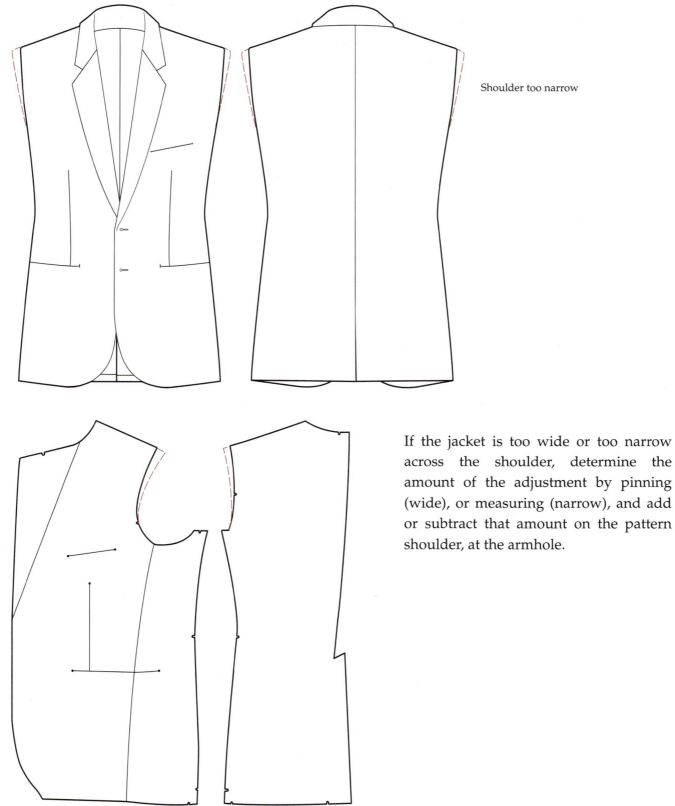

Shoulder too narrow

If the jacket is too wide or too narrow across the shoulder, determine the amount of the adjustment by pinning (wide), or measuring (narrow), and add or subtract that amount on the pattern shoulder, at the armhole.

If your client has sloped shoulders, and the jacket has been cut for normal shoulders, diagonal creases will appear, on front and back, at the bottom of the armhole. These creases can most often be eliminated by increasing the amount of shoulder padding.

When padding cannot solve the entire problem, open the shoulder seam and re-pin it to eliminate the creases. Measure the amount of the pinned correction at the armhole edge of the shoulder.

On the pattern front and back apply that measurement from the neck edge of the shoulder. The **lapel** is also raised by the amount of the pinned correction. The center back neck is raised by that amount plus ⅛" (3 mm).

Square Shoulder

If your client has square shoulders and the jacket has been cut for normal shoulders, circular creases will appear at the base of the collar, on front and back. Decreasing the amount of shoulder padding will sometimes solve the problem but not always.

Remove the collar and re-pin the shoulder seam, eliminating the creases. Measure the amount of the pinned correction at the neck edge of the shoulder.

On the pattern front and back, apply the amount of the correction down from the neck edge of the shoulder. Also, lower the **lapel** and the back neck by that amount.

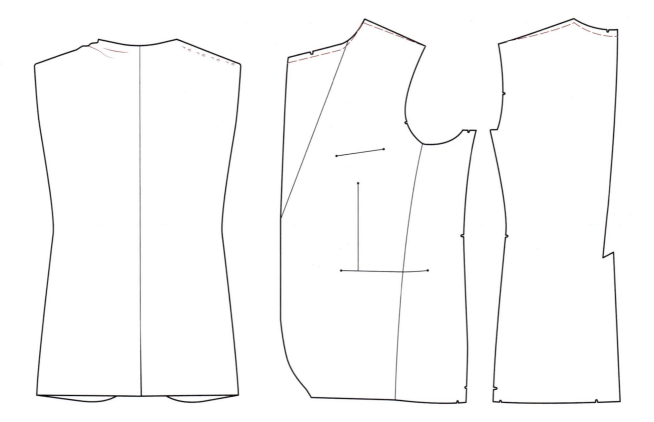

Neckline – Too High/Too Low

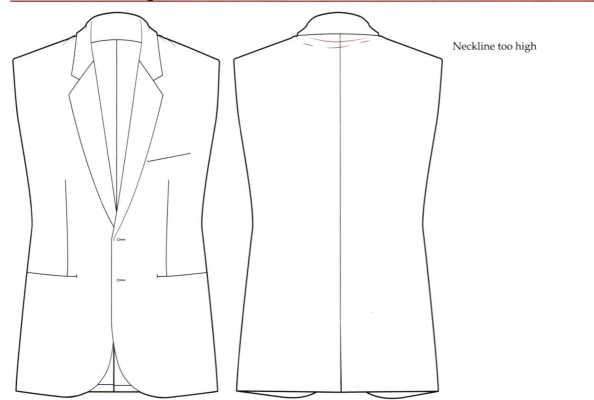

Neckline too high

Neckline too low

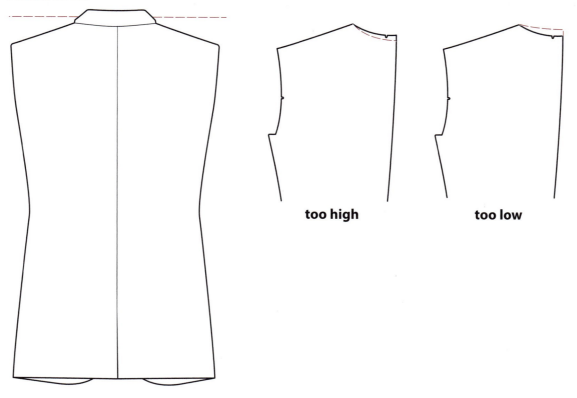

too high   **too low**

If the bottom of the collar does not sit on the shoulder at the back, but sits above or below shoulder level, the collar must be removed and the back neckline raised or lowered.

The amount of the adjustment can be determined easily if the fitting is done over a shirt that fits well at the neckline. Raise or lower the jacket neckline at the back to allow about ½" (1.3 cm) of the shirt collar to be visible above the jacket collar.

Apply the depth of the adjustment to the pattern neckline at center back.

If the jacket neckline is too tight, the armhole seam at the shoulder will show signs of pulling towards the neck. There will be creases on the front shoulder, reaching out from the neck towards the armhole.

The collar will be a bit high if the neckline is too tight, but the height of the collar will be less obvious than the pulling of the fabric in the shoulder and neckline area. Once the neckline is released, the collar should settle to a comfortable height.

Remove the collar. Open the toile shoulder seam at the neck and the top of the center back seam, and let the jacket settle at the neckline.

The adjustment should be distributed equally at the neckline between the shoulder seam and the center back seam.

Loose Neckline

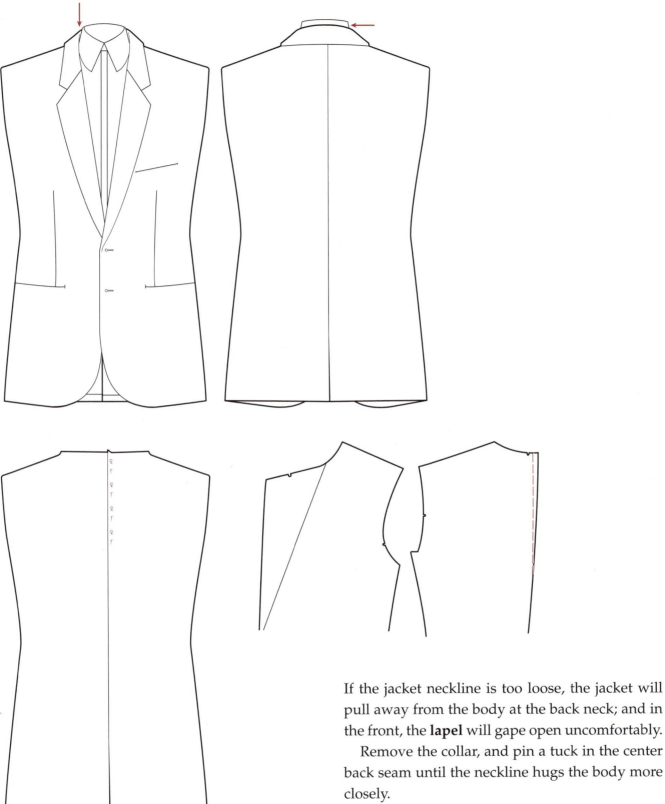

If the jacket neckline is too loose, the jacket will pull away from the body at the back neck; and in the front, the **lapel** will gape open uncomfortably.

Remove the collar, and pin a tuck in the center back seam until the neckline hugs the body more closely.

Apply the depth of the adjustment at the neck edge of the center back seam.

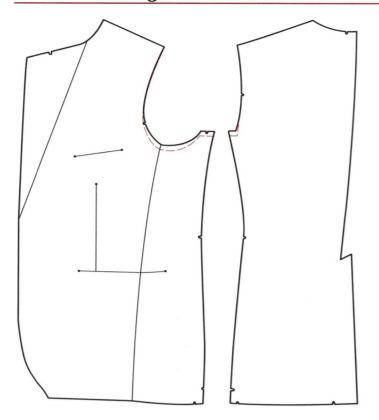

Armhole too high

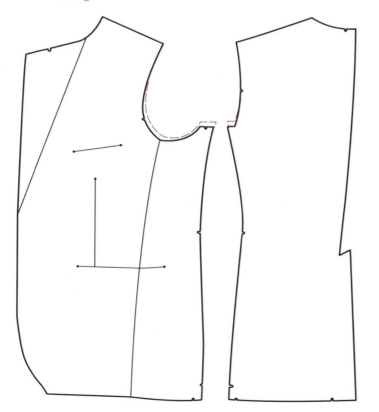

Armhole too low

Contrary to popular belief, the most comfortable armhole for a sleeve is one which is cut as high as possible without restricting the forward movement of the arm. A low-cut armhole is only comfortable if a sleeve is not attached. With a sleeve set into a low-cut armhole, raising one's arm involves raising the entire side of the jacket.

The cutting edge of the fabric should be about 1" (2.5 cm) below the center underarm.

Raise or lower the pattern the depth of the adjustment at mid-underarm, and at the top of the side seam, back and front. This adjustment at the top of the side seams is necessary to maintain the contour of the armhole.

The armhole should also be "scooped" slightly in the front notch area, if wrinkles develop when the arm is resting at the side. Trim the fabric, a little at a time, until the wrinkles disappear. Be very careful not to cut into your client's shirt if you attempt doing this while he is wearing the jacket toile.

Shoulder – Not Concave

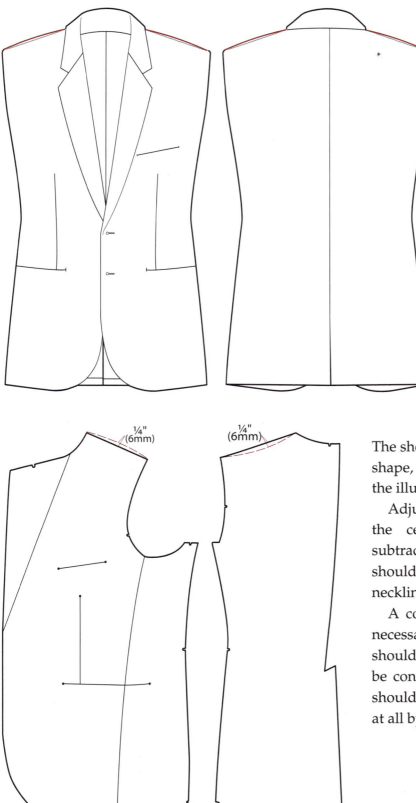

¼"
(6mm)

¼"
(6mm)

The shoulder should have a graceful concave shape, rather than the bulky convex shape in the illustration.

Adjust the pattern by adding ¼" (6 mm) at the center of the shoulder front and subtracting ¼" (6 mm) from the center of the shoulder back, tapering to the armhole and neckline seams.

A correctly shaped shoulder pad is also necessary in order to achieve this concave shoulderline (page 165). The padding should be concentrated at the armhole edge of the shoulder, tapering to *no* thickness in the pad at all by mid-shoulder.

THE PANTS

Waistline – Too Loose/Too Tight

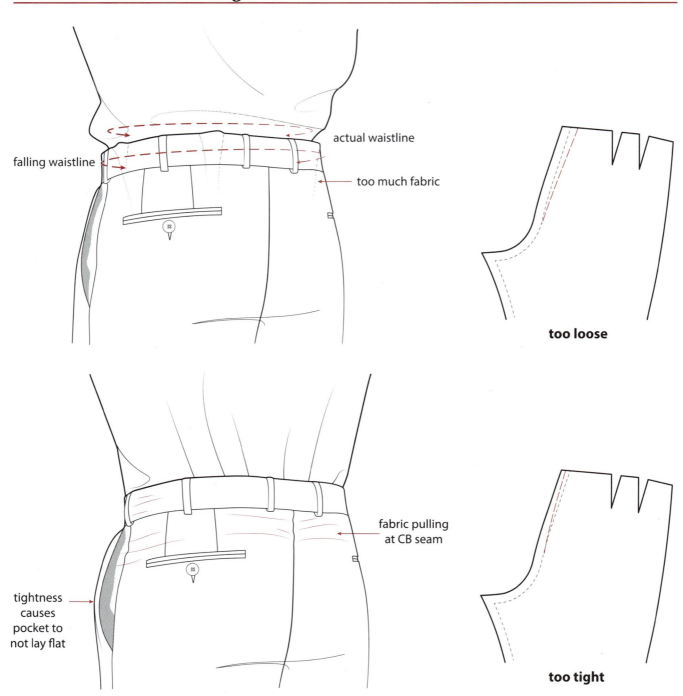

actual waistline

falling waistline

too much fabric

too loose

fabric pulling at CB seam

tightness causes pocket to not lay flat

too tight

The first point to check in the fit of the pants is the **waistline**. Only when the **waist** fits comfortably can the pants settle into place on the body. If the **waist** is too loose, pin the center back seam to a comfortable fit. Note the amount of the correction.

If the **waist** is too tight, open the center back seam and re-pin it, using as much of the seam allowance as necessary.

Add or subtract the indicated amount on the pattern at the center back seam.

Too Tight Across Hips

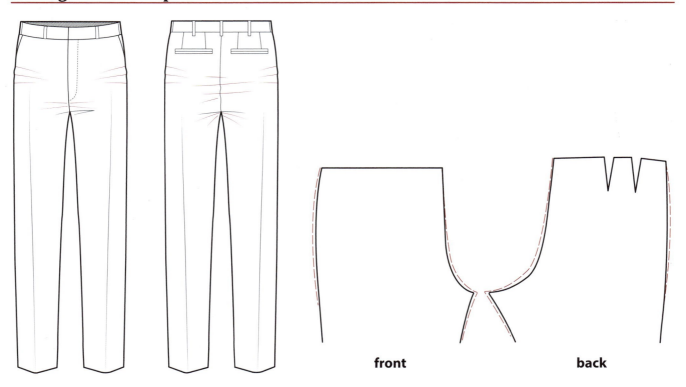

front   **back**

If the pants are too tight across the hips, ½″ (1.3 cm) is the most we can add without disturbing the balance of the pants. The ½″ (1.3 cm) is added at three points on the pattern pants front and back.

The adjustment is out at the top of the inseam, out at the **crotch** at hip level, and out at the side seam at hip level.

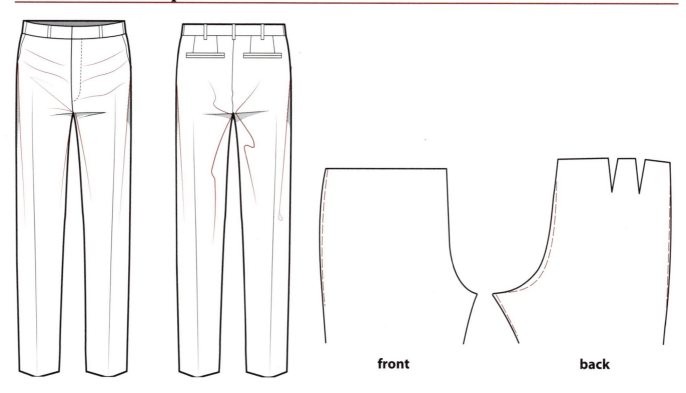

front   **back**

If the pants are too loose across the hips, ½" (1.3 cm) is the most we can subtract without disturbing the balance of the pants. The ½" (1.3 cm) is subtracted from the pattern at one point on the pattern front and at three points on the pattern back.

The adjustment is in at the side seams at hip level, in at the top of the back inseam, and in at the back of the **crotch** at hip level.

Crotch – Too Short/Too Long

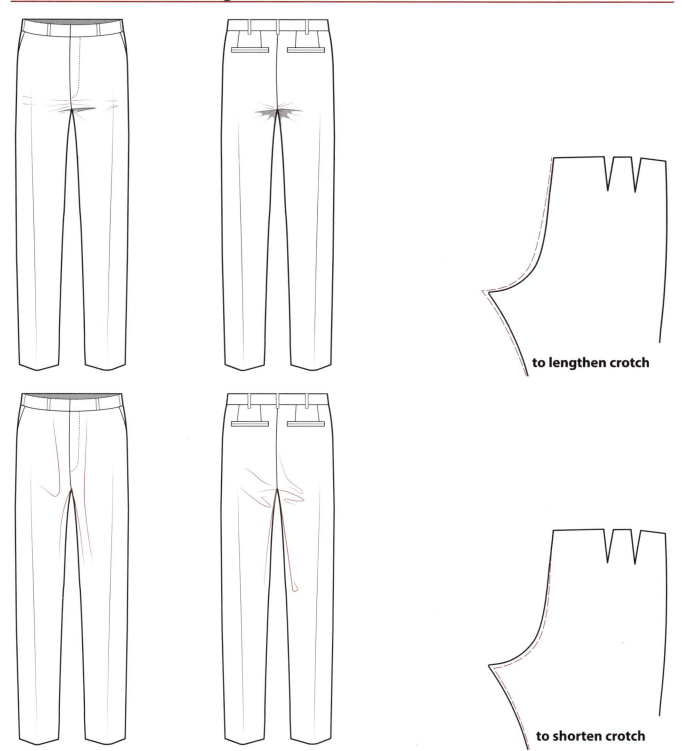

to lengthen crotch

to shorten crotch

If wrinkles are concentrated in the **crotch** area, the hips are probably fine, but the **crotch** length must be corrected. Tight, pulling creases radiating from the **crotch** indicate a short **crotch**. Sagging, loose creases indicate a **crotch** that is too long.

Depending upon the amount of wrinkling, adjust the **crotch** between ¾" (1.9 cm) and 1" (2.5 cm). Add or subtract this corrected amount on the pattern back only, by extending out or in from both the top of the inseam, and the center back seam at hip level.

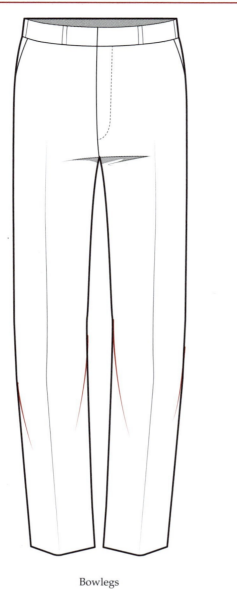

Bowlegs

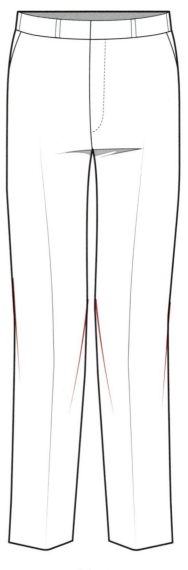

Knock-knees

The pants will wrinkle noticeably at the knee if the client has bowlegs or knock-knees. A simple correction of ½" (1.3 cm) to 1" (2.5 cm) will usually allow the pants to fall smoothly, despite the knee problem.

Bowlegs

Knock-knees

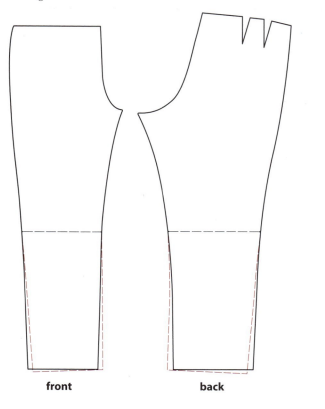

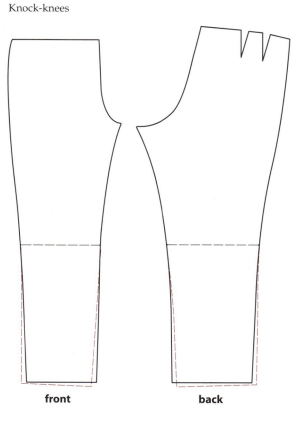

front   **back**

front   **back**

Apply the same adjustment amount in and down at the bottom of the outseams, and out at the bottom of the inseams.

Apply the adjustment amount in and down at the bottom of the inseams, and out at the bottom of the outseams.

Flat Seat

Semi-circular wrinkles or folds will appear at the back of the pants if the client has very flat buttocks, or if he stands with his hips thrust forward. In both cases the pants will also hit the calf of the leg at the back, rather than fall smoothly to the floor.

Determine the amount of the correction by the volume of the folds. A ¾" (1.9 cm) correction is about average.

Apply the adjusted amount at three points on the front of the pants pattern and at four points on the back. If, for example, you use ¾" (1.9 cm) as the corrected amount, measure out ¾" (1.9 cm) at the hip, down ¾" (1.9 cm) at the center back **waistline**, and in ¾" (1.9 cm) at both the **crotch** hip level and the top of the inseam. The correction on the pants front pattern involves measuring in ¾" (1.9 cm) at the **waistline** side seam, and both out and up ¾" (1.9 cm) at the center front **waistline**.

A hip curve ruler will be essential in tapering these new points to meet one another. All of the new lines except for the center front seam are curved lines.

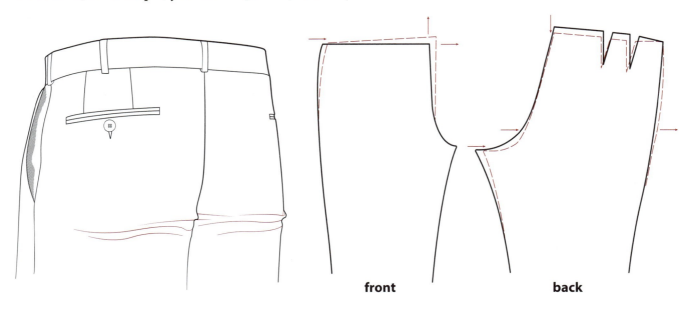

front   back

Prominent Seat

Pulling occurs across the back of the pants if the buttocks are full, or if the client's overly erect posture causes the hip to be thrown backward and upward. The pants are also distorted by hitting the bottom of the leg in the front rather than falling smoothly to the floor.

Determine the amount of the pattern correction by the amount of the pulling at the back – ¾" (1.9 cm) is about average.

Apply this corrected amount at three points on the pants back pattern: out from the top of the inseam, and from the **crotch** at hip level, and up at the center back **waistline**. The pants must also be extended out at the side seam at hip level. However, ¾" (1.9 cm) additional shaping would be too much at the hip for most men. Add ½" (1.3 cm) at the side seam at the hip level and taper the line.

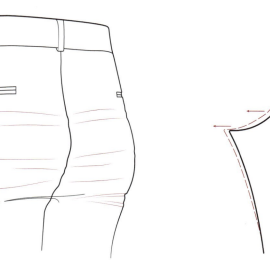

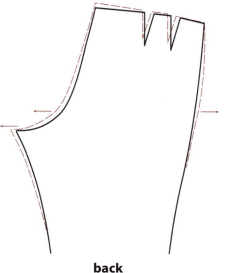

back

THE VEST

Vest Front – Too Low/Too High

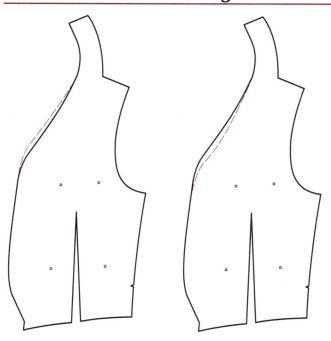

Only one vest button should be visible when both vest and jacket are buttoned. Too much vest distracts from the cut of the jacket **lapel**. However, if the vest is not visible, it may as well be eliminated. If necessary, taper your vest front pattern using the hip curve.

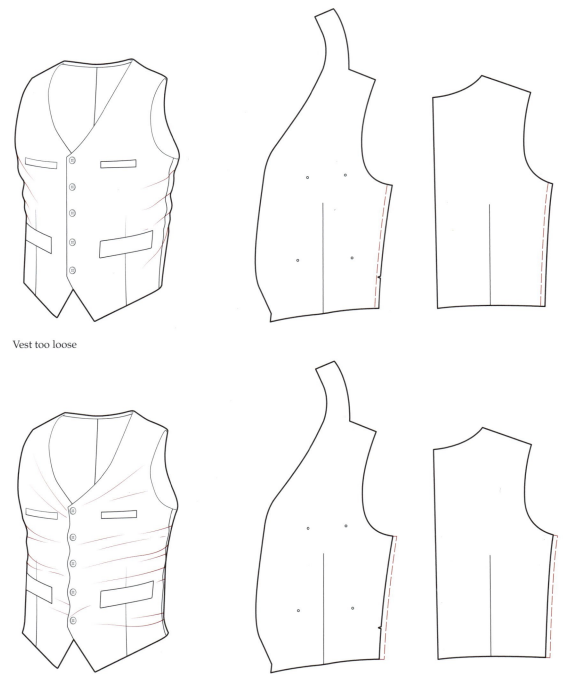

Vest too loose

Vest too tight

If the vest is too loose or too tight distribute the amount of the adjustment equally between the front and back side seams.

If the amount of the adjustment is significant, it may be necessary to move the pocket placement line so that the pockets remain centered on the vest front.

4 FABRIC

SELECTING THE FABRIC

If you want the very finest fabric for classic tailoring, choose wool. There is an endless variety of beautiful fabrics available to us today, most of which will respond favorably to certain tailoring features. There is no reason to limit your wardrobe to one fabric. However, full tailoring procedures (canvas, haircloth, tape, etc.) will produce their best results for wool. Silk and linen are close seconds.

Wool fabric has a distinctive personality which relates better with tailoring procedures than any other fabric. There is no disagreement among tailors on this.

The tailoring techniques described in this book direct you at times to stretch the fabric, or to shrink it, to mold it to fit the contours of the human body. Wool fabric is somehow able to take on this newly molded shape and to hold it as if it had always been its own. This is unique among fabrics.

Wool comes in a variety of weights and characteristics, which can be worn comfortably from the tropics to the Arctic, year-round. It is durable, has a long life expectancy, and handles beautifully at the sewing machine.

There are two major wool categories:

- Worsteds
- Woolens

Worsted fabric is woven from long, finely combed wool fibers which have been twisted tightly, and then woven tightly. The effect is a fabric with a firm, flat surface, as in a serge, or a gabardine. The traditional tailored business suits are made from worsteds rather than from woolens.

Woolens are woven from relatively short wool fibers, which have not been combed smooth. These fibers are twisted loosely and then woven much less tightly than the worsteds. The effect is a soft, easy fabric, such as a Harris tweed, or a flannel. Woolens are more suited to comfortable, sporty garments than they are to business suits.

Fabric Weights

It is essential that the novice tailors be very careful in the choice of cloth for their first forays into the techniques outlined in this book. While an experienced tailor may be highly capable to shape, mold and manipulate a difficult lightweight suiting, we recommend students start off with heavier suiting cloth (around 12 ounces per square yard, or 400 grams per square meter), woven with woolen fibers. Worsteds, silks, fiber blends and tropical-weights are to be avoided until the student has gained confidence in their tailoring abilities.

Tropical-Weight Suitings

The lightest tailoring cloths are called tropical-weight suitings. These fabrics are constructed from highly twisted fibers, often blended with linen or cotton for improved breathability. Topical-weight suitings usually weigh below 8 ounces per square yard (248 grams per square meter), and display an open weave, which allows better air movement. These fabrics are notoriously difficult to manipulate through the tailoring process, and require extensive expertise for accurate results.

Mid-Weight Suitings

These fabrics are suitable for all-year wear. Fabrics in this range make comfortable suits to be worn (jacket and pants) in air-conditioned office environments. Mid-weight suitings often surprise the novice tailoring student for their lightness, smoothness and flexibility (considering these are most commonly 100% worsted wool). They usually range from 8 to 12 ounces per yard (248 to 400 grams per meter).

Jacketings and Coatings

Cloths heavier than 13 ounces per square yard (440 grams per square meter) are usually not suitable for year-round suits, and preferred either for winter suits or just to be used for sport coats or separate cooler climate jackets. These jacketings and coatings are often woven in handsome checks, plaids and other patterns, using woolen yarns for added warmth.

Fabric Patterns

Plains

The word "plain" is often misleading. In the case of tailored fabrics, plain-colored cloths, which have been most likely piece dyed to achieve a uniform solid coloration, may seem at first to be an easy choice to avoid the complications of matching patterns. The solid coloration, and the matte quality of the most common plain cloths such as lawn, serge, and gabardine, have an unfortunate tendency to make any mistake in the construction of the tailored garment particularly visible.

Textured Plains

Many fine tailoring cloths are in fact not truly solid colors, but heathered or mélangé. Blending fibers of different tones of grey for example, in the spinning of yarn for a twill suiting, will give the final result much deeper dimensionality. The heathered coloration of the cloth will also enable the garment to hide small stains and defects more effectively, improving the length of time it will remain wearable. These multi-tonal fancy plains also include small geometric patterns such as pin-dot, bird's eye, sharkskin, tick weave and many more.

Stripes

Stripes are very common in tailoring fabrics. They elongate the body, create the illusion of wider shoulders, and showcase the elegant shaping of the garment. Pinstripes have single contrasting warp threads running on a plain background, while chalkstripes are made by groups of four to six threads together. There are also a multitude of stripe patterns such as boating stripes, shadow stripes, and multi-stripes. Herringbone weave can also be considered a type of textural stripe pattern, and should be treated just as carefully

when matching pockets, sleeves and garment edges. Stripe cloths are commonly woven in a twill structure, for better durability.

Checks

Checks tend to be by far the trickiest fabric patterns to work with, as they involve matching

garment pieces in both the lengthwise and crosswise directions of the cloth. Very experienced tailors often find the challenge of a complicated check pattern very thrilling, and the final result particularly rewarding. Guidance for the accurate matching of check patterns is given throughout this book. If working with a check, be sure to read the section addressing it first, before any cutting of the fabric.

PROPERTIES OF WOVEN FABRICS

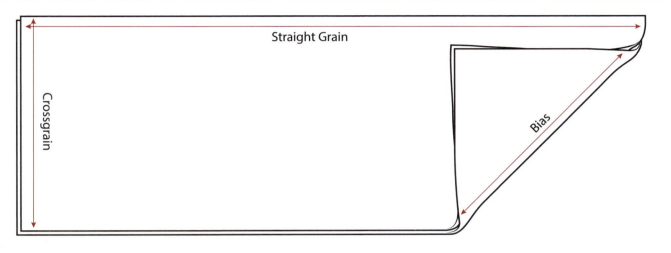

The Grain

Woven fabric is made by interlacing threads at right angles to one another, evenly or in patterns. The lengthwise thread (the wrap) runs parallel to the selvage (the finished edge along the length of the fabric at either end). The lengthwise of the fabric is called the straight grain. The crosswise thread (the weft), the crossgrain, runs at a right angle to the selvage. There is no thread running diagonally across the fabric. However, the diagonal direction of the fabric is called the bias. The lengthwise thread must be strong to withstand the workings of the loom, and to support the fabric. The crosswise thread need not be quite as strong.

Because of the strength of the lengthwise thread, and the fact that the crosswise thread will "give" or drape gently in response to gravity, most garments will hang best if they are cut so that the lengthwise thread hangs vertically. Garments cut on the crossgrain (with the crossgrain hanging vertically) hang less comfortably and somewhat stiffly. Garments cut on the bias (with the bias hanging vertically) have neither the lengthwise nor the crosswise

thread to support them directly. Therefore, the fabric finds it difficult to hold a shape. Bias-cut garments drape beautifully, *and* they stretch.

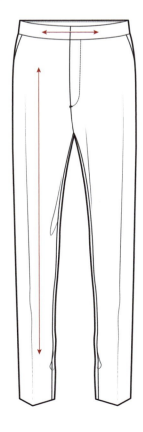

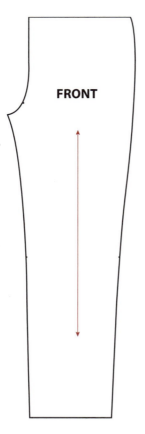

FRONT

Whether you are cutting a bias skirt, or a crossgrain waistband, or a straight grain pair of trousers, the directions for cutting are always the same. Every pattern piece should be placed on the fabric so that the arrow on the pattern is parallel to the lengthwise grain of the fabric.

To say that something is cut on the crossgrain, or on the bias, has less to do with the direction in which it is cut than it has to do with the direction in which it is worn.

The waistband and the trousers, have both been cut in the same direction. However, because the waistband will eventually be placed on the garment with the straight of the grain in a horizontal position, the waistband will be said to have been cut on the cross grain. And since the straight of the grain on the trousers will be in a vertical position, the trousers are said to have been cut on the straight grain.

The major pattern pieces of men's tailored garments are cut on the straight grain. And for various reasons, certain smaller pieces of each garment are cut on the crossgrain or on the bias.

Straightening the Grain

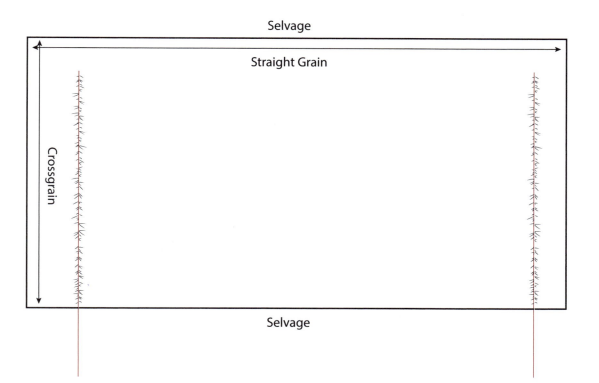

Selvage

Straight Grain

Crossgrain

Selvage

Somewhere from the loom to you, the fabric grain may have been distorted. Considering the importance the grain plays in the hang of your finished garment, it is essential to check the grain alignment before cutting the fabric. What we are doing is checking to see if the crosswise threads and the lengthwise threads are running at right angles or perpendicular to one another. If they are not, everything we have discussed about placing the arrows on the pattern parallel with the selvage, will be useless.

To check the grain alignment, pull a crosswise thread from selvage to selvage, across either end of your fabric. Do this at the very end of your fabric yardage, so that you do not waste fabric. The puckering along the pulled thread indicates the exact line of the crossgrain.

Cut the fabric along the puckered thread at either end.

Crossgrain

Straight Grain

Selvage

Fold the fabric selvage to selvage, right sides together. See if the fabric will lie comfortably in a perfect rectangle. If it will not, the crosswise and lengthwise threads are no longer running perpendicular. The fabric is off grain and must be coaxed back into place.

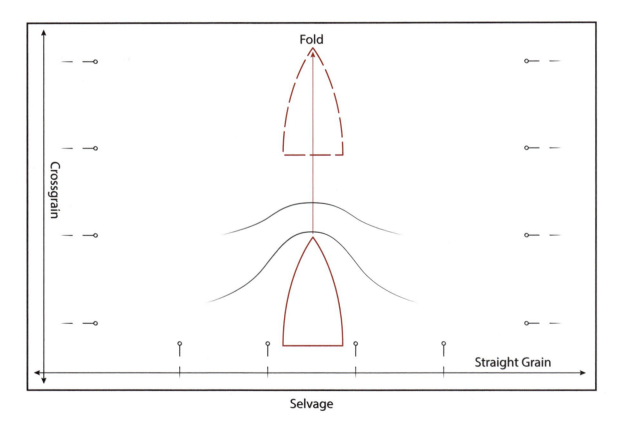

Fold

Crossgrain

Straight Grain

Selvage

To coax the fabric back into place, pin the folded fabric into the rectangular shape it should have. Steam press from selvage to fold, on the wrong side, until the ripples in the fabric disappear.

Washable fabrics which are off grain can be gently pulled back into shape while they are damp. This should be done on a flat surface, a small area at a time.

Shrinkage

Woven natural fibers are susceptible to shrinkage. All woven fabrics, which will become part of your garment such as the wool canvas **interfacing**, the twill tape, the pocketing, and the garment fabric itself, must be preshrunk. The French collar canvas and the haircloth used as stiffening, are exceptions.

Even if the label on the garment fabric says that it has been preshrunk, you are safer if, before cutting, you have the fabric steam-pressed and preshrunk professionally by a dry cleaner.

Shrink the wool canvas **interfacing** by soaking it in cool water for about one hour. Let it drip dry and then steam press well. The cotton twill tape can be soaked in cool water and ironed wet. It will not lose its shape. Pocketing fabric is sufficiently shrunk by simply steam pressing it well. The lining fabrics we have suggested will not shrink during dry-cleaning.

The Nap

When the garment fabric has been preshrunk, is on grain and ready to go, run your hand lightly over the fabric, on the straight grain, first in one direction, then in the other. If the fabric feels the same in both directions, it has *no* discernible nap. If there is even the slightest difference to the touch, the fabric has a nap, and the direction of the nap is the direction in which the fabric feels smoother.

The direction of the nap is the direction in which short fibers on the surface of the fabric have been brushed. It is not important that these fibers feel different in one direction than in the other. What is important is that they reflect light differently. Therefore, the fabric will have a different color shading when it is held up in one direction than in the other.

The difference in color shading due to nap is often slight, and not easily discernible while you are working with the fabric flat on the table. If you ignore the nap and (for example) cut the jacket body with the nap down and the sleeves with the nap up, from across the room it may look as if you have cut the sleeves from completely different fabric.

The simplest way to avoid such problems is to determine the direction of the nap before you lay out your pattern pieces; to draw arrows on the fabric indicating the direction of the nap (the direction in which the fabric feels smoother): and to cut the pattern so that the nap on all pieces of the finished garment falls in the same direction.

Most fabrics are cut with the nap down. Cut this way, the fabric feels smoother if you run your hand downwards on the front of the jacket, than it does if you run your hand upwards. It's the same principle as petting a cat from the front to back.

Velvet is sometimes cut with the nap up, because the deep pile catches the light best that way, and gives the fabric a richer color.

If the nap is so slight that you have difficulty in determining which direction is smoother, simply choose a direction, and mark arrows to that effect on the fabric. It is less important to have the direction of the nap correct than it is to cut all the pattern pieces consistently, in whatever direction you have chosen.

5 LAYOUT AND CUTTING

Most students with limited tailoring experience are unaware of the fact that professional tailors do not use tissue paper patterns. They are just too unwieldy.

The only positive quality about a tissue paper pattern seems to be that it fits neatly, or not so neatly, into a pattern envelope. On the negative side, it wrinkles, it tears and it flies away far too easily.

Tailors make their own patterns on sturdy paper or on oaktag. The oaktag pattern can be laid in place on the fabric, weighed down rather than pinned, and traced with tailor's chalk. Small holes are made in the oaktag pattern through which dart tips and pocket points can be marked. Notches are cut into the edge of the pattern at **waistline**, hemline, roll line, etc. When not in use, the patterns are hung neatly on pattern hooks.

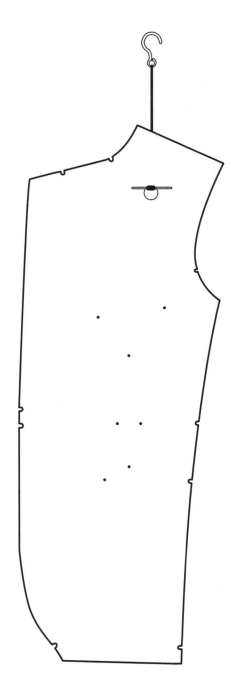

Except when cutting the sheerest dress fabrics, this method of pattern layout is faster and more accurate because it eliminates pinning the pattern to the fabric. Besides being time-consuming, the process of pinning disrupts the lay of the fabric, making it very difficult to cut the two layers of fabric identically.

If you simply don't have the patience to transfer your pattern onto oaktag at the moment, you can still avoid pinning the pattern to the fabric by weighing down the tissue pattern. Tracing will not be quite as speedy without the stiff pattern edge to guide the chalk, but it will still be more accurate, and easier than pinning.

We strongly recommend you choose the oaktag method, especially for patterns that you use over and over again.

For your first few tailoring projects, we suggest that you purchase more fabric than your pattern requires, to allow for a few small errors in judgment and skill, pocket flaps, etc.

For the jacket, lay out your main pattern pieces: the front, back, side panel, **facing** (make sure this is the revised **facing** on page 26), and sleeve. The sleeve should be traced onto the fabric along with the other main pattern pieces, as a reminder of its presence, and its demands on the fabric. However, we will not cut the sleeve until much later, when the jacket is almost completed. Until you are familiar with the construction techniques, the pockets and the collar should be cut only as you need them, following the instructions in each section.

Do the same with your trouser and vest patterns. Set to work with only the front of your vest cut, and the front and back of your trousers. Cut the facings, and pockets and waistband as you work along with the book.

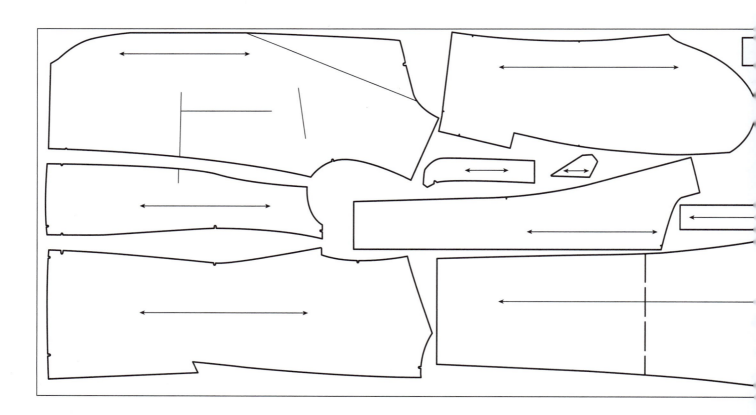

Of course, cutting everything at once allows for the most economical use of your fabric, and many tailors develop this skill to a fine art. The illustration shows a professional, nap layout of a size 40, three-piece suit. It makes good business sense as well as a good challenge to plan your work as tightly as it is illustrated here. It also takes experience.

With your fabric well prepared (preshrunk, pressed, on grain and marked for nap), lay out your main pattern pieces. Use a nap layout unless you have a good reason not to (too little fabric). It is always safer to use a nap layout especially with wool, since slight color shading may be discernible in the sunlight, and not in your workroom. Lay your pattern pieces with great respect for the fabric grain. The grain arrows on each pattern piece should be exactly parallel with the selvage. Measure to check the accuracy of your eye.

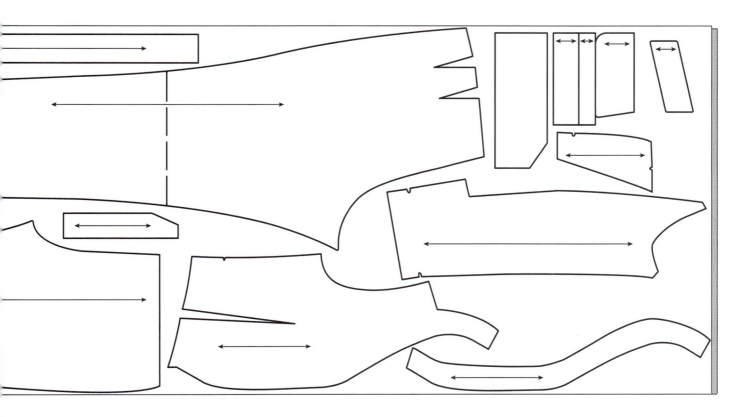

With sharpened, clay tailor's chalk, the process of tracing around each pattern piece is easily and accurately done. Sharpen the chalk, so that you can produce a thin, clean line without the necessity of pressing heavily on the chalk and the fabric. Applying pressure to the chalk instead of sharpening it, produces a thick, undetermined line, and may even disturb the lay of the fabric.

We suggest clay tailor's chalk, rather than chalk with a wax content, because with chalk you can freely mark on the right side of your fabric without ever worrying that the marks will be permanent. The clay chalklines can be brushed away easily when they are no longer needed. Pressing on top of the clay chalklines is not suggested, since this will render the marks more difficult (though not impossible) to remove.

Trace around the jacket front pattern piece indicating all notches, including the **waistline**, the collar notch, the top and bottom of the **lapel** roll line, and the front armhole notch.

Mark the dart tips and the ends of the pocket placement lines, by scratching the chalk and letting the chalk dust settle through the holes in the pattern.

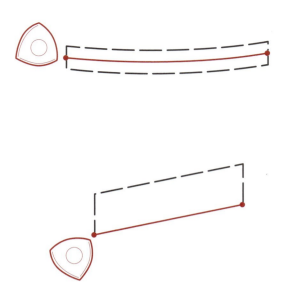
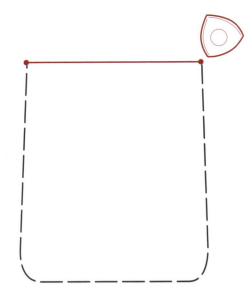

The pocket placement line for a double-piping pocket is the center line, for a **welt** pocket, it is the bottom line, and for a patch pocket, the pocket placement line is at the top.

Remove the pattern and cut the fabric, indicating border notches by a snip into the seam allowance (no deeper than ⅛" (3mm)).

The best scissors to use for cutting double layers of fabric are bent-handle shears. The bottom blade can rest on the table as the fabric is being cut. The blade is in a position to slide along with minimal disruption of the fabric.

Resist the urge to pull the fabric towards you as you cut. Any such movement might ruin your careful grainline efforts.

After each pattern piece has been cut, the chalk guidelines are preserved by tailor tacking.

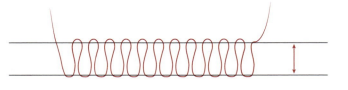

Tailor tacking is simply a running stitch through two layers of fabric, which leaves loops of extra thread on the top layer (as illustrated).

When the two layers of fabric are separated, the excess thread is shifted to the inside.

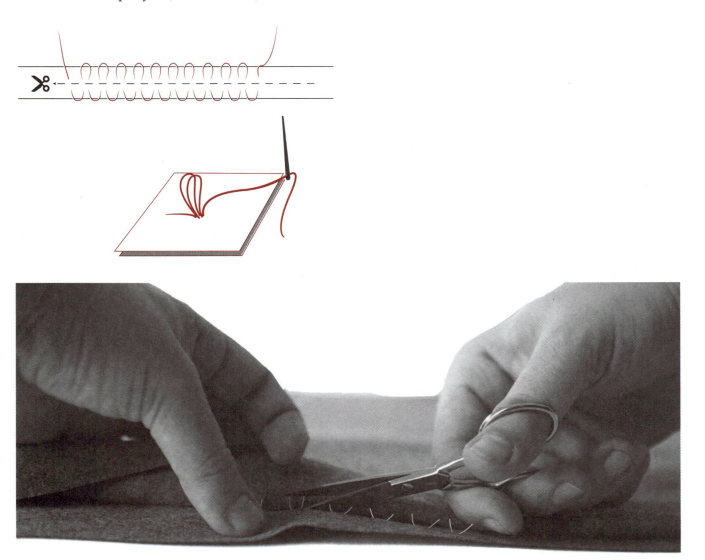

Snipping the thread down the center creates the thread markers – neat loops on the wrong side of the fabric, and hair like protrusions on the right side.

To tailor tack points or ends rather than lines, two stitches are taken on top of each other, leaving the loose thread loop on the top layer of fabric.

Dart tips and the ends of each pocket are point-tacked in this way.

Chalkmark the hemline and roll line. Tailor tack the full length of the hem, and only the beginning and end of the roll line.

The procedure for cutting pants is essentially the same as for cutting the jacket. The grain of the fabric is vital, and all pertinent pattern information should be tailor-tacked into the fabric. The short time spent on tailor tacking now will save hours of guessing and correcting later on.

The procedure for marking the vest front pattern is slightly different. Because a layer of fusible material will be applied to the wrong side of the vest front, the pattern information should be chalkmarked on the right side of the fabric, rather than preserved by tailor tacking. Threads caught in the fusible would be very difficult to remove.

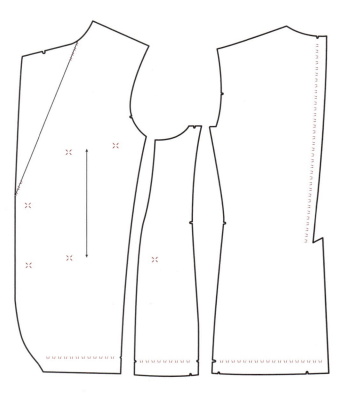

PLAIDS OR STRIPES

Sleeves

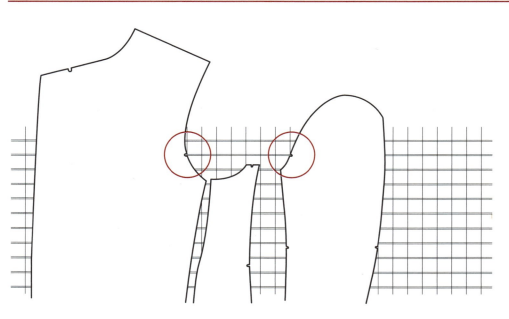

The layout for a plaid or striped fabric requires added attention.

The horizontal lines at the top of the sleeve front should match those on the body of the jacket. Place the notch on the top sleeve pattern and the front notch on the armhole at identical points on the plaid design. (See page 197.)

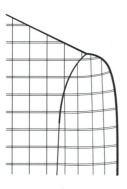

Facing

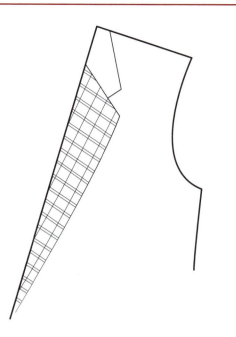

The outer edge of the **lapel** on the **facing** should be on the straight of the grain, between two prominent vertical stripes. The stripe should run the whole length of the **lapel**, without veering off along the way.

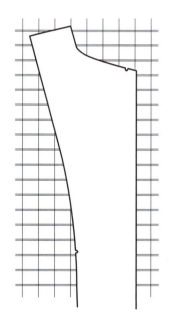

Place the revised facing pattern (page 26) so that the notch at the top of the **lapel** falls between two prominent vertical stripes. The **facing** on a plaid or striped jacket should be applied by hand (page 146) rather than by machine, for the most control in matching the lines.

Back Neck and Collar

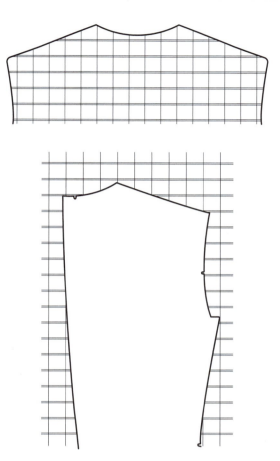

The center back seam, at the neck edge, should not interrupt the pattern of the plaid.

Place the stitchline of the center back neck edge at the very center between two vertical stripes on the plaid.

The collar, viewed from the back, should not create any interruption in the plaid design of the jacket back.

Therefore, the topcollar, which is cut after the undercollar is set, should be attached to the undercollar with an eye to continuing both the horizontal and vertical design lines present on the back of the jacket. (See page 181.)

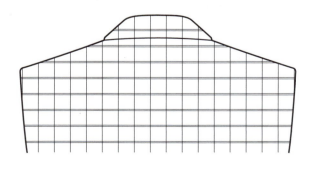

Jacket Front

The seamline at the straight part of the jacket front, below the **lapel**, should not fall on a prominent vertical stripe. (This also applies to the straight part of the vest front seamline.)

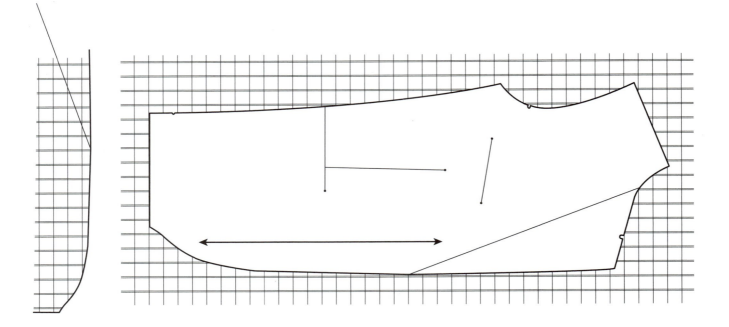

Place the straight portions of the jacket (and vest) front patterns on the plaid so that the stitchline falls between two prominent vertical stripes.

Jacket Seams

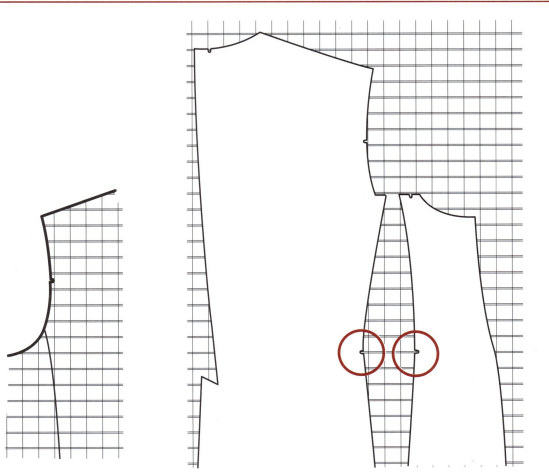

All horizontal bars in a plaid must match at the seamlines.

Place the notches of all seams, which will be joined, at identical points on the plaid design.

Jacket Hem

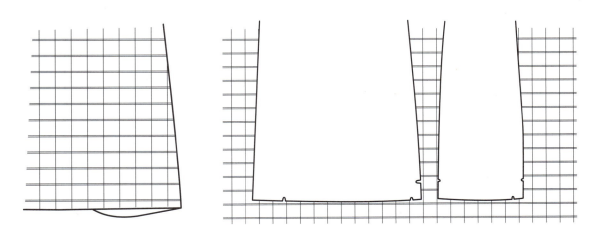

The hem foldline on the jacket should not fall on a prominent horizontal stripe.

Place the hem foldline of the jacket front, back and side panel midway between two prominent horizontal stripes.

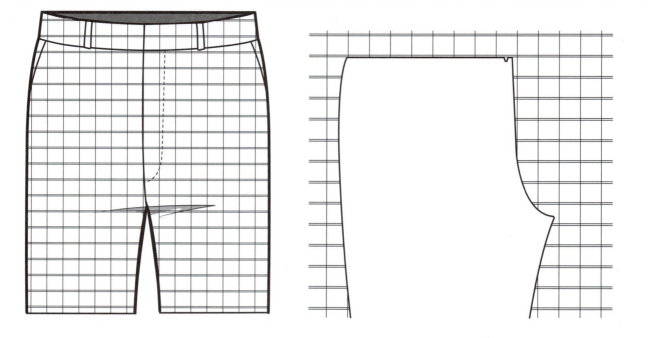

The fold at the top of the pants fly should be between two prominent vertical stripes. Place the notch at the center front **waistline** between two prominent vertical stripes.

The information needed for constructing pockets on a plaid or stripe fabric is discussed with the individual pocket directions.

6 | THE JACKET

DARTS AND SEAMS

If there is a dart on the jacket, at this point in your tailoring procedure it is indicated by four tailor tacks.

On the wrong side of the fabric, draw a chalkline from top to bottom at the center of the dart.

On one side of the dart, draw a slightly curved line from the top of the dart to **waist**, and from **waist** to bottom of the dart. Use the hip curve to taper line gradually into the dart ends. An abrupt curve at the dart ends will create puckering on the right side of the fabric which will be impossible to press out.

Remove the tailor tacks and press the dart in half, using the center chalkline as foldline.

Machine stitch the dart from top to bottom. Sewing the fabric in the direction of the nap is an added courtesy to the fabric. In velvet or pile fabrics, it is an absolute necessity.

It is better to tie the threads at the dart ends, rather than backstitching to tack. Backstitching adds unwanted bulk and stiffness into the delicately thin area of the dart tips.

Slit the dart on the center chalkline, beginning and ending the slit ½" (1.3 cm) away from top and bottom. Press the dart open using a tailor's ham.

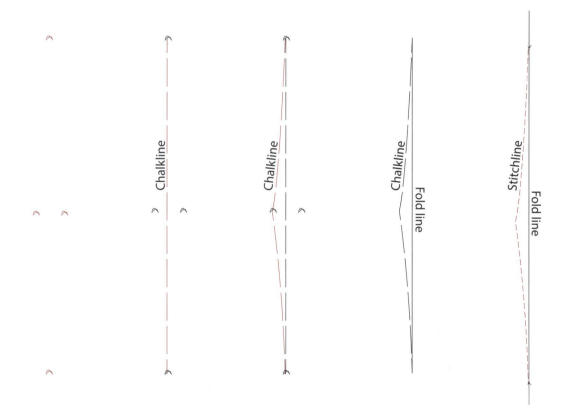

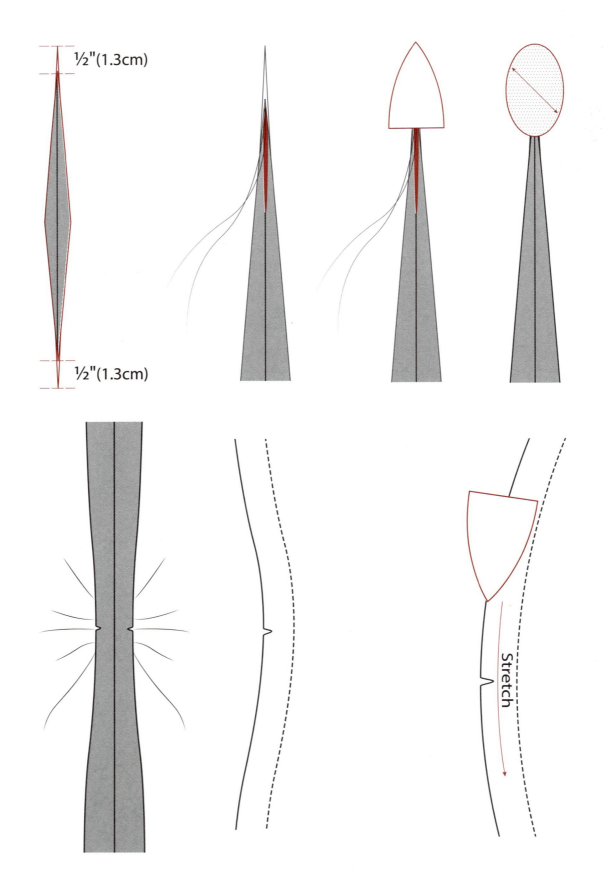

½"(1.3cm)

½"(1.3cm)

Stretch

The fabric at the dart tip is somewhat difficult to control, since it may pull to one side rather than allowing itself to be pressed flat at the center. When this happens, it becomes obvious on the front of the jacket by a slight wavering of the dart seamline, instead of a perfectly straight seamline, at the dart tip.

Before pressing, control the fabric at the dart tip by inserting the eye end of a threaded needle as far into the dart tip as it will go. This will hold the seamline straight as you press the dart seam allowance flat in the center. Remove the needle (by the thread, the needle is hot), and press the dart tip flat once more. On the front of the jacket, the dart line should now be perfectly straight.

A bias-cut, oval-shaped, very lightweight, nonwoven fusible can be used to reinforce the dart tip and maintain the fabric's body in this area. Use only a fusible which presents no competition in weight with the garment fabric. Try a sample on a fabric scrap. If there is any indication of the fusible from the right side of the fabric, it is too heavy. If in doubt, leave it out.

Baste and sew your side panel to the jacket front, matching notches, and press the seam open. If the jacket has significant **waistline** shaping, there will be some constriction in the **waistline** area at the seam. Stretch the seam allowance in the **waistline** area by steam pressing it into a curve opposite to its shape. When the seam allowance is then pressed open, the constriction will have been relieved.

Slashing the seam allowance at the **waist** to relieve this tightness weakens the garment unnecessarily in this area, and it's always wise to keep seam allowances intact for possible future alterations.

Gently press the jacket front from the wrong side. You are now ready for the construction of the jacket pockets.

IRONWORKING THE JACKET

Traditional tailoring is much more complex than just sewing flat pieces of fabric. The value of all the hand sewing we will undertake can be lost if we do not shape our fabric pieces first. The craft of tailoring rests in the way the tailor will manipulate, shape and form the cloth with a

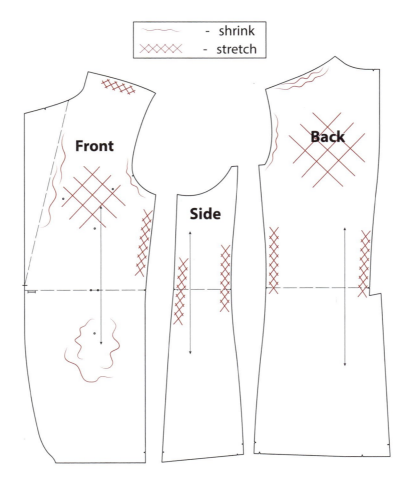

multitude of techniques, the most important of which is iron work. Ironworking the cloth involves careful use of heat, steam and pressure, to stretch and shrink the fabric at specific places on the garment. This creates a curved, three-dimensional object, instead of a flat surface, which will fit much more elegantly and comfortably over the client's body.

Shrinking and stretching the fabric in the areas indicated above will result in a fuller **chest** and shoulder blade area, a more comfortably-fitting armhole, a gracefully concave shoulder with ample room to accommodate the protruding collar bone, and flat and inconspicuous seam allowances and fabric inlays.

As mentioned in the previous section, seam allowances can be stretched once the seams have been sewn, although tailors often find it preferable to preemptively address this problem by stretching the **waist** seam allowances and fabric inlays that will require this treatment before sewing them together.

Front

Before starting to work on the **chest** area, it is important to reduce any excessive volume caused at the hip if your pattern has a double-ended dart.

This is done by shrinking the area, using steam liberally, and moving the iron on the cloth in increasingly small concentric arcs.

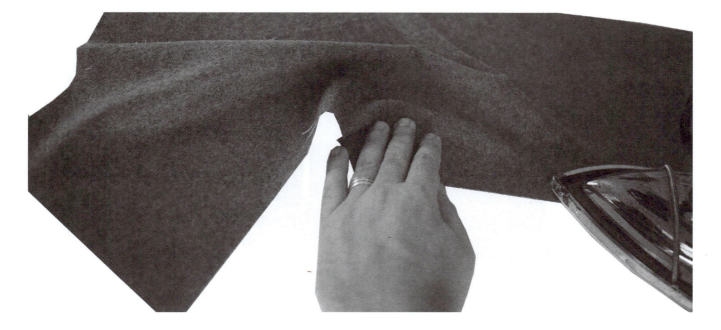

Working on the jacket front, start just under the **waist** level, at the sideseam, and stretch the

concave section of the seam allowance working upwards towards the armhole.

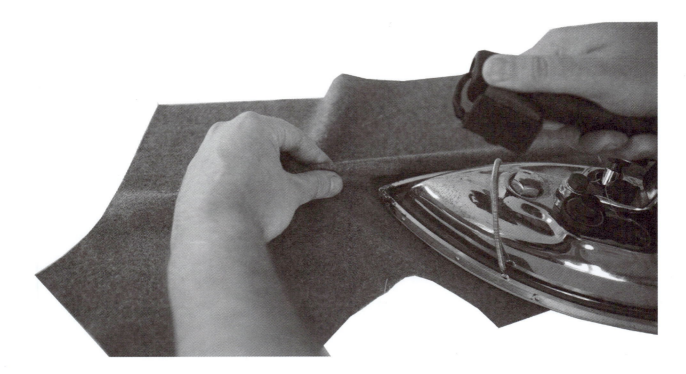

From the **waist** allowance, on the front, bring the iron to stretch the fabric in the **chest** area. As you

bring the iron towards the **chest**, use your free hand to hold the **chest** fullness.

The stretching of the **chest** area can result in unnecessary lengthening at the front armhole as well. To remedy this problem, shrink the unnecessary length out of the armhole, using steam and pressure liberally. Shrinking the lower portion of the armhole will help further define the volume you created on the **chest**. Allow the iron to rest over this area for a short while, to preserve the shape created.

Lift the iron and bring it to the center front, at **waist** level. As you move the iron towards the **chest**, following a diagonal line somewhat parallel to the **lapel** roll line, gently stretch the fabric ahead of the iron with your free hand.

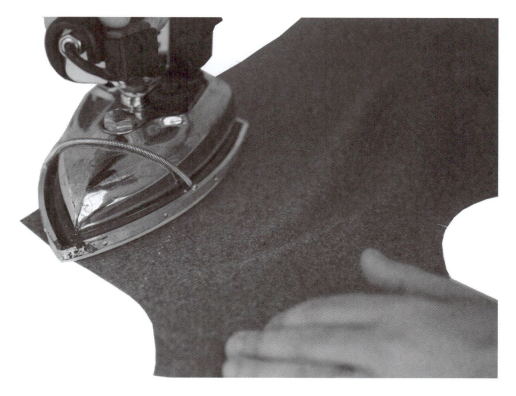

The **lapel** is then pressed flat on the table, reducing any additional stretching that may have occurred when ironworking the **chest** area.

The front of the shoulder also needs to be stretched in order to create the gently concave shape tailors and discerning customers will look for in the shoulder line. This is done by stretching the **gorge** line between the collar notch and the shoulder seam. This added length is then pressed to the middle of the shoulder. If using a striped cloth, be careful to correct any overly aggressive distortions you may have caused in the stripe pattern.

Once ironwork is completed on the front panel, we can check its effectiveness by laying the entire front panel on a flat surface. It will be obvious that, while the hip volume has been reduced, the **chest** area presents ample **ease**, which will give graceful form to the finished garment.

Side

The side panel does not usually require much ironwork. Commonly, the side panel will only see its concave seam allowances and inlays stretched, in order to avoid causing tension lines and puckering in the completed garment.

Back Panel

The back panel will also require some ironwork, although not as pronounced as on the front. The purpose of this is to generate additional room for the shoulder blade, while reducing unnecessary fabric length in the shoulder area.

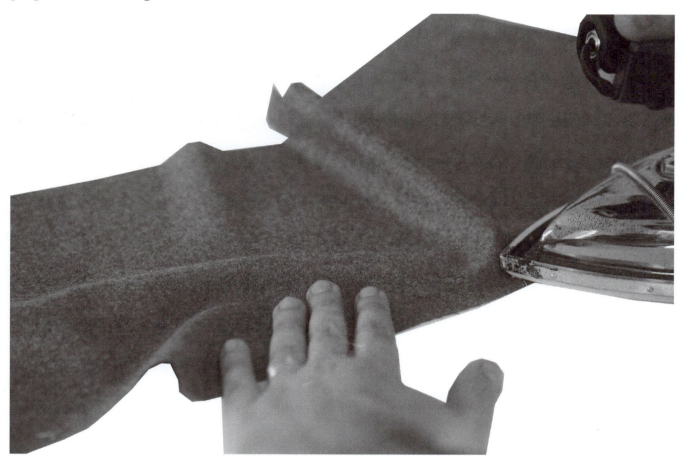

As with all other panels, inlays and seam allowances are stretched to allow them to lay without obstruction to the finished garment. Start below the **waist**, on the side seam, and stretch the seam allowance as you move upwards.

In a manner similar to the one we used to stretch the **chest** area, draw the iron across to the shoulder blade, moving the extra fullness ahead of the iron with your free hand. The stretching of the seam allowance and blade area is repeated, this time starting below the **waist** on the center back seam.

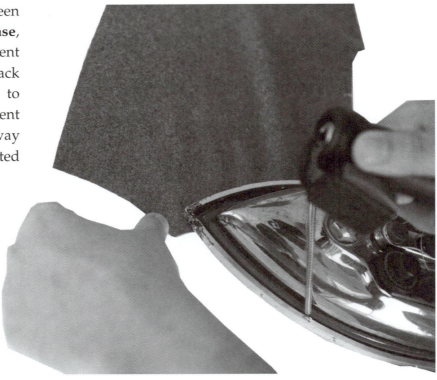

Once the shoulder blade has been given the necessary additional **ease**, shrink the additional length present along the back shoulder and the back armhole. Do not allow the iron to extend more than 1" on the garment piece, so as to avoid shrinking away the added volume we just created through the ironworking process.

THE JACKET POCKETS

The most popular types of jacket pockets are:

- **Welt** Pocket;
- Double-Piping Pocket;
- Double-Piping Pocket with **Flap**; and
- Patch Pocket.

The construction of these pockets is presented here in great detail. Therefore, you need not limit yourself to the style of the pocket given on your commercial pattern. Feel free to substitute a double-piping pocket for a patch pocket, or to add a **flap** if you wish. The only guidelines seem to be that patch pockets are usually restricted to casual wear, and that the **welt** pocket on men's jackets is generally used only as a breast pocket and not at hip level.

The perfection of the pocket construction says much about the skill of the tailor. Because of the prominent position of the pockets on the front of the jacket, any distortion in the pocket line will call attention to itself, and detract from the overall beauty of the jacket. We suggest that you practice the pocket construction on a fabric scrap before constructing them in your jacket fabric.

The Welt Pocket

The breast **welt** pocket is 4½" (11.4 cm) long and about 1" (2.5 cm) wide, placed on the left side of the jacket at approximately the level of the front

sleeve notch. The placement line is usually on a ½" (1.3 cm) slant, lower right to upper left when the jacket is worn.

Chalkmark the placement line on the jacket front. If you have adjusted your pattern at the front armhole, check to see that the pocket placement line is at least 1½" (3.8 cm) away from the armhole stitchline.

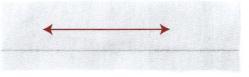

Cut a piece of woven fusible, on the crossgrain, 4½" (11.4 cm) by 1⅜" (3.5 cm). Draw a ⅜" (1 cm) margin along the bottom edge on the unglued side. This line will eventually be the stitchline for attaching the **welt** to the jacket.

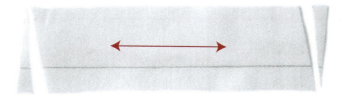

Trim away ¼" (6 mm) diagonals from the upper right and lower left of the rectangle. This will create the slant for the **welt**.

Press the fusible to the wrong side of a piece of the garment fabric, leaving ⅜" (1 cm) fabric at each side and ⅝" (1.6 cm) at the top. It is important that the side of the fusible be parallel with the straight grain on the garment fabric, and that the nap be down.

Cut two pieces of pocketing, 6" (15.2 cm) by 6" (15.2 cm) on the straight grain, and cut a ½" (1.3 cm) diagonal off the top of each piece.

Use a ¼" (6 mm) seam to sew the top edge of the garment fabric to the top of the pocketing, and press the seam open.

Fold the garment fabric, using the top edge of the fusible as a guideline.

At either end of the fusible, baste the **welt** to the pocketing, easing the **welt** slightly towards the center. This easing creates a slight bulge in the **welt**, which will ensure that the pocketing edges will be hidden when the **welt** is turned to the right side.

Machine-stitch just beyond the edge of the fusible. Tack the top, but not the bottom of each stitchline.

Press the seams open and turn the **welt** to the right side.

Slash the pocket to the bottom of the stitchlines. Trim the seam allowances to ¼" (6 mm) and trim the top corners.

To assist in turning the corners, take one stitch and gently pull both ends of the thread. This is a safer procedure than poking the corners from the inside with the point of the scissors. Press the **welt** on the right side.

Carefully open the **welt** seam just enough to expose the stitchline which is drawn on the fusible.

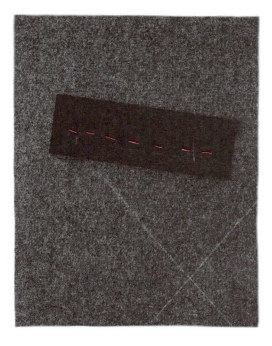

Place the **welt** face down on the jacket front, matching the stitchline which is drawn on the fusible with the placement line drawn on the jacket. Don't be concerned if you notice that the **welt** is upside down at this point; it should be.

Baste, and then machine stitch the **welt** to the jacket, tacking well at either end.

Cut a piece of pocketing 2″ (5 cm) by 6″ (15.2 cm) on the straight grain, and place it on the wrong side of the jacket. The lower edge of the pocketing should fall about ½″ (1.3 cm) below the **welt** placement line which is drawn on the jacket front. Baste or pin the pocketing in place. This piece of pocketing is called a reinforcement since its purpose is to strengthen the fabric in the area in which we will be working.

Trim corners of the **welt** seam allowance.

 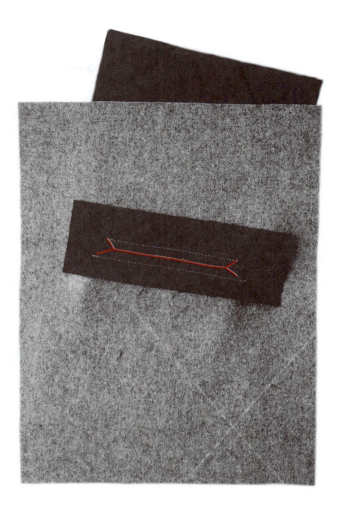

Insert the second piece of pocketing under the **welt** seam allowance and stitch on the pocketing, very close to the **welt** seam allowance. This stitchline should be about ⅜" (1 cm) shorter that the **welt** stitchline at either end. Tack well at either end.

From the wrong side of the jacket the two stitchlines will be clearly visible on the reinforcement. Begin at the center and slash through the reinforcement and the jacket fabric, directly between the two stitchlines. While you are cutting, hold the **welt** seam allowance and the pocketing safely out of the way. Cut prongs about ⅜" (1 cm) long at each end. Slash very close to the last stitch on each line, but not close enough to cut the threads. Cutting the prongs correctly is a simple, but essential step in the construction of a perfect pocket.

If the prongs, especially at the bottom, are not snipped directly to the last stitch, your pocket corners will pucker.

If, however, the cut overshoots the last stitch, you will have a hole on the front of your jacket at the ends of the pocket. Avoid any puckers and holes by simply giving this step your full attention.

On the front of the jacket, the **welt** should now be sitting upright. Baste the pocket closed.

Reach through the opening and pull the pocketing to the wrong side. Press open the seam that attaches the **welt** to the jacket.

The sides of the **welt** are attached to the jacket by a diagonal handstitch from the wrong side. The stitches should not be visible on the outside.

Machine-stitch the pocketing pieces together, and trim the seam allowance. Do not trim the reinforcement piece. It will be used later for attachment to the canvas.

You may wish to add a decorative bartack at either end of the top of the **welt**. If you wax the buttonhole twist thread and press it between two pieces of paper, the wax will melt into the thread and give it a better body. Take one stitch at either end of the **welt**, and anchor the stitch on the inside. The **welt** pocket is complete.

Welt Pocket (Plaids/Stripes)

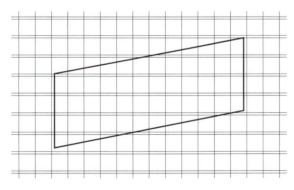

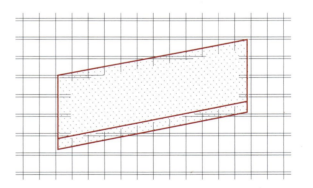

Because there are no darts or seams in the area of the breast **welt** pocket, the plaid or stripe should be able to run uninterrupted from the jacket, through the **welt**, both vertically and horizontally.

The best way to guarantee an accurate match of fabric is to draw the plaid design on the fusible, during the construction of the **welt** (page 93).

Place the trimmed fusible, glue side up, on the jacket front, with the **welt** stitchline at the pocket placement line. Draw the plaid design lines on the edges of the fusible.

Place the marked fusible, glue side down, on the wrong side of a piece of garment fabric, matching the plaid. Be sure to match the plaid at the sides of the **welt**, as well as at top and bottom.

The Double-Piping Pocket

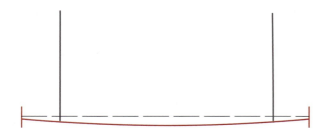 

The double-piping pocket on a man's jacket is approximately 5¾" (14.6 cm) to 6" (15.2 cm) long. The visible **piping** is ¼" (6 mm) at top and bottom.

Draw the pocket placement line on the jacket front using the hip curve. A slight curve, less than

⅛" (3 mm) deep at center, will be almost imperceptible in the finished pocket, but will help prevent the pocket from gaping open when not in use. Remove the tailor tacks at either end of the pocket placement line and chalkmark the ends.

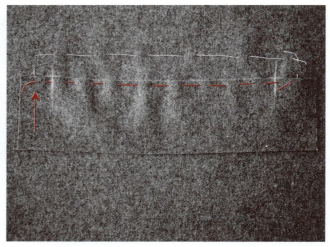

For each pocket cut two pieces of garment fabric to be used as **piping**; one 8" (20.3 cm) by 1½" (3.8 cm), the other 8" (20.3 cm) by 2" (5 cm), straight grain, nap down.

Cut a piece of pocketing to be used as reinforcement, 8" by 2½" (20.3 by 6.4 cm), straight grain. On the wrong side of the fabric, center the reinforcement along the pocket placement line. Baste or pin in place.

Place the wider piece of **piping** face down on the jacket front, nap up. The top edge of the **piping** should be flush with the placement line. Baste very close to the edge, catching the **piping**, the jacket, and the reinforcement. Because the placement line is on a slight curve, some rippling will appear at the center of the **piping**. Chalkmark on the piping, indicating either end of the pocket placement line.

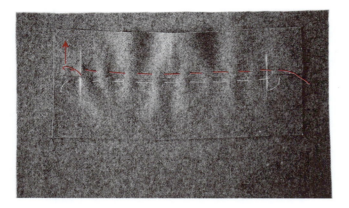

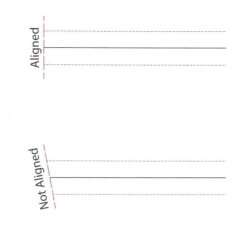

Place the second piece of piping face down on the jacket front, nap up, the edges of both pieces of piping touching. Baste very close to the edge.

Chalkmark on the top piping indicating either end of the pocket placement line.

Steam press the piping on the flat surface to eliminate the rippling in the **piping**.

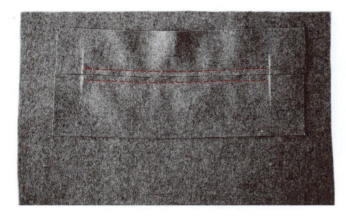

Machine-stitch the **piping** to the jacket ¼" (6 mm) above and below the placement line. These stitchlines should not be exactly parallel. The center of each stitchline should be slightly closer to the placement line than the ends are. Refer to the illustration as your guide for what we mean by "slightly." This contour of the line will not be visible in the finished pocket, and will help prevent the pocket from gaping open when not in use.

It is very important that the ends of the two stitchlines be directly aligned. If they are not, the sides of the finished pocket will slant rather than stand straight, and the whole effect will be unprofessional.

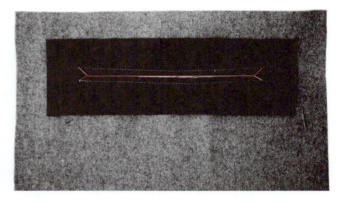

Working on the wrong side of the jacket, begin at the center and slash through the reinforcement and the garment fabric. Be careful to hold back the **piping** to that it is not snipped in the process.

Cut ⅜" (1 cm) prongs at either end of the slash, snipping as close as possible to the last stitch in either line. It is very important to slash correctly here.

If the prong is not snipped up to the last stitch, there will be puckering on the right side of the jacket at either end of the pocket.

If, on the other hand, the slash overshoots the last stitch, you will have a hole on the front of your jacket at the ends of the pocket. Avoid the puckers and the hole by simply giving this step your full attention.

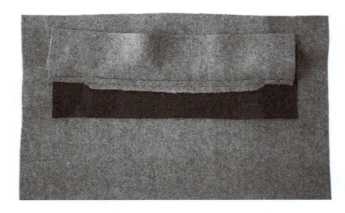

Pull the **piping** to the wrong side and press the seams open.

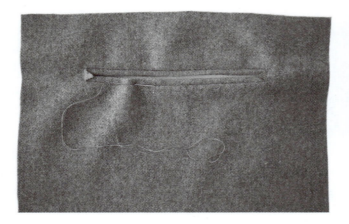

Using the seam allowance as a guide, and ignoring the prongs for the moment, backstitch by hand in the **piping** seam, using silk finishing thread. The **piping** must be kept even on top and bottom, and the stitches should not be seen.

The pocket is now steam pressed on the right side using a ham and covering the fabric with a presscloth.

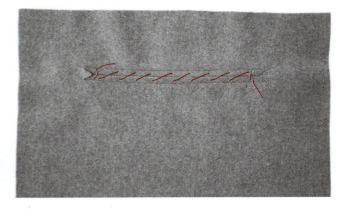

Whip-stitch the **piping** closed so that it will not shift while we attend to the prongs.

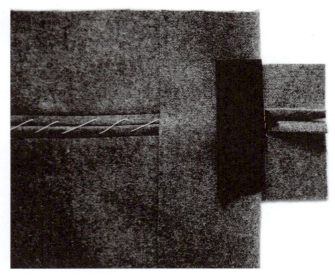

Push the prong to the wrong side and hold it so that the end of the pocket is a straight line, not a slanted one. Backstitching the prong to the **piping** by hand can provide greater control, but also be very challenging due to the small work area. Alternatively to hand stitching, you can secure the prongs by using a small machine stitch. Be very careful to start and stop this stitch *exactly* at the end of the prong.

Cut a piece of pocketing, straight grain, 8″ (20.3 cm) wide and 2″ (5 cm) longer than twice the depth of the pocket. The pocket depth varies with the length of the jacket, but the pocketing should extend no lower than about 1″ (2.5 cm) above the top of the finished jacket hem.

Cut a piece of garment fabric to be used as **facing**, straight grain, nap down, 2″ (5 cm) by 8″ (20.3 cm). Topstitch a folded edge of the **facing** to the top of the pocketing, leaving about ½″ (1.3 cm) pocketing above the **facing**.

With the **facing** placed on the wrong side of the jacket, sew the bottom edge of the pocketing to the edge of the bottom **piping**. Use a ¼″ (6 mm) seam.

Pull the pocketing down and thumbnail press the seam. Match the top edges of the pocketing and the top **piping**.

Machine-stitch on the reinforcement as close as possible to the garment fabric. Stitch the length of the pocket opening, pivot to catch the prong area, and continue out and around the pocketing.

Trim the seam allowance, but not the reinforcement. Layer the fabric above the top stitchline and snip away the excess fabric in the seam allowances to reduce the bulk.

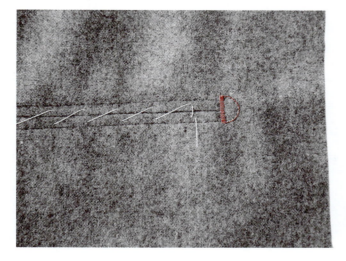

If you wish, bartack one stitch at either end of the pocket, using silk buttonhole twist. If you wax the buttonhole twist and press it between two pieces of paper, the wax will melt into the twist and give it a better body.

Many custom tailors will choose to use a D-tack instead of a bartack, as it provides better control for the edges of the pocket opening as well as the prongs.

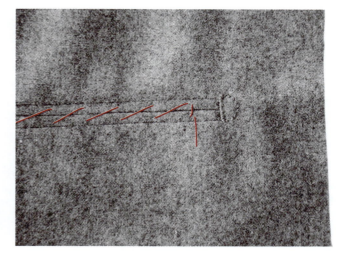

The pocket remains basted closed until the jacket is ready to be worn.

Steam press the finished pocket on the right side of the fabric, using a ham and a presscloth.

The Double-Piping Pocket (Plaids/Stripes)

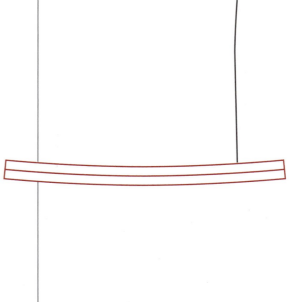

In almost all instances, two seams cut into the top of a hip-level, double-piping pocket – the front dart and the side panel seams. Depending on the pattern, either one seam or no seam will continue below the pocket.

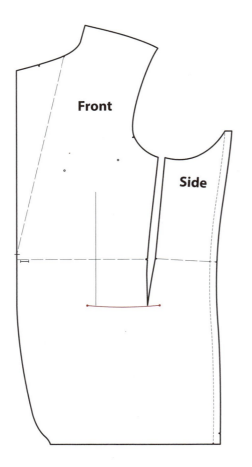

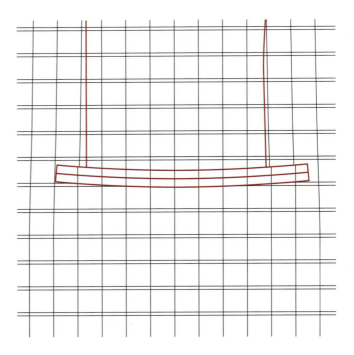

The best pattern to use for a plaid or striped fabric is one which eliminates the seam below the pocket by using a dart instead of a separate side panel. The plaid below the pocket is then undisturbed by seamlines. Above the pocket, you can't avoid seams if proper shaping is to be achieved.

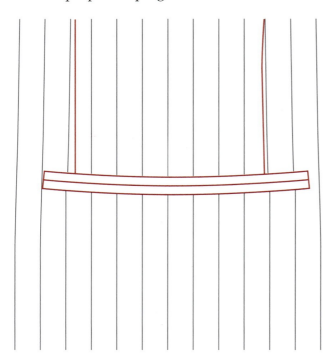

In a striped fabric, cut the **piping** on the crossgrain and place it on the jacket so that the visible **piping** falls between the stripes, in the solid area of the fabric. Cutting the **piping** in this way avoids the question of matching a stripe on the **piping** with a stripe on the jacket.

On a plaid fabric, the vertical matching cannot be avoided. You can, however, cut the **piping** to eliminate any horizontal lines on the finished pocket.

Cut the **piping** on the straight grain, and match the plaid lines at the center of the pocket. The plaid on the jacket at the end of the pocket will have been slightly distorted by the darts. Simply match the **piping** at the center, and ignore the slight mismatch at the ends of the pocket. Even the most expensive custom-tailored plaid jackets are not matched at the end of the pocket.

We do not suggest cutting the **piping** on the bias. This would avoid the matching problem by introducing a completely different line, but it would also leave us with bias, stretchable **piping** which would cause the pocket to gape open.

The Cash Pocket

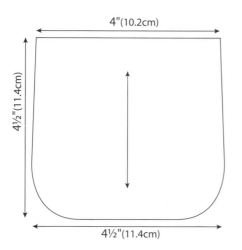

Once you are familiar with the construction of the double-piping pocket, it is simple to add, during construction, a smaller inner pocket, used most commonly for loose change – a cash pocket.

In addition to the fabric needed for the double-piping pocket, you will need a piece of pocketing, straight grain, 4" (10.2 cm) by 4½" (11.4 cm) by 4½" (11.4 cm), rounded slightly at the bottom edges.

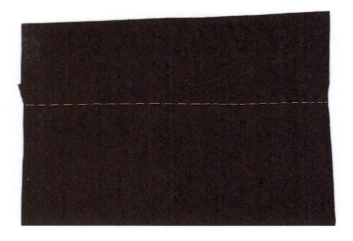

Press the seam open. Fold the bottom seam allowance under, and topstitch it in place.

Cut about 2½" (6.4 cm) from the top of the main piece of pocketing, and then stitch the pieces together, using a ⅜" (1 cm) seam.

The garment fabric **facing** is now placed on the right side of the pocketing. Place the folded edge of the **facing** along the pocketing seamline, and topstitch the **facing**.

If there is a **flap** on the double-piping pocket you are making, there will be no **facing**. In this case, simply topstitch just above the seamline, holding the top seam allowance in place.

Place the cash pocket fabric on the wrong side of the pocketing, with the top edge of the cash pocket just above the top seam allowance. Stitch around the edge of the cash pocket using a ⅜″ (1 cm) seam.

The seam at the top edge of the cash pocket is now snipped open to allow access, and the construction of the cash pocket is complete.

The construction of the double-piping pocket now continues.

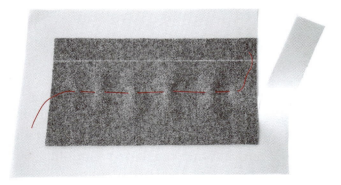

To make a pattern for the **flap**, draw a rectangle equal to the dimensions of the finished **flap**. For a 6″ (15.2 cm) pocket opening, this would be 6⅛″ (15.6 cm) by 2½″ (6.4 cm). At the lower right corner, extend the rectangle by ¼″ (6 mm). Add ¾″ (1.9 cm) seam allowance at the top edge and ¼″ (6 mm) around the three sides. Use this pattern to cut **flap**s from your garment fabric, straight grain, nap down.

The **flap** added to the double-piping pocket is about 2½″ (6.4 cm) wide, finished. A **flap** which extends out slightly at the lower back edge compensates for the contour of the body and is more graceful than a perfect rectangle.

The top edge of the **flap** should be ⅛″ (3 mm) larger (a slight ⅛″) than the opening of the pocket into which it will be placed. The extra **ease** is taken by the body contour, and allows the **flap** to fall comfortably. It is easier to be accurate concerning the amount of **ease** in the **flap** if you make the **flap** first, and then the pocket.

Baste the **flap** face down on the right side of a piece of lining, straight grain. Trim the lining even with the **flap**.

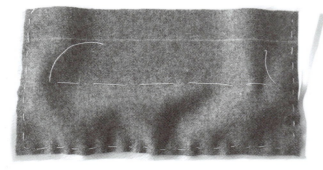

Baste around the **flap** close to the edge easing the garment fabric in from the lining about ⅛″ (3 mm). This will make the lining slightly smaller than the **flap**, and will ensure that the lining will not show at the edges of the finished **flap**. Trim the excess lining.

For a crisp finish, prick-stitch along the edge of the **flap** using silk finishing thread.

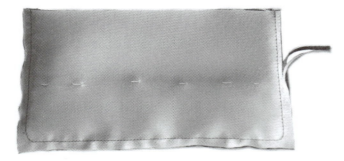

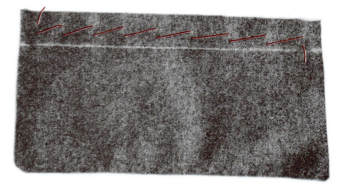

Machine stitch around the three sides using a ¼″ (6 mm) seam allowance. Stitch from the lining side to avoid slippage. Trim the seam allowance to ⅛″ (3 mm) and turn the **flap** to the right side.

Press the **flap** from the right side, and baste across the top of the **flap** to hold the lining in place.

Measure up 2½″ (6.4 cm) from the bottom of the **flap** and draw a chalkline. This is the guideline for inserting the **flap** into the pocket opening.

A thin border of garment fabric should be visible from the lining side.

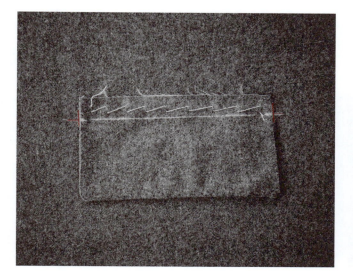

is more than ⅛″ (3 mm) larger than the pocket opening, the finished effect will be puckered and quite unprofessional.

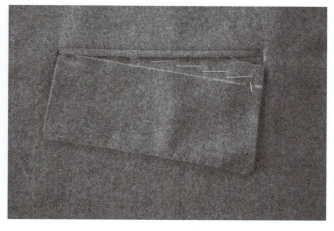

Place the **flap** on the jacket front. Match the chalkline on the **flap** to the pocket placement line on the jacket. Indicate the exact length of the **flap** by chalkmarking the jacket at either end of the **flap**.

The double-piping pocket is now constructed according to the instructions given above. When the prongs have been secured to the **piping** (page 102), open the pocket and insert the **flap**, using the chalkline on the **flap** as a guide.

Baste through the top **piping** to hold the **flap** in place. The ⅛″ (3 mm) **ease** in the **flap** should be drawn towards the center.

The pocket opening should be made ⅛″ (3 mm) smaller than the **flap**. Therefore, chalkmark ¹⁄₁₆″ (1.5 mm) in from either end of the pocket placement line. Take these measurements carefully. If the **flap**

From the wrong side of the jacket, baste the pocket closed, catching one layer of the top **piping** through the **flap**.

Using a ham, steam press the **flap** from the wrong side. The ripples at the top of the **flap** should disappear. If they do not, steam press once more, this time from the right side of the pocket.

The inside of the pocket is completed according to the instructions for the double-piping pocket, with the exception of the **facing**. Since the **flap** covers the pocket opening, the garment fabric **facing** is not necessary at the top of the pocketing. It may be eliminated completely, or replaced by a less bulky **facing** of lining fabric.

When the pocketing is being machine stitched to the top **piping** (page 104), the **flap** is also caught, and thus attached to the garment.

Double-Piping Pocket with Flap (Plaids/Stripes)

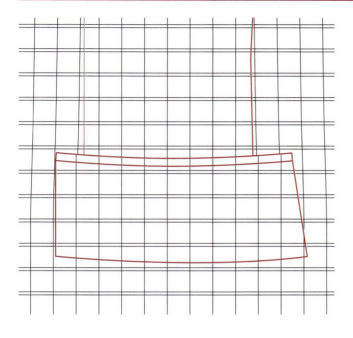

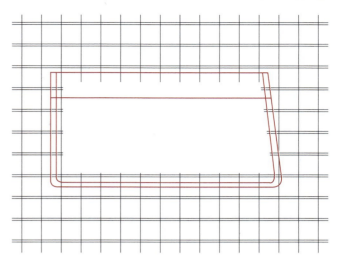

The best jacket pattern to use for a plaid or striped fabric is one which eliminates the seam below the pocket by using a dart instead of a separate side panel (page 22). If there is no seam to distort the plaid lines below the pocket opening, it is possible to cut the **flap** for a double-piping pocket so that it matches the jacket fabric at the sides and bottom of the **flap** as well as matching the **piping** at the top.

Place the **flap** pattern (page 109) on the jacket front, matching the **flap** placement line and pocket placement line.

On the pattern draw lines around the edges indicating the placement of the plaid design. This procedure must be done for each pocket, since the lines may differ slightly.

Place the **flap** pattern on the right side of the plaid fabric so that the lines around the edges of the pattern coincide with those on the fabric.

Cut the fabric and proceed with the construction of the pocket (following the instructions given previously).

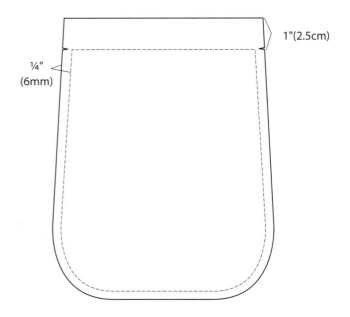

Cut a piece of garment fabric in the dimensions of the desired pocket plus 1″ (2.5 cm) extra fabric across the top and ¼″ (6 mm) seam allowance on the other sides.

Notch both ends of the 1″ (2.5 cm) fabric extension.

The patch pocket is used on men's tailored jackets when a more causal effect is desired.

For a hip-level patch pocket, the width at the top edge is 5¾″ (14.6 cm) to 6″ (15.2 cm). The depth is approximately 9″ (22.9 cm), however this will vary according to the length of the jacket. The patch has a more graceful line in the width at the bottom is about 1″ (2.5 cm) larger than at the top.

A breast-level patch pocket runs from 4½″ (11.4 cm) to 5″ (12.7 cm) at the top edge, and is approximately 5½″ (14 cm) deep.

Chalkmark the pocket placement line (the top edge of the patch) on the front of the jacket.

Apply a lightweight woven fusible, bias cut, to the wrong side of the pocket, leaving ¼″ (6 mm) margin of fabric free all around.

Cut a piece of lining, straight grain, slightly larger than the garment fabric. Press down ½" (1.3 cm) towards the wrong side at the top edge.

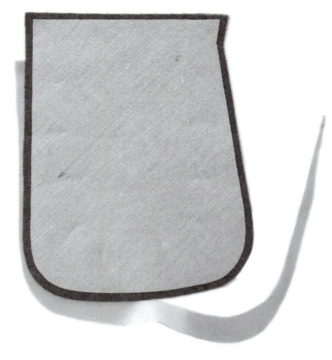

Trim the lining even with the patch.

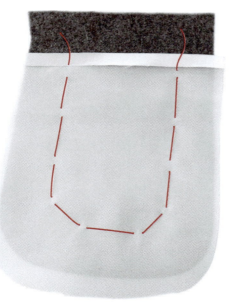

Place the lining and pocket together, right sides touching; the folded edge of the lining should be ½" (1.3 cm) below the notches at the top of the pocket. Baste around the pocket, about 1½" (3.8 cm) in from the edge.

Working from the fusible side, baste around the patch once more, this time easing the patch in from the edge of the lining about ⅛" (3 mm) all around. This step ensures that the finished patch will be slightly larger than the lining and that the lining will not show at the edges.

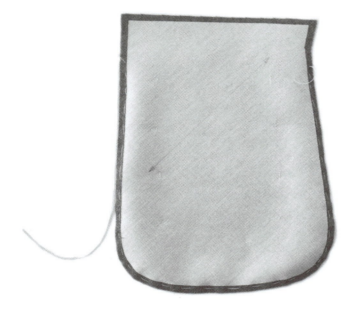

Trim the lining even with the patch.

Using a ¼" (6 mm) seam, machine stitch around the pocket, tacking well at the top corners. Sew from the lining side to avoid slippage. Trim the corners, remove the basting, and turn the pocket to the right side.

Fold the 1" (2.5 cm) extension back onto the lining and baste the ends down.

Baste around the edges of the patch once more, and then steam press on the right side. Use a handstitch to secure the folded edge of the lining at the top of the pocket. The patch is ready to be attached to the jacket.

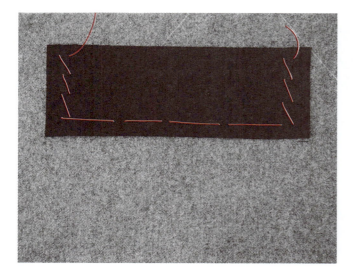

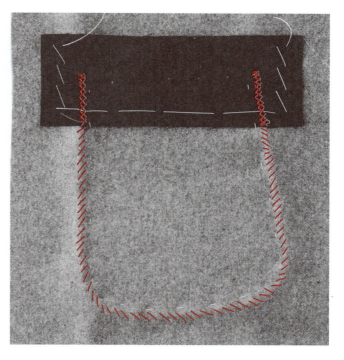

Cut a piece of pocketing to be used as reinforcement, straight grain, 3" (7.6 cm) wide and 2" (5 cm) longer than the top of the finished patch. Place the reinforcement on the wrong side of the jacket, centered over the pocket placement line. Baste or pin in place.

On the wrong side, secure the patch to the jacket by hand, using a diagonal stitch and silk finishing thread. Double the stitch in the reinforcement area.

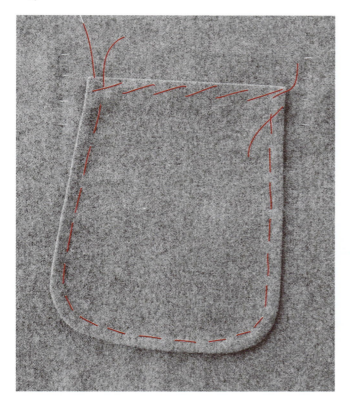

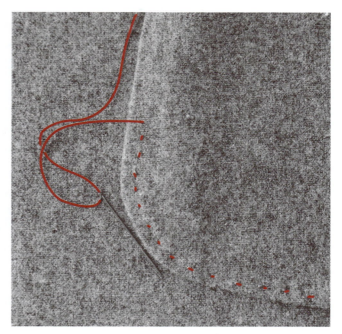

On the right side, place the top of the patch at the pocket placement line. Baste the patch to the jacket.

You may choose to add a row of hand topstitching to the front of the pocket. If so, use buttonhole twist which you have waxed, and then pressed between two pieces of paper. The heat will melt the wax into the twist and give the thread a better body. If you wish, add a single bartack at each corner of the pocket as a finishing touch.

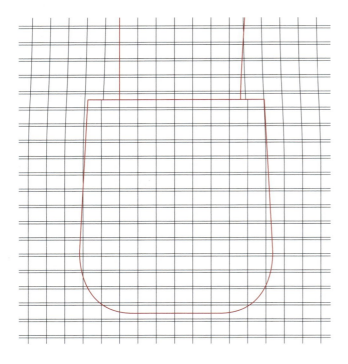 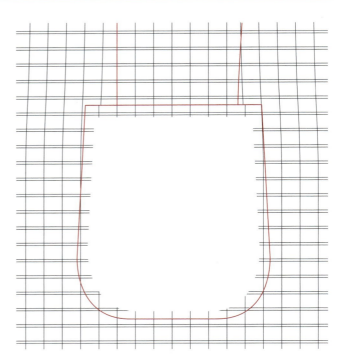

The plaid on the patch pocket should match the plaid on the jacket perfectly along both sides and at the bottom of the patch. There will, however, be slight distortion in the plaid on the jacket at either end of the pocket at the top edge, due to the darts.

In order to cut the patch so that the plaid lines match, place the patch pocket pattern (page 114) on the front of the jacket. Fold back the 1" (2.5 cm) extension at the top of the patch and place the notches, which are at the top of the patch, at the pocket placement line on the jacket. Draw lines on the pattern, around the edges, indicating the placement of the plaid design. This procedure must be done separately for each pocket, since the lines may differ slightly.

Open out the 1" (2.5 cm) extension which was folded at the top of the patch, and place the pattern on the right side of the plaid fabric, so that the lines around the edges of the pattern coincide with those on the fabric.

Cut the fabric and proceed with the construction of the pocket, following the instructions given above.

THE CANVAS

Preparing the Canvas

"Canvas" is the name given to the understructure of the jacket, which is constructed from wool canvas **interfacing**, haircloth, and French collar canvas; and covered in part by flannel.

These layers of fabric, heavily concentrated in the **chest** area of the jacket, are meant to give the jacket a body that does not depend completely for its life on the human body wearing the jacket. The purpose of the canvas is to control the fabric and reduce its susceptibility to wrinkling and stretching.

It is possible to purchase pre-padded, fully constructed canvas fronts at tailoring supply stores. They are sold according to average suit sizes. Although many tailors use these ready-made canvas fronts, we offer you instructions for cutting and preparing the canvas yourself, because we strongly believe that an "average" size canvas will never fit as well as one which is made specifically for your jacket.

The wool canvas **interfacing** is cut on the straight grain using the jacket front pattern as guide. Trace around the pattern, ½" (1.3 cm) from the edge at the armhole, shoulder, neck, **lapel**, and jacket front. Leave a bit of extra fabric at the hem curve and across the bottom of the pattern. Extend the underarm line about 2" (5 cm) out at the side, to approximately the center of the underarm.

Indicate on the canvas, the top and bottom of the roll line and the dart points. Remove the pattern.

Draw the roll line. It is preferable to use a suppression, instead of a double-pointed dart, in the canvas, so as to avoid unnecessary volume on the hip area. The suppression is drafted according to the following instructions:

- Extend the center line of the dart upwards by 3" (7.6 cm). Mark point A.

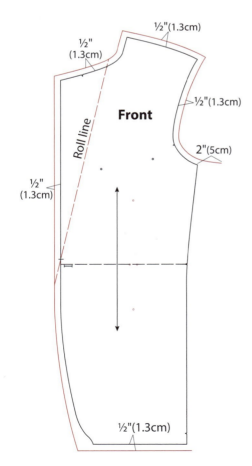

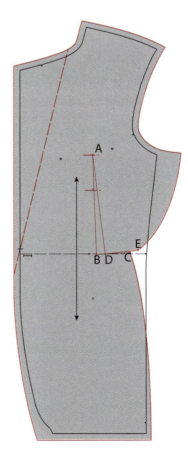

- Extend the **waistline**, from the widest part of the dart, towards the sideseam. On this line, position point B, ¾" (1.9 cm) outwards from the dart point closest to center front.
- Connect points A and B. From Point B, draw a perpendicular line towards the side. Mark point C, 2½" (6.4 cm) from point B on this new line.
- Mark point D, between B and C. The distance between B and D should be equal to the widest part of the dart on the front pattern, plus ¼" (6 mm).
- Connect points A and D. From this new line, draw a perpendicular from point D, towards the sideseam. On this new line, mark point E, 2½" (6.4 cm) away from point D.
- Draw a curved line from the underarm to point E.
- Gently curve from point C to the hem.

Note that, when the dart is closed, the wedge between points C, D and E will be removed and sewn flat, butting the raw edges together.

Cut out the canvas. There is no right or wrong side of the canvas fabric, however, for purposes of construction, indicate with an "X" the wrong side of each piece.

Cut out the dart, using the dart stitchline as a cutting line.

Divide the shoulder into thirds, and mark each section. On the mark closest to the neck, cut a 3" (7.6 cm) slit into the canvas.

Cut a bias strip of wool canvas **interfacing** 1½" (3.8 cm) by 4" (10.2 cm) by ½" (1.3 cm). Topstitch it to the wrong side of the canvas, so that the slash in the shoulder is held open ½" (1.3 cm) at the top.

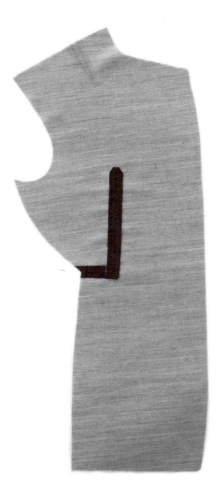

Measure your jacket front pattern at center shoulder, from 1″ (2.5 cm) below the stitchline to 2″ (5 cm) above the **waistline**. Cut the haircloth to this length, and trim away the fringe along the edge.

Fold the haircloth in half. Draw a diagonal line running from 1″ (2.5 cm) to the right of the center at the top to 1″ (2.5 cm) to the left of the center at the bottom. Cut the haircloth along the diagonal line.

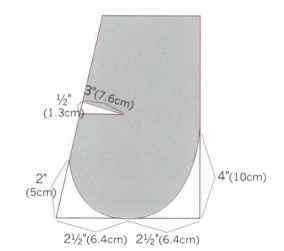

The **waistline** suppression is closed by top-stitching a bias strip of pocketing to the wrong side of the canvas, and butting the raw edges of the suppression closed. The suppression is reinforced by a row of zigzag stitching on top of the pocketing strip.

Place the two pieces of haircloth together, narrow edges at top (there is no right or wrong side to the haircloth). Trim the bottom edges of the haircloth as illustrated. At the center of the longer side of the "plastron" or shield, which we are now constructing, draw a dart 3″ (7.6 cm) long and ½″ (1.3 cm) wide. Cut out the dart.

Using the plastron as a pattern, cut two pieces of covering flannel, straight grain, ½″ (1.3 cm) larger than the plastron all around. Do not put darts in the flannel.

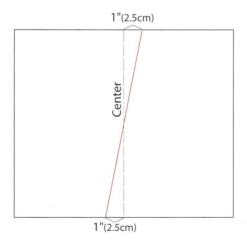

Haircloth is usually sold in 18-inch (45.7 cm) widths with a fringe of hair along the width.

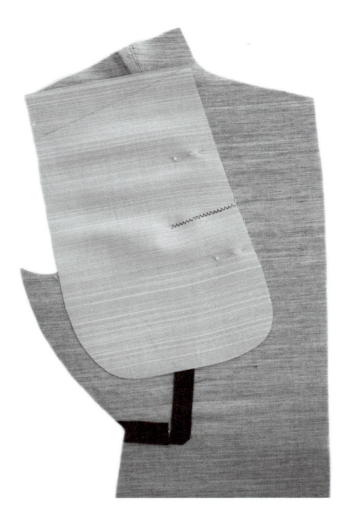

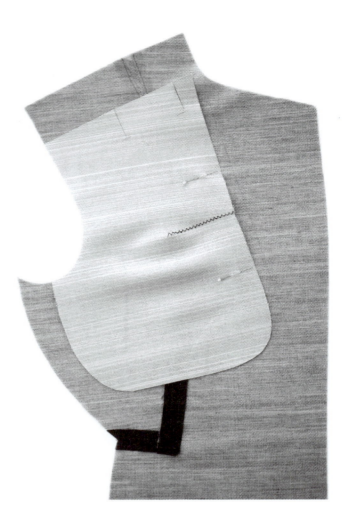

Close the dart on the haircloth with a zigzag stitch (the dart sides butted together). Pocketing is not needed here as reinforcement for the dart.

When the dart has been closed, place the haircloth plastron on the canvas, ½″ (1.3 cm) back from the roll line. The top of the haircloth should be trimmed so that it lies parallel to the shoulder, about 2″ (5 cm) below the top of the canvas.

Trim the haircloth flush with the canvas at the armhole.

Cut two slashes into the haircloth – 1½″ (3.8 cm) to either side of the center of the shoulder dart, and 1½″ (3.8 cm) deep.

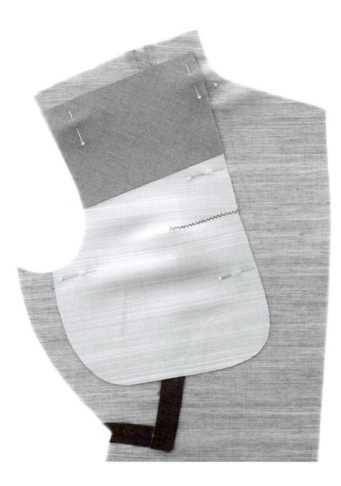

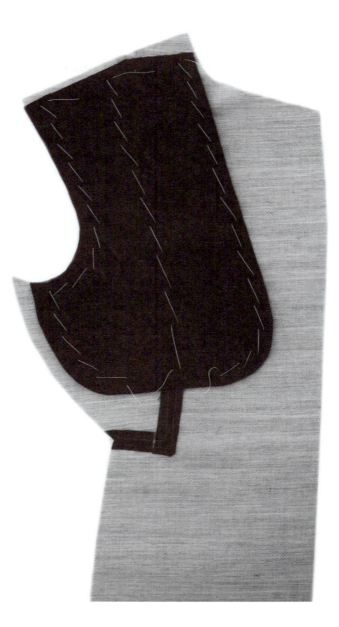

Place a 5″ (12.7 cm) wide bias cut of French collar canvas across the top of, and extending 1″ (2.5 cm) above, the haircloth.

Trim it flush with the canvas at the armhole.

Place the flannel covering ¼″ (6 mm) in from the roll line. Trim it flush with the canvas at the shoulder and armhole. Baste all layers together (as illustrated).

The flannel side of the canvas will be worn towards the body, and will prevent the haircloth from scratching your client through the lining.

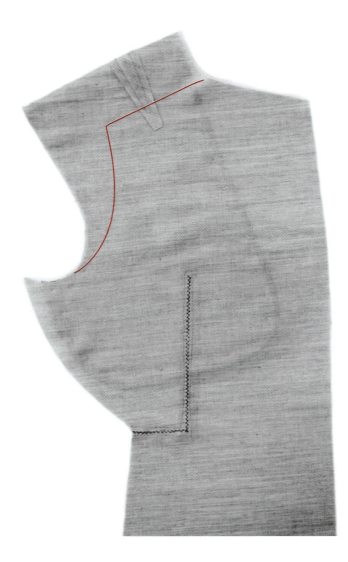

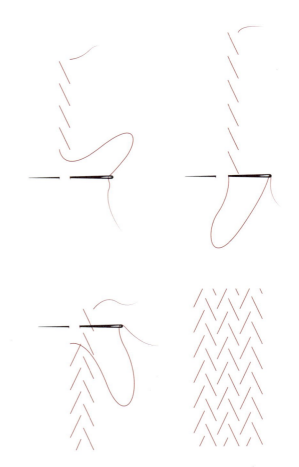

On the right side of the canvas, draw a chalk guideline, below which the haircloth, the French canvas, and the flannel covering will be pad-stitched to the canvas **interfacing**. This guideline, drawn about 2½″ (6.4 cm) below the shoulder and 3″ (7.6 cm) in from the armhole, tapers into the underarm curve.

The pad stitch is a diagonal stitch which is staggered from one row to the next. It is used to join two or more layers of fabric, so that they act as one, while maintaining their individual characteristics. If the stitches are pulled too tightly while padding, the fabric will pucker and create bulky ridges between the rows. We will be using the pad stitch at several points during the construction of the jacket.

Here, because the stitch will not be visible in the finished jacket, it can be done in basting thread and the amount of fabric picked up by the needle (the size of the stitch on the underside) can be a generous ⅛″ (3 mm). The size of the diagonal is a good ⅜″ (1 cm). Do not spend time measuring your stitches. Just get a general sense of the size, and proceed.

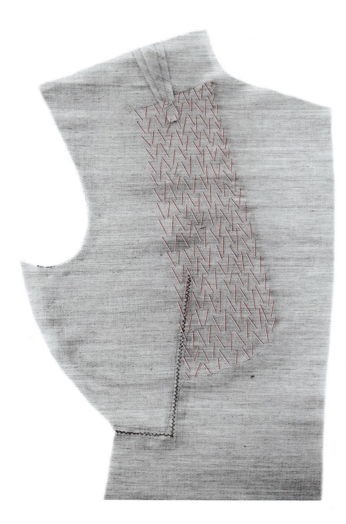
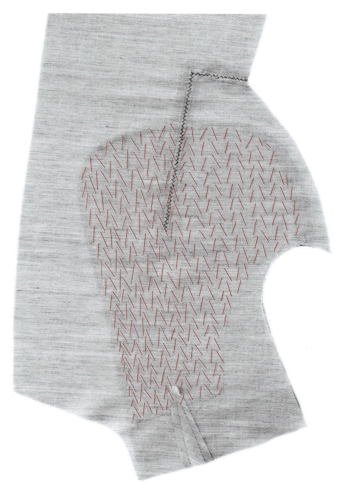

Since the plastron area is now somewhat bulky, it is easier to padstitch half of the area at a time. Begin at the center and stitch in vertical rows, working your way over to the end of the flannel at the roll line; then from the center out to the end of the flannel at the armhole. Padstitch only in the area covered by the flannel and below the chalk guideline.

It will be easier to work with the canvas upside down on one-half of the plastron. Which half this happens to be depends on which hand you sew with, and which side of the jacket you are preparing. The padstitching is done on the right side of the canvas, because stitching on this side will produce the correct contour in the plastron. The wrong side of the plastron will be facing the body in the finished garment. Padstitching on the right side will contour the canvas correctly, towards the body.

On the wrong side, slipstitch the edges of the flannel to the canvas.

The canvas is now pressed gently, and is ready to be basted to the jacket front.

The canvas and jacket front are now basted together so that they may be handled as one unit during the construction of the jacket. It is important that the jacket front lay smoothly over the canvas. Any rippling visible on the garment fabric, after it has been basted to the canvas, will be impossible to press out. Therefore, several rows of stitching are used to control the two layers of fabric, and great care is taken to gently smooth the fabric ahead of the needle as you baste. The arrows in the sketches indicate the direction in which the fabric is smoothed.

On a flat surface, place the jacket front and canvas together with the wrong side of the jacket to the right side of the canvas. The canvas and jacket darts should be offset by ¾" (1.9 cm). Since the canvas suppression is longer than the top part of the jacket dart (page 119), it will extend above the jacket dart point. A ½" (1.3 cm) margin of canvas should be visible around the outer edges of the jacket.

Beginning above the front dart, about 3" (7.6 cm) below the shoulder, baste down the front of the jacket, catching the canvas and smoothing the garment fabric gently ahead in the direction of the arrows. The stitches are about 1½" (3.8 cm) long and are left comfortably without tension. Baste through the pockets, using the dart as guideline, and finish at the hem foldline.

Carefully fold back the garment fabric until the ends of the pockets are visible. Baste one edge of the pocket seam allowance, and the reinforcement ends into the canvas using diagonal stitches.

Before proceeding with the outside basting, the pockets must be secured into the canvas. With one hand on the hip pocket to prevent the garment fabric from shifting, tug gently upwards at the tip of the canvas **lapel**. "Gently" is the word. This should eliminate any rippling in the canvas on the diagonal from the hip pocket to the **lapel** tip.

Fold the garment fabric back in place. Smooth and baste the fabric across the **waistline** from the dart to 1″ (2.5 cm) from the edge of the jacket.

Below the **waistline**, at approximately midway on the second stitchline, baste down from **waist** to hem smoothing the fabric as indicated by the arrows.

Approximately 1″ (2.5 cm) from the jacket edge, baste down from the **waist** to just above the hem, and continue across the end of the canvas.

Above the **waist**, the fabric is smoothed up and out, as stitchline #5 rises from the **waist** to 3″ (7.6 cm) below the shoulder.

Using the tailor tacks as a guide, chalkmark the roll line on the right side of the jacket. Stitchline #6 moves up from the **waist** into the roll line. The fabric is smoothed up and out between stitchlines #5 and #6 as the roll line is basted.

If you are working on the left front of the jacket, carefully fold back the fabric until the inside of the **welt** pocket is visible. One side of the pocket has already been basted into the canvas (page 127). Now, following the same procedure as above, baste the second side of the pocket into the canvas. The side of the hip pocket cannot be basted, since it overshoots the canvas. Fold the garment fabric back in place.

Stitchline #7 runs across the top of the other stitchlines, and traces the armhole, remaining 3" (7.6 cm) away from the edge. The basting curves into the **waist**, then out and down to the hem. Smooth the fabric gently, following the direction of the arrows.

The bias curve of the jacket armhole is basted into the canvas. Care should be taken not to stretch the fabric in this area.

Trim the canvas even with the jacket front.

With the basting completed, hold the jacket front up and check that there is no ripping in the garment fabric between the lines of basting. Slight rippling is to be expected on the canvas side, and serves as **ease** for the garment fabric.

Cross-stitch the canvas into the seam allowance at the top of the pocket.

The assembly of canvas and jacket front is complete.

Padstitching the Lapels

In order to give the jacket **lapel** the crisp body it will need in the finished jacket, the canvas **lapel** is now padstitched (page 124) into the jacket **lapel**.

Since these stitches will show through on the underside of the **lapel** in the finished jacket, use silk thread in a color that matches the garment fabric. The stitches on the canvas side should be about ⅜" (1 cm) long. On the jacket side, they should be tiny pinpricks.

As previously discussed, if the stitches are pulled too tightly while padding, the canvas will pucker and create ridges which will be obvious through the **facing** on the finished garment.

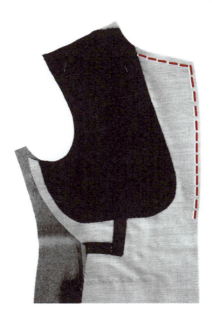

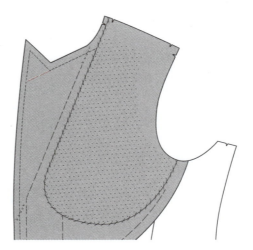

Draw a chalkline on the canvas **lapel** indicating the seam allowance. If you are working on a peak **lapel**, add a line across the bottom of the peak.

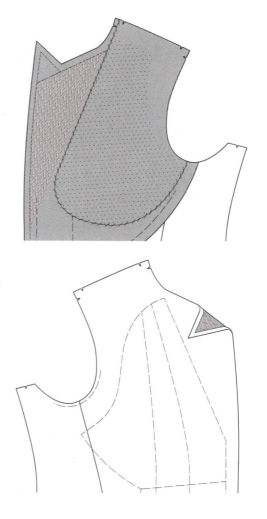

From the canvas side, begin padstitching along the very edge of the flannel, working across the **lapel** in rows parallel to the roll line. To give the **lapel** a soft natural roll, you should place the jacket on the edge of your work table, aligning the table edge and **lapel** roll line, and letting the **lapel** hang down.

If you are working on a peak **lapel**, a second rolling is suggested. To prevent the peak from drooping forward in the finished garment, it is padstitched while held rolled towards the jacket body.

About 1½" (3.8 cm) past the roll line, turn the **lapel** so that it takes the position it will have in the finished jacket. Continue to padstitch with the **lapel** held in this position. This procedure of rolling the **lapel** while padstitching ensures that the garment fabric **lapel** will end up slightly smaller than the canvas **lapel**, and will, therefore pull towards the jacket. It is exactly this inclination or pulling towards the jacket that we are trying to create for a natural roll of the **lapel**.

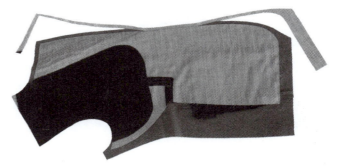

Beginning ½" (1.3 cm) past the roll line, draw the seam allowance on the canvas – across the top of the **lapel**, down the jacket front, and across the hemline at the bottom of the canvas.

Trim away the canvas in the seam allowance. Be very careful as you cut the canvas, not to cut the garment fabric.

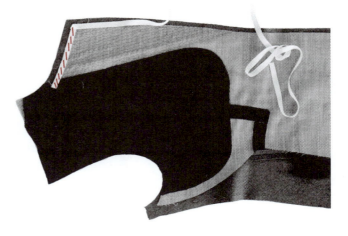

The Taping

If your jacket is double-breasted, the right front must be shortened at this point to prevent it from hanging below the left front when the jacket is buttoned. Shorten the front edge of the jacket at the hem, by ⅜″ (1 cm), tapering to nothing 7″ (17.8 cm) in from the edge.

Tape is now applied along the outer edge of the lapel and jacket front to give a crisp, defined edge to the jacket. The tape is also run along the bias of the roll line, as additional support.

Use ⅜″ (1 cm) cotton twill tape which has been soaked in cool water and pressed. Beginning ½″ (1.3 cm) past the roll line, baste the tape along the top of the **lapel** with the top edge of the tape flush with the top edge of the canvas.

At the tip of the **lapel**, slash the tape almost to the end, and bring it down along the edge of the **lapel**.

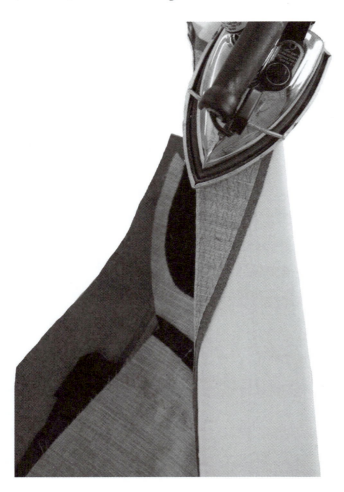

The **lapel** is now pressed from the canvas side. Be sure not to flatten the natural roll we created while padstitching.

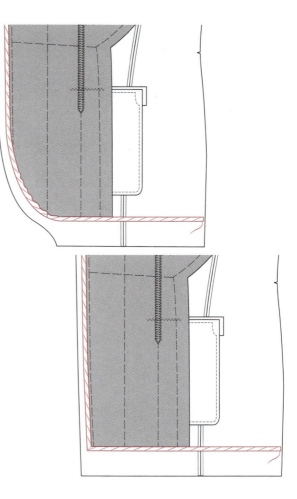

Snip away the overlap of tape at the **lapel** tip, and baste down the **lapel** and the jacket front. The tape should be placed inside the edge of the canvas, about $\frac{1}{16}$" (1.5 mm), this will help keep the edge of the finished **lapel** thin and crisp.

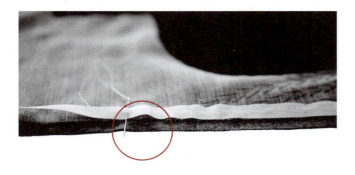

At the bottom of the roll line, place $\frac{1}{4}$" (6 mm) **ease** in the tape, so that the **lapel** will be free to fold over without restriction.

Tape across the top of the hem foldline with the bottom edge of the tape *on* the hemline.

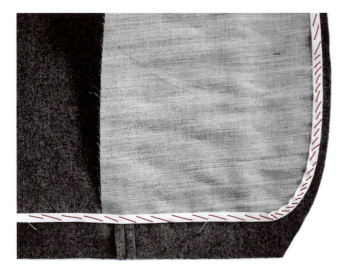

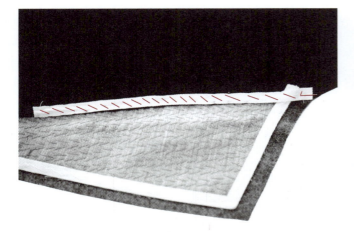

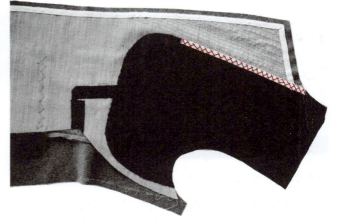

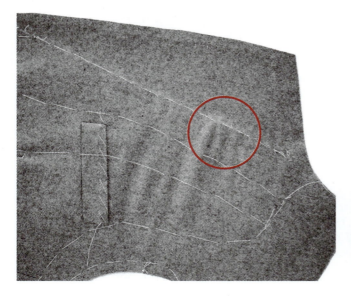

Using silk thread, cross-stitch along the roll-line tape, stitching through all layers of fabric. The stitches should be along the very edge of the tape to prevent it from curling up. You will notice that the rippling in the jacket at the center of the roll line disappears as the tape is cross-stitched to the jacket.

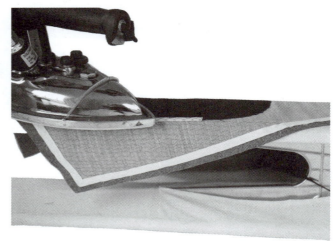

Press the roll-line tape, allowing the **lapel** to fall free.

Tape is also applied at the edge of the flannel, ¼" (6 mm) beyond the roll line. Baste the tape, through all layers of fabric, from the neck edge down for about 3" (7.6 cm). Take a couple of backstitches, and then begin pulling the tape as you baste for the next 3" (7.6 cm) or so. Rippling should appear on either side of the tape. Take a couple of backstitches at the end of the 3" (7.6 cm) span to keep the rippling in place and continue basting without pulling the tape.

Only the top two-thirds of the roll line area is taped. The bottom third is left free to allow the **lapel** to roll easily.

Pulling the roll-line tape creates the equivalent of a dart through the roll line. In the finished jacket, the effect is a roll line less inclined to pull away from the body.

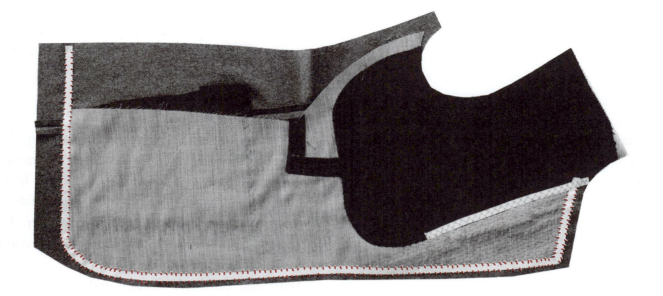

The rest of the tape is secured by the slipstitching along both edges, using silk thread. Along the outer edge of the tape, stitch through to the right side of the fabric. The stitches should be very small and sewn without pulling. On the inner edge of the tape, stitching through all layers can only be done in the **lapel** area. Below the **lapel** catch only the canvas. If you were to stitch through all layers on the inner edge of the tape below the **lapel**, these stitches would be visible and unwelcomed down the front of the finished jacket.

If necessary, trim the seam allowance along the jacket front and at the top of the **lapel**, so that only ½″ (1.3 cm) seam allowance shows beyond the tape.

FIRST FITTING

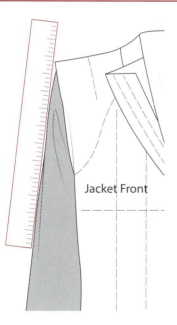

Jacket Front

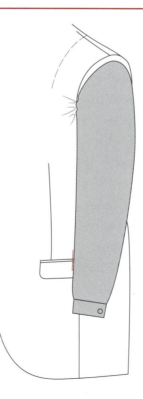

The jacket is basted together at the back and shoulder seams, and tried on by the client. Place well-constructed shoulder pads in the jacket for this fitting (page 165), so that the true contour of the shoulder, as it will appear in the finished jacket, may be observed.

With the front of the jacket pinned closed at the buttonhole markings, check the entire front, back, and side of the jacket with a keen eye for the creases we observed during the toile fitting.

Chalkmark, or pin, any minor fitting adjustments.

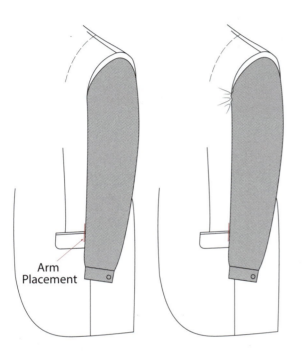

Arm Placement

Give special attention to the armhole. With the client's arm resting comfortably at his side, see if there is any wrinkling or pulling in the front notch area of the armhole. If there is, the jacket fabric must be trimmed in this area (a small amount at a time).

Check the shoulder width. If the cutting edge at the top of the shoulder extends out well beyond the shoulder edge, the fabric may need trimming. As a guide, place a ruler at the bicep and let it extend up towards the shoulder. If the fabric extends out beyond the ruler at the shoulder, the jacket shoulder is too wide and should be trimmed before attaching the shoulder pad.

With the arm still resting naturally at the client's side, chalkmark on the hip-level pocket a line indicating the natural placement of the arm. This chalkmark will be used in setting the sleeve to fall either forward or backward, in accordance with the position of the client's arm.

Remove the basting at the back and shoulder seams, and make whatever adjustments are necessary.

The back seams will not be sewn until after the **facing** is attached.

The shoulder seams will be sewn after the body of the jacket has been lined.

THE FACING

The **facing** plays a prominent role in the finished jacket. It must be carefully cut and shaped, and laid gracefully over the **lapel**, with enough **ease** to allow the **lapel** to roll freely. If the grain is off, or the **ease** is missing, there will be either ripples or strain on the front of the jacket.

The **facing** can be attached to the jacket either by hand or by machine. (Read through both procedures and decide which one you would like to learn first.) The difference in the amount of time it takes to complete either method does not seem to be significant, although one might expect this to be the case. The hand application of the **facing** seems to require a "feel" for the fabric – more confidence in one's ability to control the fabric.

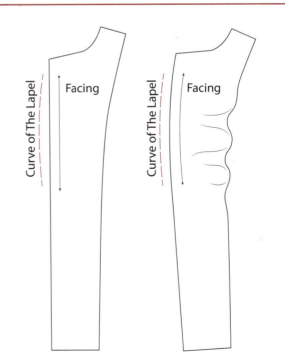

Curve of The Lapel · Facing

Curve of The Lapel · Facing

Many tailors use the hand application exclusively, because of the complete control it affords. Others use it only for a plaid or striped fabric, where matching the design requires precision. There are also tailors who consider the hand application inferior to the machine application, because a **facing** seam, stitched by machine, may be a more definite line, and more secure than one stitched by hand. You decide which method to use.

The outer edge of the **facing**, which you have cut using the revised **facing** pattern (page 26), is a straight line, and, therefore, not shaped to match the front of the jacket. Before attaching the **facing**

to the jacket, it will be necessary to steam press the **lapel** area of the **facing** into a curve which matches that of the jacket **lapel**.

If, in the beginning, you hesitate to trust your eye to match the curve of **lapel** and **facing**, create a guideline for yourself by drawing the **lapel** curve on a piece of paper and pinning the paper to your ironing board.

Place the raw edge of the **lapel** area of the **facing** along the guideline. Rippling will appear at the center, inner edge of the **facing**, if we shrink these ripples away, the front edge of the **facing** will maintain the curve we have given it.

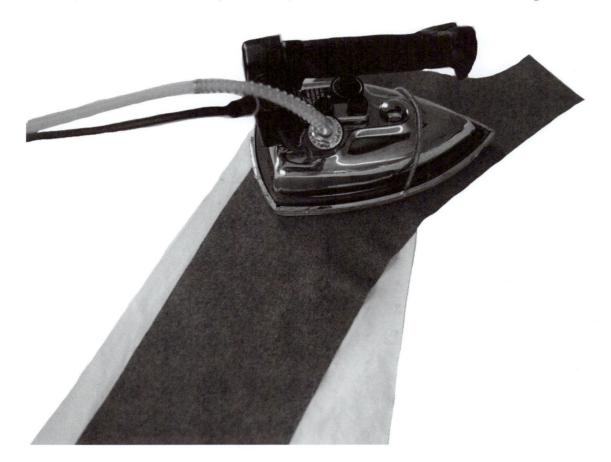

Here is where the flexibility of natural fibers can be appreciated. On the wrong side of the fabric, and using steam liberally, iron from the outer edge of the **lapel** in, using progressively smaller arcs. Depending on your fabric, this will require more or less effort; worsteds being a greater challenge than more loosely woven fibers.

The whole purpose of this effort is to maintain the straight of the grain at the **lapel** edge. The benefit of this is obvious in a striped or plaid fabric, since it allows the pattern to continue uninterrupted from the top to bottom of the **lapel**. Less obvious, but no less important, is the fact that having the strongest grain at the outer edge of the **lapel** will be a safeguard against stretching and rippling in this area.

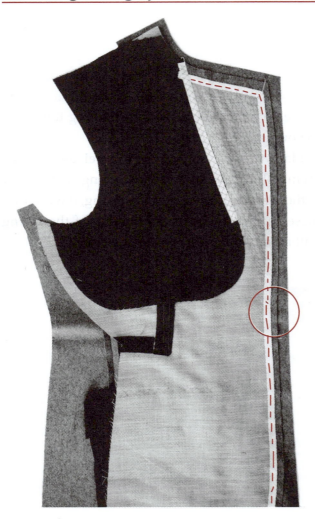

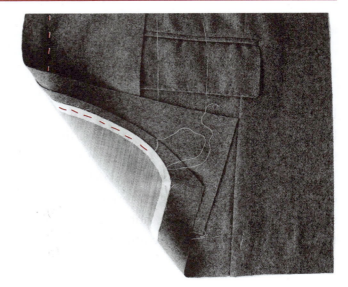

If the front of the jacket curves in at the hem, the **facing** should be based to the curve using a slightly different technique. Since this area may be inclined to curl outwards, away from the body, in the finished jacket, roll the bottom of the jacket towards the **facing** as you baste. This will shorten the **facing** slightly, and ensure that in the finished jacket the curved edge will incline gently towards the body, rather than curling outwards.

Place the right side of the **facing** to the right side of the jacket front, allowing ½" (1.3 cm) **facing** to extend beyond the jacket at the top of the **lapel** and down the front of the jacket. Beginning at the tip of the **lapel**, baste down through the center of the tape, attaching the **facing** to the jacket. Just below the bottom of the roll line, place about ¼" (6 mm) ease in the **facing** to accommodate the roll of the **lapel**. Tack the **ease** into the tape so that it will remain where you've placed it.

If the front of the jacket is straight at the hem, continue basting the tape to the bottom of the jacket.

The tip of the **lapel** in the finished jacket should also incline comfortably towards the body, rather than curling upwards. For that reason, a small bubble of **ease** is now placed in the **facing** at the tip of the **lapel**. This will prevent the possibility of the **facing** pulling the **lapel** tip forward. At the top of the **lapel**, lower the **facing** slightly to create the **ease**, about ¼" (6 mm). When the slight excess of fabric is visible at the **lapel** tip, baste across the **lapel** from the tip to just beyond the collar notch.

sharp pivot at the tip will result in a misshapen, lumpy **lapel** tip, because there will not be enough room for the seam allowance to settle in.

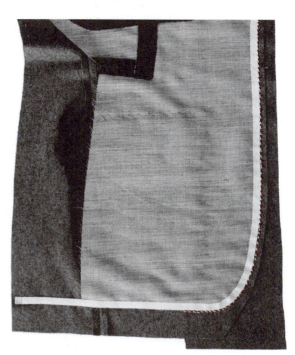

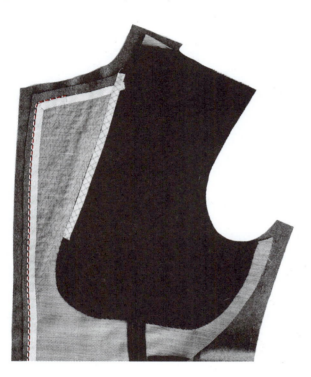

Using the tape as a guideline, machine stitch from the collar notch to the bottom of the jacket. Stitch about ¹⁄₁₆" (1.5 mm) beyond the tape, in the seam allowance.

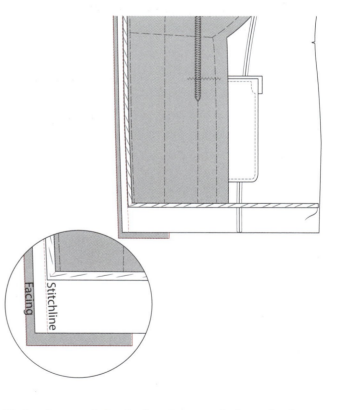

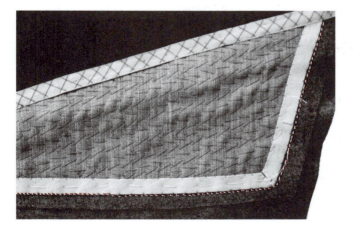

For a good point at the top of the **lapel**, take one or two stitches on the diagonal as you turn. A

If the front of the jacket is rounded at the hem, stitch with the curve to the end of the **facing**.

If the front of the jacket is straight at the hem, stitch down to the bottom edge.

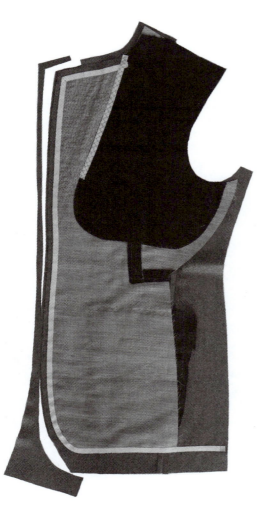

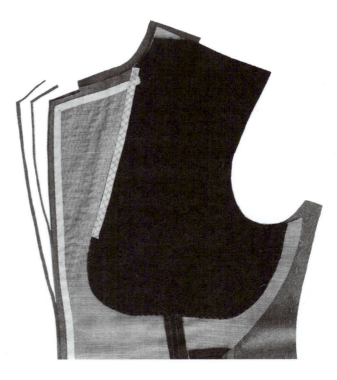

From the collar notch and around the **lapel** tip, trim a bit closer. Leave about ¼" (6 mm) jacket seam allowance and ⅜" (1 cm) facing.

Press the **facing** seam open.

Remove the basting and layer the seam allowances. Trim the jacket seam allowance to ⅜" (1 cm) and the **facing** to ½" (1.3 cm) from the bottom of the jacket to the top of the **lapel**.

The tip of the **lapel** will be flatter if the seam allowance inside is controlled and evenly distributed. To accomplish this, both seam allowances are drawn onto the tape at the **lapel** tip, one at a time. A shirring thread is first run through the seam allowance and pulled. The seam allowance is then tacked into the tape, using silk thread. These stitches should not be visible on the right side of the fabric.

The tip of the **lapel** is then pressed flat.

If the front of the jacket is rounded at the hem, the seam allowance at the curve is also tacked into the tape.

If the front of the jacket is straight at the hem, the **facing** seam allowance is tacked into itself at the hem.

The hem, on both straight and rounded jackets fronts, is now basted up with large diagonal stitches, and then stitched into the canvas with a smaller diagonal stitch. (We'll leave the hem beyond the canvas for the moment.)

Cut the collar notch almost to the stitch line. Turn the **facing** and jacket front right sides out.

Working from the jacket side, baste from the bottom of the roll line, up and across to the collar notch or from the collar notch down (depending on which hand you sew with and which side of the jacket you are preparing). As you baste, bring the **facing** seam to the jacket side, so that it will not be seen when the jacket is worn.

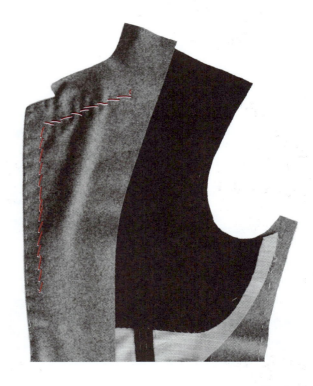

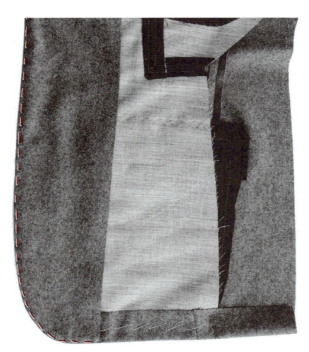

On the **facing** side, baste up the bottom of the roll line once more and continue across, about 1" (2.5 cm) below the top of the tape. These stitches are about ½" (1.3 cm) long and are placed comfortably, without pulling or tautness.

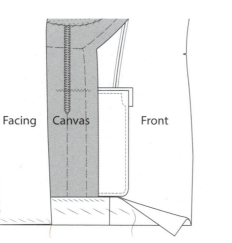

From the bottom of the **lapel** to the hem, the basting is done on the **facing** side, and the seam is drawn towards the **facing** side so that it will not be visible when the jacket is worn.

On a jacket with a straight front, make sure that the **facing** is turned up so that it is a bit shorter than the jacket, and will not be seen from the outside.

Baste on the diagonal from the tip of the **lapel**, in towards the roll line.

Chalkmark a straight line across the top of the **lapel** from the collar notch to ½″ (1.3 cm) past the roll line. The top of the tape should be directly under this chalkline.

Slash the **facing** (not the jacket) from the neck edge to this ½″ (1.3 cm) point.

From the jacket side, baste the length of the roll line, catching the **facing** underneath.

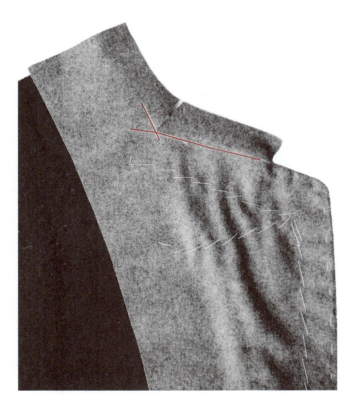

Fold the **facing** along the chalkline and baste it in place, just covering the tape underneath. Trim, if necessary, before folding.

Press the top of the **lapel** and slip stitch from the collar notch to ½″ (1.3 cm) past the roll line. The **facing** is now pressed before continuing.

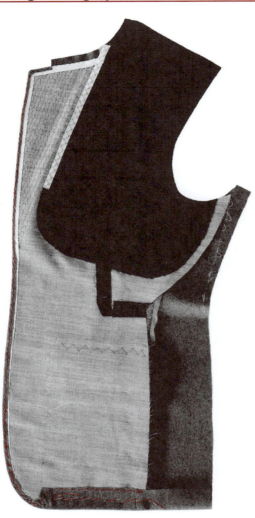

Be gentle with the fabric. The seam allowance should simply fold onto the tape, and not be pulled tightly.

The hem is also folded up, using the tape as a guide, and diagonal-stitched into the canvas.

To attach the **facing** by hand, the seam allowance at the outer edge of the **lapel** and down the front of the jacket should be trimmed to ⅜" (1 cm). The seam allowance from the tip of the **lapel** to the collar notch should be ¼" (6 mm).

Snip the collar notch "almost" to the tape, and using the edge of the tape as a foldline, begin stitching the seam allowance onto the tape. Use a diagonal stitch, with silk finishing thread, catching the tape and the canvas.

Place the wrong side of the **facing** (which has been steam pressed into shape, page 138) to the wrong side of the jacket front, leaving a generous ½" (1.3 cm) of **facing** visible around the outer edge of the jacket. Baste the **facing** and the jacket together, following the stitches that mark the length of the roll line, and then down the front edge of the jacket. At the bottom of the roll line, place ¼" (6 mm) **ease** in the **facing** to facilitate the roll of the **lapel**.

If your jacket is straight at the hem, continue basting down the entire front. If your jacket curves in at the hem (as illustrated), stop basting about 8" (20.3 cm) or so from the bottom.

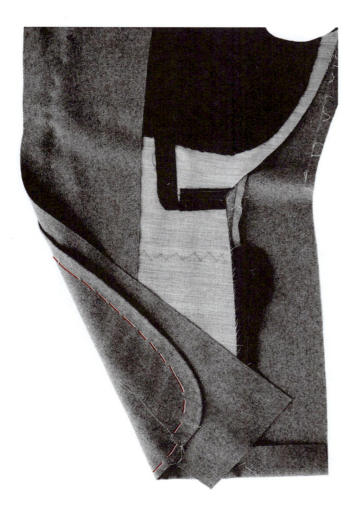

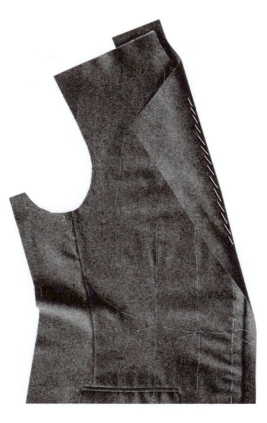

With the **lapel** rolled in the position it will take in the finished jacket, baste a row of diagonal stitches, parallel to the roll line.

Jackets which are shaped at the bottom front will be inclined to curl outwards, away from the body, unless the **facing** is manipulated to prevent this. If the bottom edge of the jacket is curled inwards, and basted to the **facing** while held in this position, the finished jacket will incline gently towards the body at the front edge.

Baste across the top of the **lapel**, and down to the bottom of the roll line, keeping the stitches about 1" (2.5 cm) away from the edge of the jacket **lapel**.

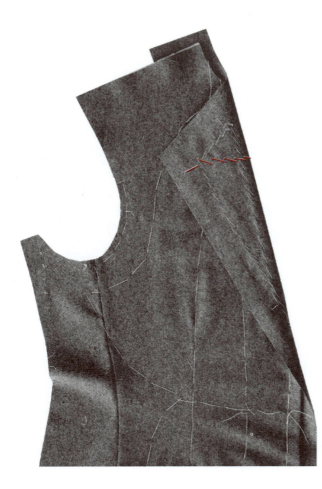

Trim **facing** seam allowance to ⅜″ (1 cm) from collar notch to the bottom of the jacket. The **facing** from collar notch to shoulder is just about even with the jacket.

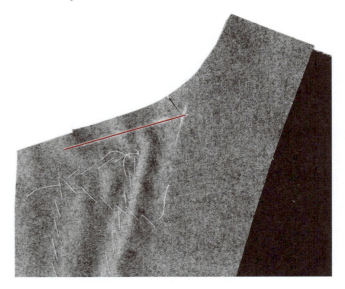

On the **facing**, chalkmark a line which extends from the collar notch to ½″ (1.3 cm) past the roll line. The chalkline is exactly where the top of the tape is on the jacket. This line is called the **gorge** line.

Snip the **facing** to a point on the **gorge** line ½″ (1.3 cm) past the roll line.

With the **lapel** still rolled, baste a diagonal line of stitches from the tip of the **lapel** basting stitches, to just past the roll line.

Fold and baste the **facing** seam allowance along the **gorge** line and down the front of the **lapel**. Allow facing to extend about $\frac{1}{16}$" (1.5 mm) beyond the jacket **lapel**, so that the **facing** seam will not be visible when the jacket is worn.

The **facing** seam, from the bottom of the roll line to the bottom of the jacket, should not be visible on the right side of the jacket. Therefore, as you baste on the **facing** side in this area, allow about $\frac{1}{16}$" (1.5 mm) of the jacket to extend beyond the **facing**.

Using silk finishing thread, slipstitch along the edge of the **facing** seam. The stitches should be quite small, and carefully placed, so that they are not visible from the outside. The **facing** should now be pressed (page 201).

THE LINING

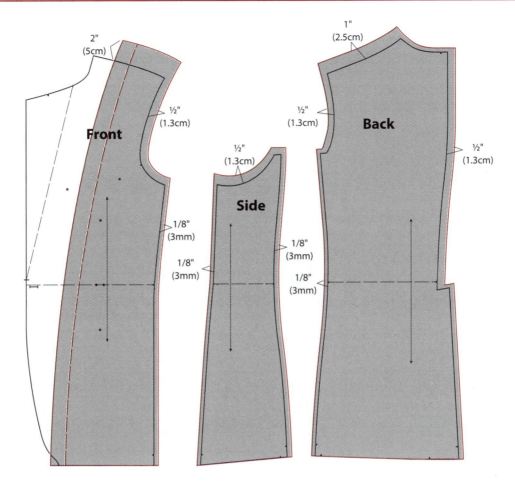

The purpose of a lining is to hide all the threads and seams and layers of padding that have gone into the jacket's construction to this point. It also helps in sliding the jacket on and off without difficulty, and feels much better through a shirt than wool canvas does.

The lining should be cut slightly larger than the jacket, in both length and width, even though it is placed inside. The constant pulling and friction, which the lining is subject to, will cause tears in the lining fabric if there is not sufficient living **ease**.

Using the front, back and side panel pattern pieces, cut the lining larger than the pattern by the amount indicated in these illustrations. The broken line on the jacket front pattern piece represents the point to which the **facing** extends. Draw this line on your jacket front pattern so that you will be able to mark the lining to overlap the **facing** by 1" (2.5 cm).

Machine-stitch the front and side panels of the lining together, and press the seams open.

We have allowed 2" (5 cm) of lining above the pattern at the shoulder front, 1" (2.5 cm) of which we'll now use to create a pleat in the front lining at mid-armhole level. The pleat is ½" (1.3 cm)

deep and is basted towards the right side of the lining. Its purpose is to reduce the pressure on the lining caused by the lining pocket.

The Barcelona Pocket

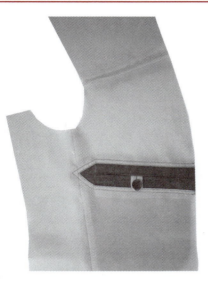

There are usually two pockets in the front lining of a man's tailored jacket, one on either side. They may be placed at breast level or at hip level. It is also not uncommon to see jackets with just one pocket on the inside left **chest**, or alternatively, jackets with multiple inside pockets of differing sizes and placements, each of which carries a specific purpose (pen pocket, ticket pocket, passport pocket etc.).

The pocket styles vary. Here we show a lining pocket known as the *Barcelona*.

The front of the pocket is made from two pieces of garment fabric, 1½" (3.8 cm) by 8" (20.3 cm), nap down. With right sides touching, machine-stitch the pieces together, lengthwise using a ½" (1.3 cm) seam allowance. Begin and end the seam with a permanent-length machine-stitch, but for 5" (12.7 cm) at the center of the seam use a larger, basting stitch. Tack well at the beginning and end of the basting stitch. We will eventually be

removing the stitches from the 5" (12.7 cm) area to open the completed pocket.

Press the seam open.

Cut two pieces of pocketing fabric, straight grain, 7" (17.8 cm) by 7" (17.8 cm) for the inside of the pocket. Cut a ½" (1.3 cm) diagonal strip from the top of each piece. The pocket shown here is designed on a ½" (1.3 cm) slant. Therefore, the inside pocketing must be cut at a slant in order to fall straight after construction. If you choose to eliminate the slant in your pocket design, then eliminate the slant at the top of the pocketing also.

One of the pieces of inside pocketing will be visible when the pocket is being used. Therefore, a piece of **facing** will be needed to cover the top of that pocketing piece. Cut the **facing** from lining fabric about 2½" (6.4 cm) by 7" (17.8 cm) and press up a ½" (1.3 cm) hem on one side.

Topstitch the folded edge to the top of one of the pocketing pieces. Do *not* be concerned with the slanted side edges – you'll trim them away later.

The buttonhole tab is made from a strip of lining fabric, straight grain, 1½" (3.8 cm) by 3½"

(8.9 cm). Sew a ⅜" (1 cm) seam in the strip and press the seam allowance open. Turn and press the seam to the center of the strip. Fold the strip into an arrow shape, and topstitch the point.

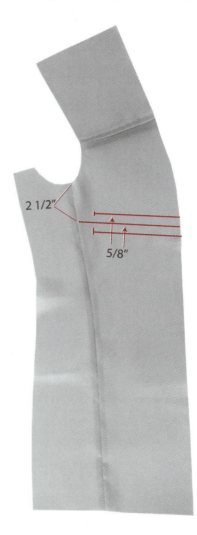

On the right side of the front lining, the pocket placement line is drawn on a ½" (1.3 cm) slant, the higher end of which falls about 2½" (6.4 cm) below the cutting edge of the lining underarm.

Draw the pocket placement line 7" (17.8 cm) long from the front edge of the lining towards the side panel seam. From the center of the line, mark off a 5" (12.7 cm) span to represent the actual pocket opening.

Draw two parallel lines, 6" (15.2 cm) long, beginning at the lining front edge, ⅝" (1.6 cm) above and below the pocket placement line. If you would prefer a narrower pocket front, use a ½" (1.3 cm) measurement.

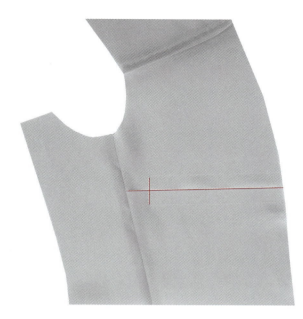

Slash the pocket placement line; and then above and below to the ends of the two parallel lines.

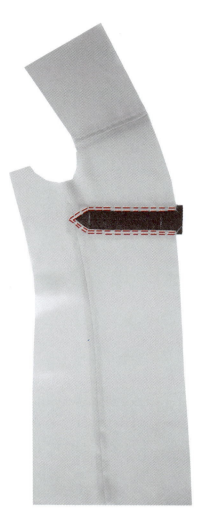

In the arrow-shaped opening created by the folded lining, place the garment fabric pocket front. The seam should run down the center of the opening. Topstitch a double row on the lining, attaching garment fabric pocket front to the lining. Chalkmark the ends of the 5" (12.7 cm) pocket opening area at the center of the garment fabric seam.

Fold the lining along the 6" (15.2 cm) lines and then diagonally at the ends. Press the lining flaps towards the wrong side.

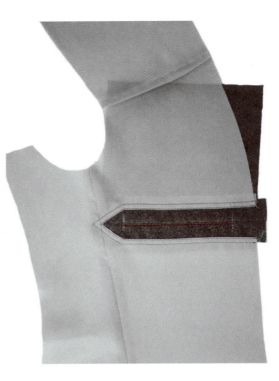

On the wrong side, trim away the excess garment fabric at the point of the arrow.

On the right side, machine-stitch just below the garment fabric seam, from beginning to end of the 5" (12.7 cm) pocket opening. With this stitch-line you will be catching the pocketing which is on the wrong side.

Baste the unfaced pocketing piece to the wrong side of the lining. The slanted edge of the pocketing should be flush with the bottom seam allowance of the garment fabric pocket front.

On the wrong side of the lining, pull down the pocketing and thumbnail press its seam. Baste the pocketing in place.

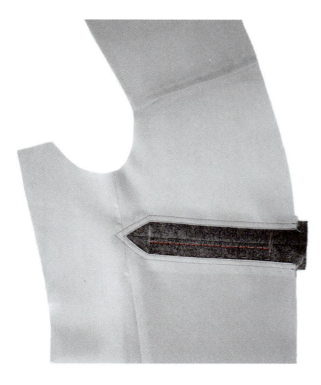

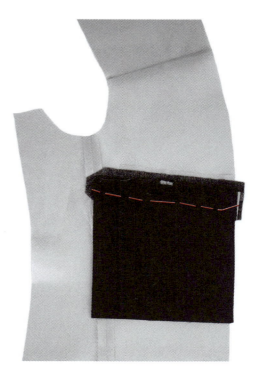

On the right side, machine-stitch a second row about ¼" (6 mm) below the first, catching the pocketing again.

Place the second pocketing piece (the one that has been faced) on top of the first. The top edge of the pocketing should be flush with the top seam allowance of the pocket front.

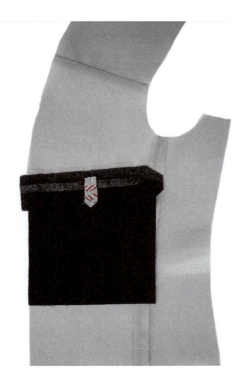

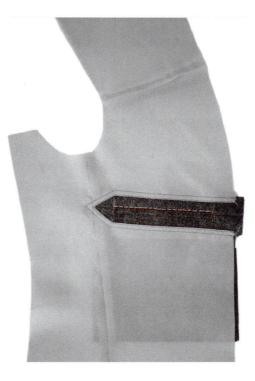

Baste the buttonhole tab at the center of the 5" (12.7 cm) pocket opening on the wrong side. The distance from the garment fabric seam to the horizontal stitchline on the tab should be about ⅝" (1.6 cm). This buttonhole is for a ½" (1.3 cm) button.

On the right side, machine-stitch just above the garment fabric seam, catching the pocketing *and* the buttonhole tab. Tack well vertically at either end of the 5" (12.7 cm) pocket opening.

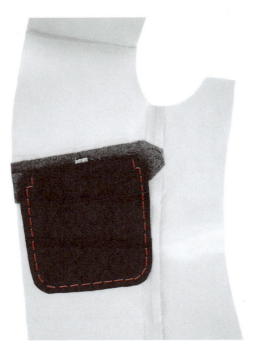

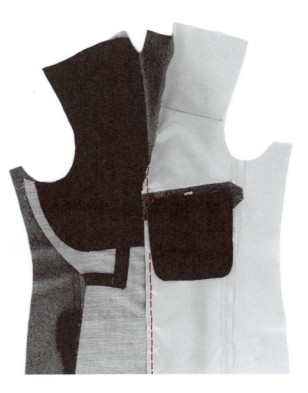

Sew the two pocketing pieces together. Trim the seam allowance to ⅜″ (1 cm).

With the pocket complete, attach the front lining to the **facing**, using a ⅜″ (1 cm) seam allowance. Stitch to just past the top of the jacket hem. The pleat in the lining faces downwards. Trim away the garment fabric bulk in the seam allowance.

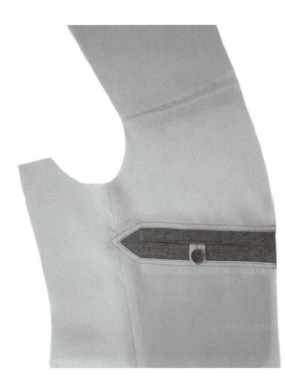

Slit the garment fabric seam from beginning to end of the 5″ (12.7 cm) pocket opening area, and pull the buttonhole tab to the outside. When the jacket is completely finished and pressed, a ½″ (1.3 cm) button is sewn on the pocket front, and the *Barcelona* pocket is complete.

With the seam allowance towards the lining, baste along the edge of the **facing**, attaching the **facing** to the canvas.

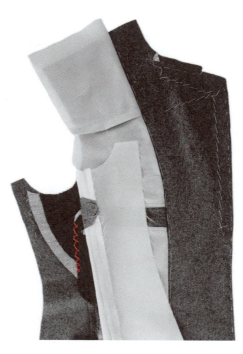

Turn the lining back once more, and cross-stitch the seam allowance of the lining pocket into the canvas. We're simply working our way across the lining, securing it in place.

Beginning about 4" (10.2 cm) below the shoulder and continuing to just above the hem, cross-stitch the lining and **facing** seam allowance into the canvas.

With the lining back in place, baste down through the center of the front lining panel, catching the canvas. Stop well above the hem.

From the right side of the jacket, baste through, catching the lining, begin at about center armhole level, 3" (7.6 cm) in from the edge. Baste down the length of the side panel and then across the jacket, about 5" (12.7 cm) above the hem fold.

To afford added **ease** in the back lining, the seam at the center back is sewn in a scalloped fashion. This creates a controlled pleat which will open out only when required to by the body's movement. The seamline begins at the lining neck edge, at what was the seamline on the jacket pattern.

Sew down approximately 2" (5 cm) and then begin a series of three or four scallops, about 3" (7.6 cm) in length each, extending back the depth of your jacket seam allowance. The ½" (1.3 cm) extra lining, which we added at center back, serves simply as seam allowance for the inner edges of the scallops. The pleats are needed only above the **waist**.

The stitchline ends about 1" (2.5 cm) below the top of the lining vent. If there is no vent, the stitchline below the **waist** continues along the jacket seam allowance.

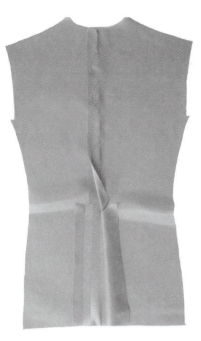

Above the vent, press the center back lining seam allowance to the left. Slash the top of the right vent almost to the stitchline. Trim away 1" (2.5 cm) lengthwise from the left vent.

Before stitching the jacket center back seam, we'll reinforce the vent area with crossgrain strips of pocketing, about 2" (5 cm) wide, from the top of the vent to the hem foldline. Draw a chalkline from the bottom of the center back stitchline to the vent notch at the bottom of the jacket. Use the chalkline as a guide for the placement of the pocketing reinforcement pieces.

Because the left side of the vent will fold and the right side will lie flat in the finished jacket, the pocketing pieces are placed in slightly different positions on either side, to accommodate that difference. (You will note that left and right sides of the jacket are reversed in the illustrations, since we are viewing the jacket from the inside.)

On the right side of the jacket back, place the reinforcement on the vent extension, flush with the chalkline. Leave $3/8$" (1 cm) of the garment fabric visible at the edge.

On the left side of the jacket back, the reinforcement is placed, not on the vent extension, but directly to the right of it, flush with the vent chalkline.

Baste the reinforcement pieces in place and slip-stitch the sides using silk finishing thread. The stitches should not be visible on the right side of the garment fabric.

On the right vent, fold over the ⅜″ (1 cm) of garment fabric at the vent edge, and diagonal stitch it in place. The stitches should not show through on the right side.

Trim away the left vent extension completely, so that the seam allowance down the center back is even from top to bottom.

Machine-stitch the center back seam to 1″ (2.5 cm) below the top of the vent. At the top of the right vent, slash the garment fabric almost to the stitchline.

On the left side of the jacket, baste up about half the hem, leaving enough room for you to sew the side seams without obstruction later on. The left side seam allowance at the vent edge is folded onto the vent reinforcement, basted and then stitched in place using small diagonal stitches and silk finishing thread.

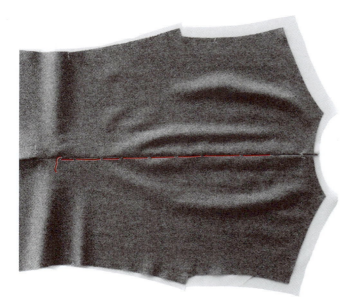

From the right side, baste around the back of the jacket, catching the lining. The illustration shows the approximate distance the basting stitches should remain from the edge of the jacket, in order not to interfere with work still to be done.

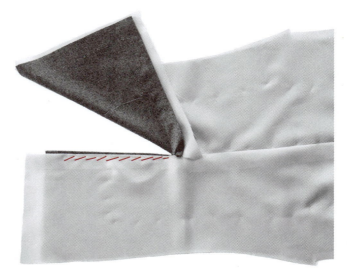

With wrong sides touching, place the lining and jacket backs together, matching **waistline** notches. There will be ½" (1.3 cm) of lining above the jacket neck edge. Baste down the center back seam from the neck edge to the vent opening.

Fold the lining over the left vent, leaving about ¼" (6 mm) of garment fabric showing at the edge. Baste the lining in place to just above the top of the hem.

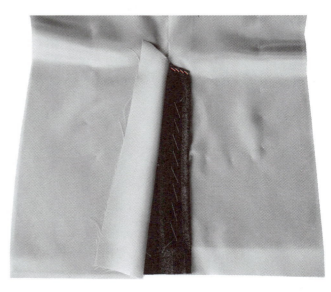

The right vent is now placed on top of the left and back-stitched securely along the top. Stitch through the top of the left vent which is underneath, but do not go through to the right side of the fabric.

Fold and baste the right vent lining over the right vent, so that only a narrow edge of garment fabric is visible at the vent edge.

Since the vent is now completed, we'll machine-stitch the back of the jacket to the side panels and press the seams open. Also press back ½" (1.3 cm), or ⅜" (1 cm) depending on your jacket seam allowance, on either side of the back lining.

The folded edge of the back lining is basted on top of the side panel lining, and is finished with a slip-stitch. A few basting stitches are now added, connecting the front and back underarm basting.

The raw edge of the **facing** is double-cross-stitched to the hem.

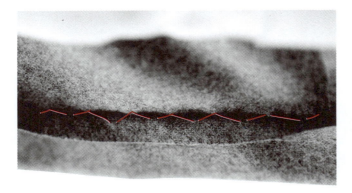

Fold the top edge of the jacket hem forward and hem-stitch it in place.

Baste up the lining hem so that it ends about ¾" (1.9 cm) above the jacket hem. Place your stitches about 1" (2.5 cm) above the lining hem fold, so that you will be able to lift the lining and hem-stitch one layer of it into the jacket hem. The procedure creates a fold at the lining hem, which affords the lining lengthwise **ease**.

The lining at the edge of the vent is finished with a prick-stitch.

SHOULDERS

The Shoulder Seams

Before stitching the shoulder seams, the front shoulder must be reinforced with a strip of lining. Cut a semi-bias strip of the lining to be used as reinforcement, about ¾" (1.9 cm) wide and the length of the front shoulder seam.

Baste the lining strip to the wrong side of the garment fabric, at the front shoulder edge. Catch the garment fabric only, allowing the canvas and the lining to fall freely.

Baste the front and back of the jacket together at the shoulder seams. Since the back shoulder edge is about ½" (1.3 cm) longer than the front (page 24), there will be rippling along the edge of the back seam when the shoulder is basted. Bring the **ease** to the center of the shoulder, leaving 1" (2.5 cm) or so at either end without rippling.

The extra **ease** at the back of the shoulder is there to provide added room for the curve of the back in the shoulder blade area. We can eliminate the rippling at the seam, and still retain the **ease** in the shoulder blade area, by steam pressing carefully, before the shoulder seam is machine-stitched.

Steam press on a flat surface, allowing the iron to extend onto the fabric no more than 1½" (3.8 cm) or so. Bring the iron flat down on top of the ripples at the shoulder edge. The combination of heat and moisture on the flat surface should cause the ripples to shrink away.

If the iron is allowed to extend further onto the shoulder area, while still on a flat surface, the **ease** in the shoulder blade area will also shrink away, and the whole process will have been useless.

It is essential that this pressing be done while the shoulder seam is basted, and not yet machine-stitched. Once the seam has been machine-stitched, it will be impossible to eliminate the ripples.

Machine-stitch the shoulder seam, remove the basting, and press the seam open. Use a tailor's ham for pressing here, in order to protect the shape you have created.

The Shoulder Pads

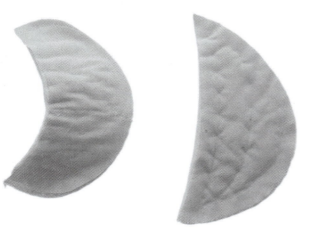

The shoulder pad at the right in this photograph is the best ready-made shoulder pad available. As you can see, it is flat and heavy, and does not coincide with the natural contour of the shoulder.

The shoulder pad at the left can be constructed quite simply, using cotton wadding as the filler, and bias muslin as the top and bottom covering. (Use the shoulder pad pattern on page 269 to cut the muslin coverings.)

Cotton wadding is available in bulk at upholstery supply stores; or, if you prefer, simply take the wadding from a pair of ready-made shoulder pads and reshape it.

Separate the wadding into thin layers, and create on the muslin shoulder-pad pattern, a smooth, sloping mound which tapers to nothing at the sides and back.

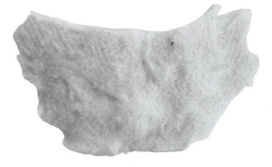

Press down gently at the front centermost edge of the pad and measure the thickness. The amount of padding most flattering to your shoulder has been determined at the toile fitting.

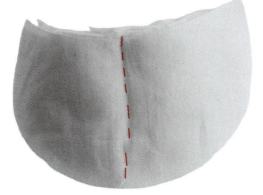

Cover the wadding with a second piece of muslin and baste across the top of the pad to anchor the layers together. By pulling the bottom layer of the muslin cover down a bit, and tacking at either end, the pad begins to take shape.

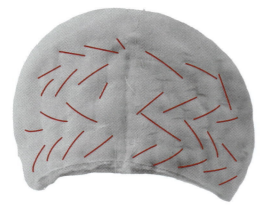

Pad-stitch the shoulder pad from end to end, beginning at the center and working in rows, first towards the front, and then, from the center, towards the back. The stitches go right through all layers of the filling, and should be left comfortably without pulling.

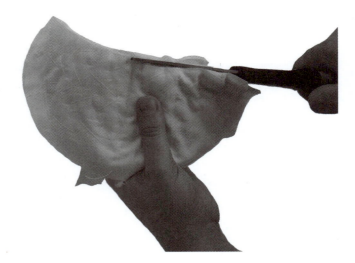

Trim slightly across the front of the pad and around the edges.

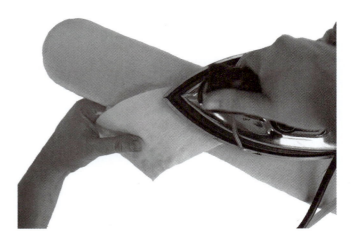

Press the shoulder pad, maintaining the curve you have created.

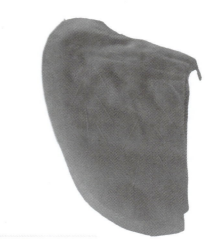

Inserting Shoulder Pads

Before the shoulder pad is sewn into the jacket, check the shoulder width once more, with the pad in place. If the cutting edge at the top of the shoulder extends out beyond the shoulder edge, the fabric may need trimming. As a guide, place a ruler at the bicep and extending up towards the shoulder (see page 137). If the fabric extends out beyond the ruler at the shoulder, the jacket shoulder is too wide and should be trimmed before attaching the shoulder pad.

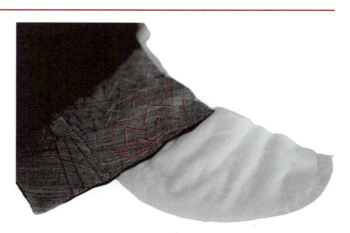

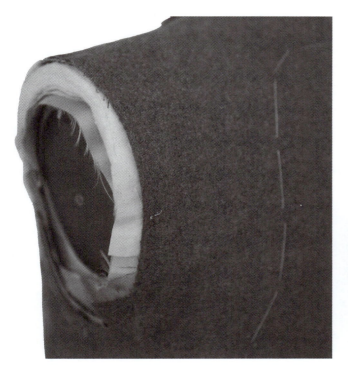

The shoulder pad is placed into the armhole of the jacket, so that the pad reaches to about mid-armhole on the back shoulder. If this tilts the pad too far backwards, you may need to use a larger pad. The front shoulder does not require quite as much of the pad, as the client's musculature will naturally fill the shoulder in this area.

The pad should be between the lining and the canvas, at the armhole cutting edge.

Sometimes, when the top of the shoulder pad is at the armhole cutting edge, the ends of the pad are not. Pull the shoulder pad out until the ends of the pad are at the armhole cutting edge. You can trim the excess later.

With the shoulder pad exactly in place, reach into the armhole and pin the shoulder pad to the canvas. The shoulder pad is now padstitched to the canvas, the stitches covering the entire area of the canvas touched by the pad. Stitch through all layers of padding.

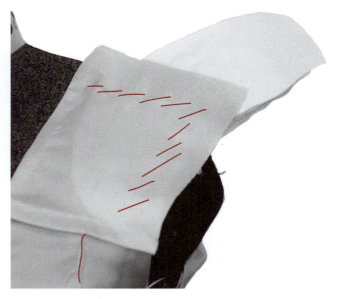

Smooth the front lining up over the shoulder pad and baste the lining to the pad along the armhole and across the top of the lining.

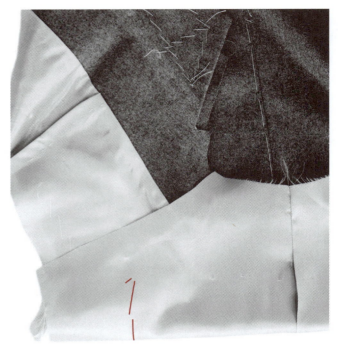

With one hand inside the shoulder area, give the shoulder a concave shape and baste along the front neck edge of the jacket, catching the **facing**. This step is essential in creating the concave shape of the shoulder, a telling detail in a fine-tailored jacket.

The lining at the back of the jacket is still hanging loose at the shoulder. Smooth the back lining up over the shoulder pad and baste from the outside, right through the shoulder pad, to catch the lining. Baste from the bottom end of the shoulder pad up, stopping about 1" (2.5 cm) from the shoulder seam; and bring the needle through to the inside.

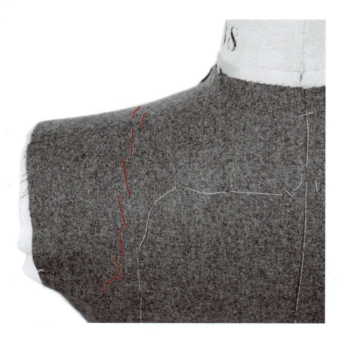

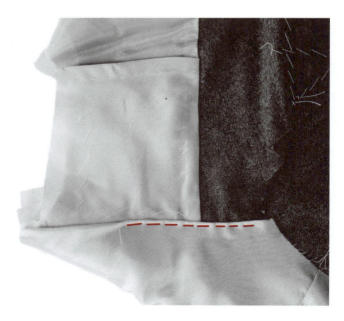

Smooth the jacket fabric out towards the armhole, and baste the entire length of the shoulder pad, about 3" (7.6 cm) in from the armhole edge. Catch the top layer of the shoulder pad as you baste.

Fold the back lining across the shoulder, and baste across the fold, towards the neck edge. Place a bit of **ease** into the back lining as you baste. The lining is left loose, 3" (7.6 cm) in from the armhole edge.

THE COLLAR

The collar can be constructed by following the design lines of your pattern, or in a way that leaves room for a bit of your own designing. Essential to both methods of construction is the fit of the undercollar at the jacket neckline, from collar notch to collar notch.

If, during the toile fitting, you adjusted any of the seams that extend into the neckline, you are already aware that your undercollar pattern needs adjusting. You may, however, have "unintentionally" adjusted some of the neckline seams. The first step is to check the fit of the undercollar pattern.

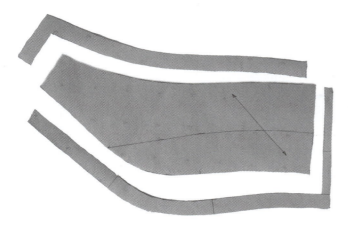

To do this, first trim away the seam allowance on the undercollar paper pattern. You will eventually need this seam allowance, but it is much easier to check the fit of the paper pattern if the seam allowance is not in the way.

Chalkmark the neck edge seam allowance on the jacket, and match the undercollar pattern, stitchline to stitchline, from collar notch to center back seam, first on one side of the jacket, and then on the other.

If you need an extra ⅛" (3 mm) or so, to help the pattern reach the entire distance comfortably, add to the collar pattern at the center back seam. If you are in doubt, remember that it is much easier to work with a collar which is slightly larger than necessary, than it is to work with one which is slightly too small.

It is possible, in checking the pattern, to find that it fits well on one side of the jacket, but not on the other. Whatever the cause (slight inaccuracies in stitching the shoulder seams, or the center back seam), you must now make a collar that is larger on one side than on the other. This is not a problem. Simply prepare both sides of the collar using the larger dimensions, and we'll adjust it later.

If you have made extensive alterations in your jacket pattern at the neckline and shoulder, it may be necessary to discard the collar pattern and to draft a completely new one. Instructions for drafting a collar, using the jacket neck edge as guide, are found below.

Once you are content with the fit of your undercollar pattern, consider the design. At this point you are still free either to redesign the collar, or to go with the collar design of the commercial pattern.

Many tailors leave the question of design until the undercollar has been attached to the jacket. They leave themselves room for designing by cutting the top and the ends of the **melton** undercollar much larger than necessary. When the undercollar has been attached to the jacket, they simply draw a collar which looks good with the existing **lapel**, and trim the excess

away. This is a simple procedure, and quite exciting if you have the desire to branch out a bit on your own.

On the other hand, the collars designed by commercial patternmakers are usually in tasteful balance with the jacket **lapel**, and you may have chosen this pattern largely because of this style. Know your options, make your choice and forge ahead.

Our instructions for the construction of the undercollar will assume that you are following the lines of the commercial pattern. However, the instructions are appropriate for both methods of collar construction. The careful measurement of seam allowances at the top of the collar is not important if you are designing your own collar; however, the shape and seam allowances at the neck edge of the undercollar should be adhered to carefully.

The Collar Draft

If you have made extensive pattern alterations involving the jacket neckline, it may be necessary to draft a new collar pattern, using the jacket neck edge as a guide.

With the jacket folded flat on the table and the neckline in full view, draw a chalkline indicating the neckline seam allowance, from collar notch to collar notch.

Place a folded piece of paper inside the jacket, large enough to reach just below the **lapel**.

On one side of the jacket place a ruler along the **lapel** roll line, and draw on the paper, a short line indicating the extension of the roll line into the neck area. It is important that the jacket not be shifted at all once this guideline has been noted.

Trace around the **lapel** as far as the collar notch. Be careful not to mark the fabric.

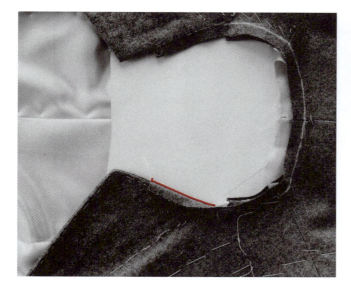

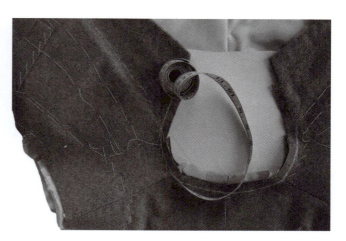

Gently fold back the seam allowance at the **gorge** line. Mark the collar notch, and the **gorge** line.

Measure the back neck stitchline from shoulder to center back. Use a ruler which you can curve, or a tape measure standing on end, to get an accurate measurement.

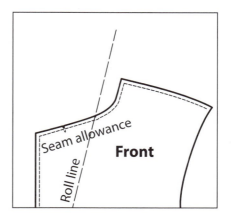

Remove the paper and open it out so that there is enough room to draft a collar. The information on the paper should look something like the markings in the illustration.

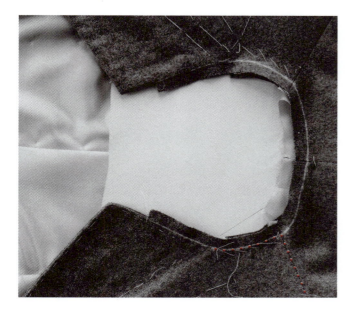

Pinprick through the fabric and the paper along the neckline seam allowance from the roll line to the shoulder seam. Continue a few inches across the shoulder seam.

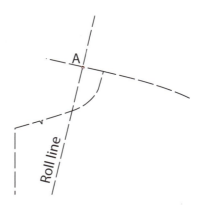

Extend the roll line and the shoulderline so that they intersect. Label the point of intersection *A*.

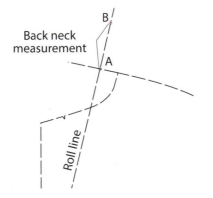

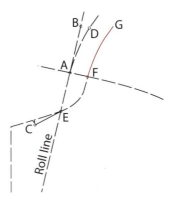

Measure up from A to a distance equal to the back neck measurement. Label *B*.

Draw a curved line, F to G, parallel to line A–D.

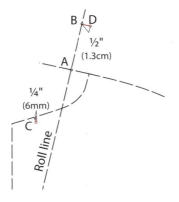

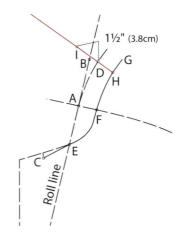

Square out from collar notch, ¼" (6 mm). Label *C*. Square out from the center back, ½" (1.3 cm). Label *D*.

On line F–G, square out going through D and beyond. Label a point (I) on the line about 1½" (3.8 cm) above point D. This measurement D–I is the width of the collar at center back above the roll line.

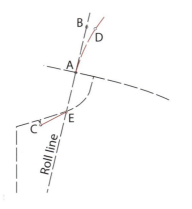

Label *E*, the point at which the neckline pinpricks meet the **lapel**. Draw a curved line, E–F, following the pinpricks. Draw a straight line from C to E, and a curved line from A to D.

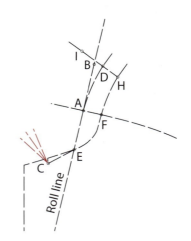

The neck edge of your collar pattern, C–E–F–H, is now complete.

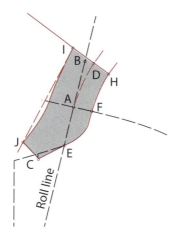

Draw out from point C, a style line for the front of the collar (J).

Draw a straight line from I to J, as a guide for the top of the collar, and then curve the line gracefully at the front.

The undercollar pattern, C–J–I–H–F–E–C, is now complete.

The collar roll line is E–A–D.

Cut out the collar draft and check the fit on the jacket.

Constructing the Undercollar

The undercollar is constructed of collar **melton** and French canvas, pad-stitched together. If you can find good quality prepadded collar **melton**, in the color that you need, by all means use it instead of pad-stitching the **melton** and French canvas together yourself. Because the quality of the prepadded collar **melton** varies greatly and the color choice is often limited, we give directions here for preparing and pad-stitching the undercollar yourself. In certain cases, particularly when using cloth that is not prone to fraying, such as good quality wool flannel, you may be able to construct the undercollar using garment fabric instead of **melton**.

Cut from collar **melton**, in a color which coordinates with your garment fabric, two bias undercollar pieces. Leave ½" (1.3 cm) seam allowance at the outer edges and ¼" (6 mm) seam allowance at the center back. Machine-stitch the center back seam and press it open.

Using the same dimensions as in the collar **melton**, cut from French collar canvas, two bias undercollar pieces. Overlap the center back seam and topstitch by machine.

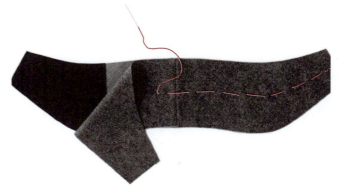

Place the French canvas on the wrong side of the collar **melton**, and between the two, at either end, place a bias piece of pocketing to add body to the front of the collar. The pocketing covers about one half of either side of the undercollar. Baste the French canvas, the pocketing, and the **melton** together.

The French canvas is now pad-stitched (page 124) to the **melton** undercollar. We want the two fabrics joined, but still flexible enough to be shaped with the iron. To maintain this controlled flexibility, we'll pad-stitch in a semi-circular pattern, which coincides with the bias cut of the fabric.

Using a radius of about 2″ (5 cm), draw a semi-circle at the neck edge stitchline of the canvas undercollar. Pad-stitch inside and then, beyond the semi-circle, maintaining the circular pattern of stitches. Use silk finishing thread close in color to the collar **melton**, so that the stitches will not be noticeable on the right side of the undercollar. Pad-stitch only within the limits of the seam allowance which is drawn on the canvas.

Press the undercollar on the canvas side, on a flat surface.

Since both the **melton** and the canvas are cut on the bias, a certain amount of stretching will occur during the pad-stitching. Our next step, therefore, is to redraw the undercollar stitchline, this time on the right side of the collar.

Sharpen the chalk so that you get a clean, accurate line. Begin at the center back, and draw first one side of the undercollar and then the other. Also mark the undercollar roll line, in chalk, and then in basting thread.

If your measurement of the jacket neck edge showed one side slightly smaller than the other, the adjustment in the collar can be made at this point. Before drawing the smaller of the two sides of the collar, fold back the necessary amount on the paper pattern, at center back. Place the folded edge of the pattern at the center back of the **melton** undercollar, and trace the outline.

From the **melton** side, trim away seam allowance completely – top, bottom, sides.

The tips of the collar, about 2″ (5 cm) from either end, are pad-stitched while held in a rolled position, **melton**-side inwards. This technique ensures that, in the finished jacket, the collar tips will incline downwards towards the shoulder, rather than curling up.

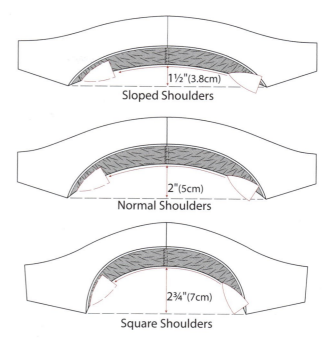

Trim a ⅛" (3 mm) margin of canvas from the top and bottom edges of the undercollar. We're doing this to prevent the raw edges of the canvas from peeking through to the outside. There is no need to trim the canvas at the ends of the undercollar, since the topcollar will eventually hide any stray canvas threads in this area.

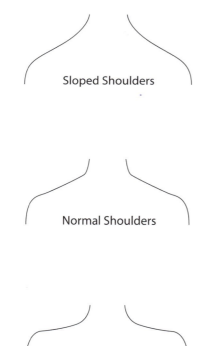

The undercollar is now pressed into shape, taking into consideration the slope of the client's shoulder.

Fold the collar on the roll line and baste it in place.

Using a moderate amount of steam, press the folded edge into an arc, the depth of which depends on your determination of the client's shoulders as sloped, normal or square. For sloped shoulders, the depth of the arc is about 1½" (3.8 cm), for normal shoulders, 2" (5 cm), and for square shoulders, 2¾" (7 cm). This shaping is a fine point in the fit of the collar and **lapel**. If, for example, a collar shaped to fit normal shoulders was set on a jacket shaped to fit sloped shoulders, the **lapel** would not lie flat. It would lift up, away from the jacket. A "sloped collar" placed on a normal neckline would cause the jacket to pull away from the body at the **lapel** roll line. These are slight inclinations in one direction or another, but they are there, and they make a significant difference in comfort and fit.

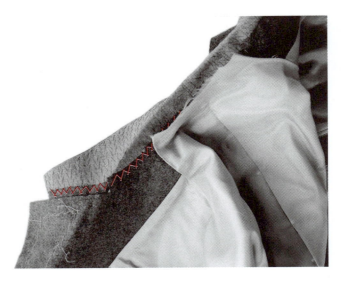

While shaping the undercollar you will have pressed a crease in the roll line. Now, remove the basting which held the neck edge back, and for a few inches at either end of the roll line, press the crease out.

Begin basting the undercollar to the jacket at the center back seam. The raw edge of one side of the undercollar is placed along the chalk guideline which you've drawn at the neckline. The front end of the collar should fall at the collar notch.

The second half of the undercollar is basted beginning at the front, and working around towards the center back. Before beginning to baste the second half of the undercollar, make sure that the distance from the tip of the **lapel** to the beginning of the collar is identical on each **lapel**.

Working on the canvas side, cross-stitch the undercollar to the jacket neckline. Use silk finishing thread, and stitch along the **gorge** line seam allowance, across the top of the **facing**, and the back neckline. Do not catch the back lining in this stitch.

If you have left extra fabric in your undercollar in order to be free to design the collar shape in reference to the **lapel** (page 170), do that now. Measure both sides of the collar accurately, as any discrepancy in length will be in full view on the front of the jacket.

It is customary to stop at this point in the construction of the collar, and to move ahead to the sleeve. Once a muslin sleeve has been set into the jacket, the client is called in for the final fitting. At the fitting, both the collar and the sleeve are checked for fit, and the collar is checked for style.

If you are making the jacket for yourself, and you are pleased with the collar shape, by all means, finish it now. If you are working for someone else, you can reduce the number of fittings by moving ahead to the sleeve at this point.

After the fitting, the collar is finished before the garment fabric sleeve is set.

Constructing the Topcollar

To create the topcollar, cut a piece of garment fabric on the fold, straight grain, nap up, 1½″ (3.8 cm) longer than the undercollar pattern and about 1½″ (3.8 cm) larger than the pattern, on top and bottom.

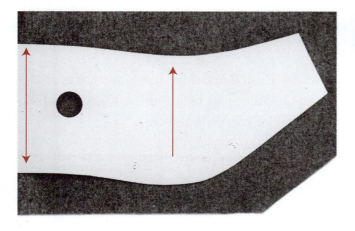

Using a steam iron, stretch the fabric top and bottom.

Place the undercollar face down on the wrong side of the topcollar, and baste the two together, from **gorge** line to **gorge** line, across the under-collar roll line.

Baste across the top of the undercollar, about ½″ (1.3 cm) from the edge.

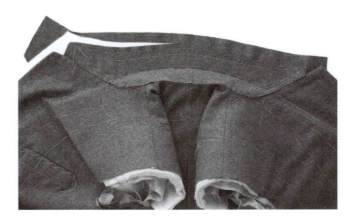

Trim the topcollar, leaving ⅜″ (1 cm) seam allowance visible above the top of the undercollar, and 1″ (2.5 cm) at the sides.

Baste across the top of the topcollar, folding the seam allowance to the inside. Allow the topcollar fold to extend about ⅛″ (3 mm) above the undercollar, so that the seam will not be visible when the jacket is worn. Both the top edge and the neck edge of the undercollar are finished with a slip-stitch, using silk thread.

With the topcollar flat on the table, baste across the undercollar just below the roll line, catching the topcollar fabric underneath.

The topcollar is trimmed, if necessary, and then folded along the **gorge** line. From the collar notch to just past the roll line, the topcollar fold meets flush with the fold of fabric on the **facing lapel**. Beginning just past the roll line and continuing to just past the lining shoulder seam, the topcollar fold overlaps onto the **facing**.

Just past the lining shoulder seam, the topcollar is slashed several times so that it will be able to take the curve of the neckline without pulling. Baste along the back neckline, catching the undercollar. Since these stitches will remain in the jacket, make sure that they do not show through to the right side, and be sure to use silk finishing thread.

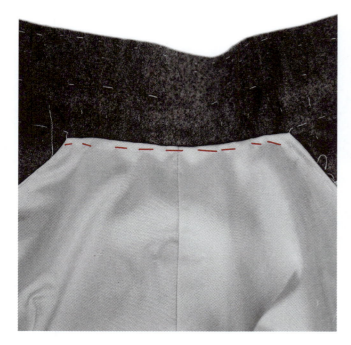

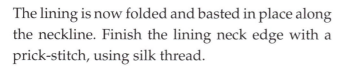

The lining is now folded and basted in place along the neckline. Finish the lining neck edge with a prick-stitch, using silk thread.

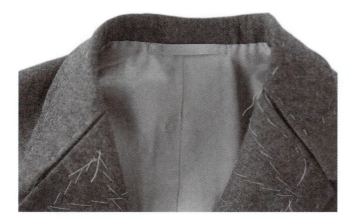

If you would like, construct a loop out of lining fabric, about 2½″ (6.4 cm) long and ⅜″ (1 cm) wide, finished. Attach the loop at the lining neck edge, back-stitching it securely through to the undercollar.

The excess fabric at either end of the collar is now folded back and pressed in place. It is finished with a slip-stitch at top and bottom, and a double-cross-stitch along the raw edge. Use silk finishing thread.

The **gorge** line is now sewn from the outside using a ladder stitch, to bring the topcollar fold and the **facing** fold together without visible stitching. The stitch is taken at the side of the fold rather than on top, and runs back and forth from **facing** to topcollar. After each three or four stitches, one stitch is taken at the center, between the two folds, anchoring the thread into the canvas.

With the collar complete, a final touch is added to the jacket front. Using # A silk thread, slip-stitch along the very edge of the collar, the **lapel**, and the jacket front, on the topside of the fabric. These stitches should be tiny and unnoticed. Their purpose is to guarantee a permanently crisp edge.

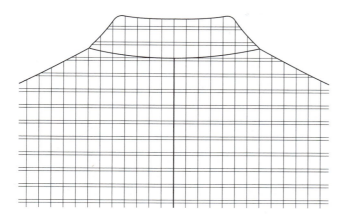

The topcollar on a plaid or striped jacket should match the design at the top of the jacket back. Note that in a plaid fabric this matching should be both horizontal as well as vertical.

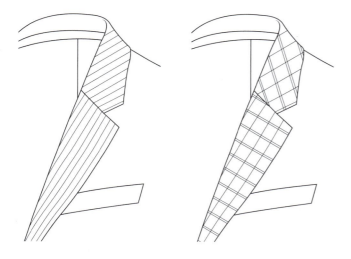

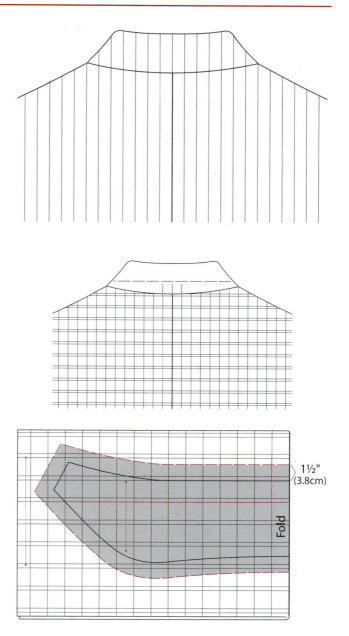

You will be able to match striped fabric at the **gorge** line if the stripes in the fabric are ³⁄₈″ (1 cm) or less apart. To match stripes, which are farther apart than ³⁄₈″ (1 cm) or so, would require excessive shrinking of the top collar at the neck edge.

In a plaid, matching the design at the **gorge** line is virtually impossible.

Chalkmark on the canvas of the completed undercollar, short vertical lines which indicate the position of the centermost vertical bars in the plaid or striped fabric design. If a plaid fabric, rather than a stripe is being used, it is also necessary to draw on the undercollar a horizontal line, indicating the next horizontal bar of the plaid design.

Transfer these guidelines to your paper undercollar pattern.

Use the undercollar pattern, from which all seam allowance has been trimmed, to cut the topcollar from garment fabric. With the fold of the fabric at center back, carefully match the design guidelines, which are on the paper pattern, with those on the fabric. Cut the topcollar 1½″ (3.8 cm) larger than the pattern all around.

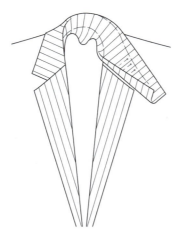

The attachment of the plaid topcollar continues according to the instructions which begin on page 177. The one point to remember is to match the design guidelines which were drawn on the canvas undercollar, with the topcollar fabric design, before beginning to baste.

The striped topcollar must be pinned in place before being basted, so that the topcollar fabric can be placed to match not only at the center back of the jacket but also at the **gorge** line. If the stripes in the pattern are not too far apart, this match of stripes at the **gorge** line can usually be accomplished by a slight movement of the topcollar fabric downwards.

THE SLEEVE

For a tailor, the fall of a well-set sleeve is a thing of beauty. There is more involved here than simply fitting the top edge of the sleeve neatly into the jacket armhole:

- The armhole is reinforced to prevent stretching.
- A muslin sleeve is prepared and set into the jacket. It is set to fall either forward or backward at the same angle the client's arm is held at rest.
- Using the information gathered from the muslin prototype, the garment fabric sleeve is cut, prepared, lined, and set.
- The sleeve head is added to produce a graceful draping of fabric out over the biceps.

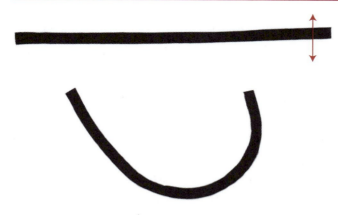

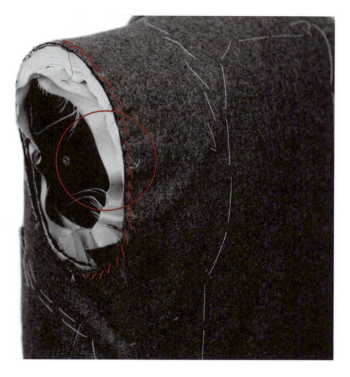

underneath. Catch *only* the garment fabric and the pocketing, avoiding the shoulder pad completely.

Before the sleeve is set, the armhole must be reinforced with a strip of pocketing to ensure against stretching. Cut a crossgrain strip of pocketing about ¾" (1.9 cm) wide and 20" (50.8 cm) long. Press it into a curve (as illustrated).

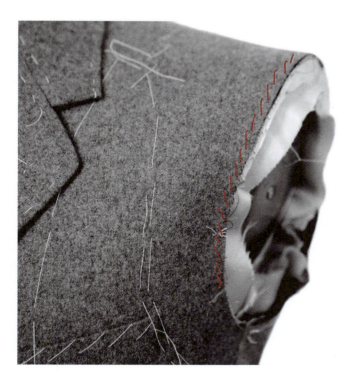

Place the pocketing strip on the wrong side of the jacket fabric, flush with the armhole cutting edge. The curved end of the strip is placed at the front armhole notch, about 2½" (6.4 cm) forward of the center of the underarm.

Working from the right side of the jacket, diagonally baste-stitch around the armhole, catching the outer edge of the pocketing strip

At a point about 1½" (3.8 cm) beyond the shoulder seam, at the back of the jacket, backstitch on the tape and then begin basting tiny ripples of **ease** into the jacket fabric. This process continues to about 1½" (3.8 cm) above the side panel seam, so that the rippled area is at shoulder-blade level on the jacket, and affords added **ease** for movement in this area.

The total amount of **ease** should not be more than ⅜" (1 cm). On gabardines, or other tightly woven fabrics, the **ease** amount should be closer to ¼" (6 mm). The **ease** is basted into the pocketing strip and tacked, top and bottom, so that it will stay where you have placed it.

Continue basting the pocketing strip down to about mid-underarm. The area from about mid-underarm forward about 2½" (6.4 cm) is not reinforced, so that there will be no restriction of the forward movement of the arm.

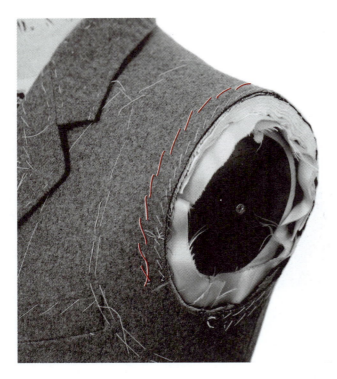

Baste around the armhole from the outside of the jacket a second time, this time catching the inner edge of the pocketing.

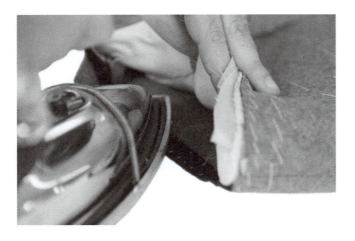

The ripples placed at the back of the armhole have brought extra **ease** beyond, to the shoulder-blade area. We can eliminate the ripples and still retain the **ease** by steam pressing carefully.

Steam press the rippled area, on the wrong side of the fabric, on a flat surface. Be careful to allow the iron to extend in from the armhole edge no more than about 1½″ (3.8 cm) or so. A moderate amount of steam, applied flat and on top of the ripples, should shrink them away.

If you were to press further in on the fabric, while still on a flat surface, you would shrink away the **ease** which the ripples represent, and render the entire process useless.

Keep the iron out and at the edge of the armhole for now.

If you have trouble getting the ripples to disappear, you have probably placed too much **ease** in the area, and are dealing with a tightly woven fabric. If necessary, remove the pocketing strip and adjust the amount of **ease**. Do take care of the problem before continuing. Once the sleeve is sewn in, the ripples will be a permanent distraction.

The Muslin Sleeve

You'll notice we haven't cut the sleeve yet. We haven't even cut a muslin sleeve. We've been waiting until the shoulder pads are placed in the jacket, and the armholes are reinforced, in order to get an accurate measurement of the jacket armholes. Once we have this measurement, we can cut a muslin sleeve with the right amount of **ease** all around.

On the right side of the jacket, measure around the armhole cutting edge. It is somewhat difficult to measure a curved area, therefore do it carefully, and double check your measurement.

Compare this measurement with that to the cutting edge around the top of your sleeve pattern. Measure both the undersleeve and the topsleeve, being careful not to include your side seam allowances in this measurement.

The cutting edge around the top of the sleeve pattern should measure 2" (5 cm) to 2¼" (5.7 cm) larger than the cutting edge around the jacket armhole. (For gabardines and other tightly woven fabrics, the measurement should not be more than 2" (5 cm). This amount of **ease** is necessary to allow the sleeve to fall gracefully from the shoulder.

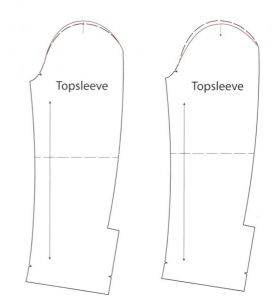

If the top edge of your sleeve pattern is not at least 2" (5 cm) larger than your armhole measurement, adjust the sleeve pattern by adding to or subtracting from the top edge of the topsleeve, tapering to nothing at the side seam allowances. The undersleeve is not adjusted. The maximum adjustment possible at the top of the topsleeve, before distorting the cap shape, is ⅜" (1 cm).

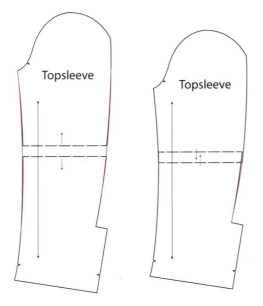

Check the sleeve length, measuring down the center of the topsleeve, from stitchline to hem fold. Using the sleeve measurement taken on page 18 as a guide, lengthen or shorten the sleeve by cutting the sleeve pattern at approximately elbow level. Separate or overlap the topsleeve pattern to achieve the correct length; and then blend the sides of the pattern using a hip curve. The undersleeve pattern is adjusted by the same amount as the topsleeve.

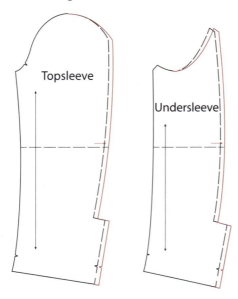

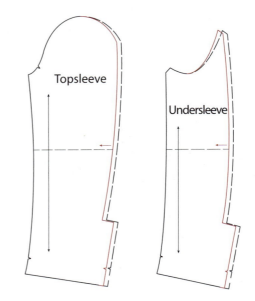

If further adjustment of the sleeve cap is necessary, it must now also involve the width of both the topsleeve and undersleeve in order to maintain the overall balance. Again, an adjustment of ⅜" (1 cm) is the maximum suggested.

Adjust the pattern according to the illustrations, using a hip curve to taper your new lines gracefully.

If this adjustment should still prove insufficient, the answer is an entirely new sleeve pattern, one size larger or smaller.

With the sleeve pattern adjusted, cut the muslin sleeve, sew the undersleeve and topsleeve together, and press the seams open.

On the right side of the fabric, press a crease in the topsleeve seam from the hem to about elbow level.

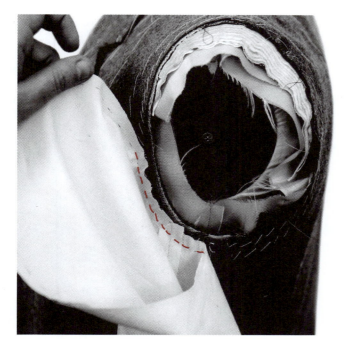

Use a ½" (1.3 cm) seam allowance to set the sleeve, even if your pattern indicates ⅝" (1.6 mm). Since we have already checked the armhole fit and the cap **ease**, this adjustment can be made without concern. It is much easier to work with a ½" (1.3 cm) seam than with a larger amount in a curved area. The bulk in the seam is reduced and the cap **ease** has more room to comfortably settle in.

It is best to use a model form to set the sleeve. With a model form, the entire armhole is in view, and the matching curves at the bottom front of the armhole and sleeve are clearly visible. This area is called the front notch, whether it is notched or not, and it is the first point at which the sleeve and armhole are tacked for a fitting.

The point at which the back seam in the sleeve falls on the armholes, is called the back notch. In order to determine this point, hold the sleeve at the top, and allow it to fall forward until the hem touches the chalk guideline on the pocket. This chalkmark indicates how far forward your arm falls when held naturally. The sleeve must hang in that same position to be without creases when it is worn. Tack the back notch into the armhole at the point which allows the sleeve to fall forward to the chalk guideline.

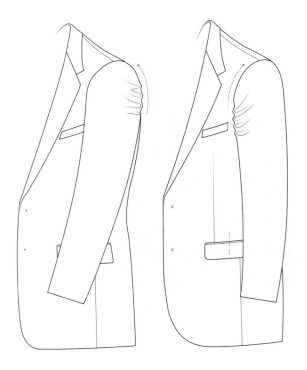

it falls a bit more forwards or back, until the creases disappear. When the sleeve falls comfortably without these creases, chalkmark the front and back notches on the jacket and the front notch on the sleeve. These notches should also be transferred to your pattern. (For plaid sleeves see page 197.)

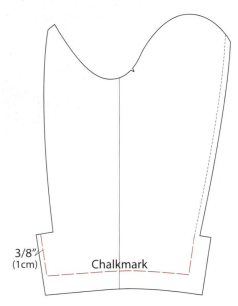

With the front and back notches tentatively tacked, baste around the armhole, distributing the 2"–2¼" (5–5.7 cm) **ease** around the entire reinforced area of the armhole. Only the 2½" (6.4 cm) area from center underarm forward is without **ease** in the sleeve. There may be some puckering at the cap of the muslin sleeve. However, if you have measured your armhole correctly, these puckers will be easy to control in the garment fabric.

Check the sleeve side view. If there are diagonal creases from the front or back of the sleeve pointing upwards, the sleeve should be set so that

The sleeve length is to some degree a matter of preference. Comfort when wearing the jacket should be your main criterion. If you choose, allow about ½" (1.3 cm) of your shirt cuff to show below the hem of the sleeve. This too, is purely preference. Adjust the muslin sleeve length, and pin in place.

Ironworking the sleeve

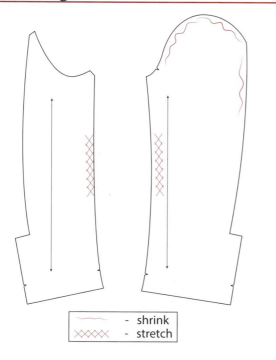

- shrink
- stretch

The sleeve, like every other part of the garment, will benefit from being shaped with iron and steam, to produce a more graceful fall. Once all the pattern corrections have made, the garment fabric sleeve can finally be cut with confidence.

There is ample easing that will be required at the sleeve cap, but this will be produced through basting, instead of preparatory ironwork.

The majority of the ironwork needed on the sleeve is located at the front seam of the topsleeve, at elbow level. To help you place the right amount of shape where it is needed, draw a chalkline from the front notch on the topsleeve, in a curve parallel to the front seam. At elbow level, stretch the fabric forward of this line. You have achieved the correct shape when, as the fabric is folded on the curved chalkline, the stretched area lays smoothly on the outer part of the topsleeve.

This process will help the sleeve curve elegantly forward, matching the natural shape of the arm.

The Sleeve Vents

Once the sleeves have been properly ironworked, machine-stitch and press open the under seam. On the right side of the fabric, chalkmark the hem and vent foldlines. The foldline on the topvent is a continuation of the sleeve seamline. On the undervent, the foldline is ⅜" (1 cm) from the edge.

the bottom of the sleeve, on the wrong side of the garment fabric.

Cut a bias piece of pocketing to be used as reinforcement, 5" (12.7 cm) wide and long enough to extend from the vent edge to vent edge at the bottom of the sleeve. Steam press the pocketing into a slight curve so that it will lie comfortably at

Baste along the chalklines at the bottom of the sleeve, catching the pocketing reinforcement, and diagonally baste-stitch across the top of the reinforcement.

Trim the sides of the pocketing very close to the basting on the undersleeve vent, and about ½″ (1.3 cm) from the basting on the topvent. Diagonal-stitch the reinforcement into the sleeve seam allowance, above the hem.

Fold and press, first the vents, and then the hem, using the basting lines as guides. Fold the bottom of the topvent into a miter, and press well. Unless the fabric is extremely bulky, we suggest that you do not trim the excess fabric in the corner. The fold will give a certain amount of appropriate body to the topvent. It will also afford you the option of lengthening the sleeve, should this be desirable sometime in the future.

Diagonal-stitch the vents and hem into the pocketing, using silk finishing thread, and slip-stitch the sides.

With the topvent ¹⁄₁₆″ (1.5 mm) longer than the undervent, baste first the vent, and then the sleeve seam closed.

The topsleeve seam should be about ⅜″ (1 cm) longer than the undersleeve (see page 186). For gabardine, or other tightly woven fabrics, ¼″ (6 mm) is better. Place this **ease** in the top third of the topsleeve seam, and steam press the puckers out, before machine-stitching the seam.

Press on a flat surface, making sure that the iron extends onto the fabric no more than about 1½" (3.8 cm).

Machine-stitch the topseam to ¼" (6 mm) below the top of the vent and press the seam open. Fold and press the seam allowance on a diagonal just above the top of the vent, instead of clipping the seam allowance here and weakening the area.

Back-stitch the tops of the vent together using silk finishing thread. The sleeve is now ready to be lined.

Lining the Sleeve

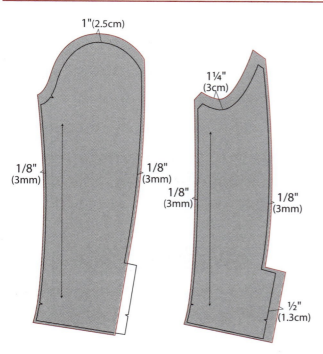

The sleeve lining is cut using the sleeve pattern. Trace around the sleeve pattern, cutting the lining larger than the sleeve by the amounts indicated. Note that the vent on the topsleeve is eliminated.

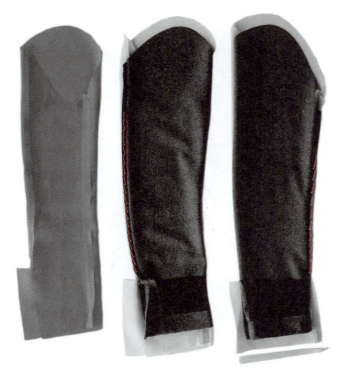

Reach into the lining, and turn the sleeve to the lining side, so that you can work on the lining hem and vent. Fold and baste the lining along the edge of the undervent (the undervent is on top when viewed from this side); and fold the lining hem about ¾" (1.9 cm) above the hem of the sleeve. Baste the lining hem about 1" (2.5 cm) above its fold, so that you will be able to lift it up for hand-stitching, shortly.

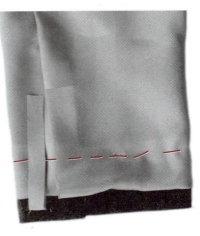

Machine-stitch the lining topsleeve and undersleeve together, and press the seams open.

With both the lining and sleeve inside out, place the two together, undersleeve to undersleeve. A ¾" (1.9 cm) margin of lining should be visible above the sleeve. Beginning about 4" (10.2 cm) from the top of the top seam, diagonally baste one layer of lining seam allowance to one layer of sleeve seam allowance. Baste to just above the top of the vent. Trim the lining to 1" (2.5 cm) below the sleeve hem fold.

Repeat the process at the undersleeve seam.

The top layer of lining is now slashed horizontally, about ½" (1.3 cm) below the bottom of the lining seam. The slash extends across, just past the edge of the undervent. This frees the lining to be folded along the garment fabric at the edge of the topvent.

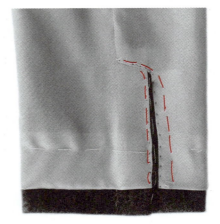

The lining is folded on the diagonal at the top of the vent and basted in place. The sides and top of the vent lining are finished with a hand back-stitch, using silk thread.

Lift the lining at the hem, and hem-stitch one layer of lining into the garment fabric hem.

Turn the sleeve to the right side, and with the lining settled in place, baste across the topsleeve about 8" (20.3 cm) or so from the top, catching the topsleeve lining. This will hold the lining in place while you set the sleeve. Press the sleeve on theright side, on a flat surface, using a presscloth. Press a light crease in the topseam from elbow to hem.

Setting the Sleeve

The garment fabric sleeve is set into the jacket just as the muslin sleeve was set. This time, however, you have the benefit of the front and back notches as guides.

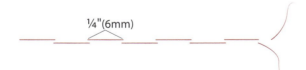

¼"(6mm)

Baste the sleeve using a straight running-stitch about ¼" (6 mm) long, with spaces of about the same length in between. If your stitches are too small, the **ease** will have no room to settle in. Do *not* be discouraged if it takes two or three attempts to baste the sleeve in so that it hangs without rippling at the cap when viewed from the outside.

Once you are pleased with the hang of the sleeve, baste around the armhole a second time,

stitching between the first stitches. This lock-stitch is done to hold the **ease** securely in place, and to prevent the possibility of the sleeve shifting during machine-stitching.

There is one more step to take before machine-stitching the sleeve. On the wrong side of the fabric, steam press on a flat surface, and shrink away the ripples at the top of the sleeve seam allowance. Be careful to press in from the armhole edge no more than one inch or so. If you steam press further, you will be shrinking the **ease** in the sleeve cap which you have so carefully created. You need the **ease**. Shrink away *only* the ripples.

Tuck the shoulder pad out of the way and machine-stitch around the armhole, catching only

the garment fabric of the sleeve and arm-hole, and the pocketing reinforcement strip.

Tacking the Armholes

The sleeve is set, but the shoulder and armhole area still needs some attention. The jacket lining is loose at the back armhole, and the shoulder pad needs to be tacked into the armhole seam allowance. With this completed, you'll be able to attach the sleeve head, and close the sleeve lining.

With one hand inside the jacket, giving shape to the shoulder area, smooth the fabric around the armhole towards the sleeve seam. Baste from the front notch up and over the shoulder, to the end of the shoulder pad. As you baste from the front notch to the beginning of the shoulder pad, catch the lining. As you continue up and over the shoulder, catch one layer of the shoulder pad.

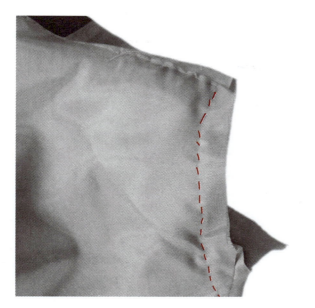

On the inside of the jacket back, the lining is still loose at the armhole. Baste from the underarm up the back of the armhole, as far as the lining shoulder seam. Use a large back-stitch, and place a bit of **ease** in the back lining as you baste.

Since you are working with the jacket inside out, be aware that the shoulder pad is now curving in a direction opposite to that which it will take when the jacket is worn. Before you baste the shoulder pad into the armhole seam allowance, force the shoulder pad into the correct curve. Experiment by turning the jacket right side out, in order to be sure of the proper direction of the curve. It is not necessary to baste though the entire shoulder pad. One layer of the padding caught in the seam allowance is sufficient.

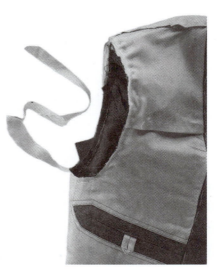

Shoulder pad, jacket lining, pocketing, sleeve, and jacket, all meet in the armhole seam allowance. Baste around the armhole, tacking all these layers together, so that the shoulder seam becomes a firm unshifting line. Tack first, the area of seam allowance untouched by the shoulder pad. The stitch is a backstitch, 1/8″ (3 mm) beyond the machine stitchline, in the seam allowance.

If necessary, the shoulder pad and lining are now trimmed flush with the garment fabric seam allowance. Be careful not to trim away the small edge of seam allowance from the side panel back seam. If you do, you eliminate the possibility of ever letting the jacket out in this area.

The Sleeve Head

The sleeve head is a strip of cotton wadding, covered with muslin and with a strip of bias canvas **interfacing**. Its job is to fill out the cap of the sleeve a bit, and to create a graceful fall of the fabric at the top of the sleeve.

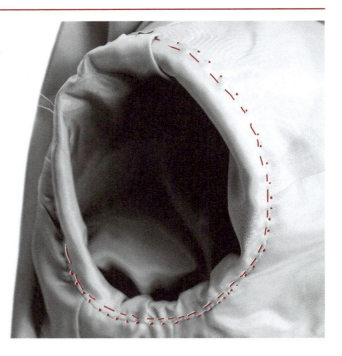

Prior to attaching the sleeve head in the garment, it should be shaped in a curve using the steam iron, as illustrated.

The sleeve lining is now brought up to be basted along the armhole edge, just covering the basting already there. Fold back about ¼" (6 mm) at the top of the lining and check that the seams in the lining are aligned with the seams in the sleeve. A twisted lining will distort the hang of the sleeve, and will be very uncomfortable to wear. Slip-stitch the sleeve lining into the armhole seam allowance using silk finishing thread.

The head is inserted into the sleeve with the canvas facing up, and hand-stitched into the seam allowance using silk thread. Place the edge of the head even with the edge of the seam allowance, from the front notch, over the shoulder and down to about 2" (5 cm) below the back notch. The sleeve head should be stitched onto the sleeve cap, using a backstitch. Be careful to place this stitch at a consistent distance from the armhole stitchline, on the seam allowance. The closer the sleeve head is attached to the armhole stitchline the more volume it will give to the top of the sleeve.

The Plaid Sleeve

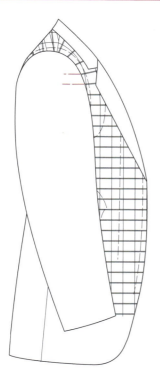

If you are working with a plaid fabric, the sleeve must be cut so that the horizontal design lines on the sleeve match those across the jacket front. (Because of the **ease** in the sleeve cap, the horizontal lines on the sleeve will not match those on the jacket back.)

With the muslin sleeve well set, draw two or three horizontal guidelines on the front of the muslin to indicate the placement of the horizontal bars of the plaid design. Transfer these guidelines to the front of your sleeve front paper pattern, and use them as a layout guide.

BUTTONS AND BUTTONHOLES

The choice of buttons for a fine tailored men's jacket should be in keeping with the high quality of the rest of the garment.

The buttons for a business or dress suit are in best taste if they are all but unnoticed on the finished jacket. Dull horn or bone buttons, close in color to the jacket fabric, are most traditional. Shiny plastic buttons are glaringly inappropriate on fine fabric. For a navy blazer, a more flamboyant silver or gold button is common; or leather buttons for sports jackets.

The jacket button is ¾" (1.9 cm) in diameter, the sleeve button is ½" (1.3 cm).

The top buttonhole on a jacket which has a **lapel**, should be placed about ⅝" (1.6 cm) below the bottom of the **lapel** roll line. If the button is placed lower or higher, the **lapel** will begin to roll just above whatever point that happens to be.

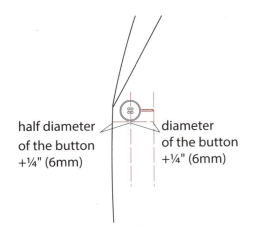

half diameter of the button +¼" (6mm)

diameter of the button +¼" (6mm)

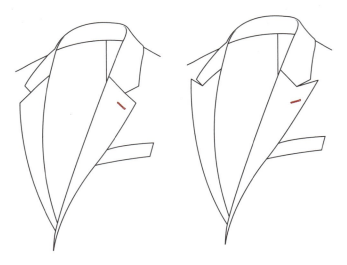

The buttonhole begins in from the edge of the finished jacket a distance equal to one half the diameter of the button, plus ¼" (6 mm).

The size of the jacket buttonhole is equal to the diameter of the button, plus a "small" ¼" (6 mm).

On the sleeve, real buttonholes are a distinctly custom touch. The buttonholes begin 1¼" (3.2 cm) above the hem fold, and ½" (1.3 cm) away from the fold at the edge of the topvent. If three buttons are used on the sleeve, the buttonholes are placed ¾" (1.9 cm) apart. If four buttons are preferred, the buttonholes are placed ⅝" (1.6 cm) apart, so that the buttons will be almost touching.

The size of the sleeve buttonhole is equal to one half the diameter of the button, plus ⅛" (3 mm).

Handworked buttonholes, reinforced with gimp, for a crisp edge, are a hallmark of custom tailoring. Machine buttonholes work as well, but are not nearly as beautiful.

If you choose to add a **lapel** buttonhole, it should be cut parallel to the top of the **lapel**. The buttonhole on a peak **lapel** will, therefore, slant upward. On a square **lapel** it will slant downward.

The length of the buttonhole is between ¾" (1.9 cm) and 1" (2.5 cm) depending on the width of the **lapel**, and since it will not actually be used for a button, there is not keyhole cut at the end.

The buttonhole is placed about 1½" (3.8 cm) below the top of the **lapel** and ½" (1.3 cm) in from the edge.

On the wrong side of the **lapel**, about 1" (2.5 cm) below the buttonhole, a thread loop is sewn. This serves to hold the stem of a small flower boutonnière.

Constructing the Buttonholes

Snip the buttonhole through the jacket front, the canvas, and the **facing**. At the end of the buttonhole closest to the jacket edge, cut a small keyhole.

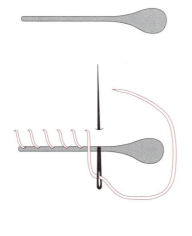

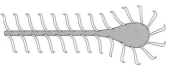

Trim away the canvas around the very edge of the buttonhole, so that stray white canvas threads do not find their way into the buttonhole stitches.

Using silk finishing thread, overcast around the buttonhole to control the fraying threads. These stitches will not be seen in the finished buttonhole.

Cut a length of buttonhole gimp, about three times the length of your buttonhole. Prepare silk buttonhole twist. Cut one yard or buttonhole twist, wax it well, and press the twist between two layers of paper. The heat will melt the wax into the thread and give it added body. The buttonhole twist is used as a single thread, knotted at the bottom.

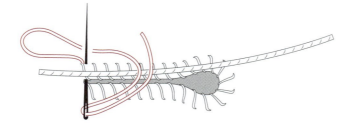

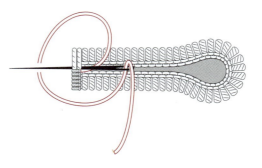

As you take the first buttonhole stitch, near the straight end of the buttonhole, insert the gimp in the loop created by your thread. Do not worry about the cut end of the gimp right now, as we will address it shortly.

Buttonhole stitches create a raised edge, at the center of the buttonhole. To achieve this, the buttonhole twist must be looped around the needle (as illustrated) and then drawn up to form a knot. A firm amount of tension will help keep your buttonhole stitches consistent. As you work the buttonhole, be sure to place these knots, as well as the gimp underneath, towards the cut edge of the buttonhole, while preventing them from falling into it. Buttonhole stitches should be about ⅛" (3mm) deep, and almost touching.

Once you have taken three or four buttonhole stitches, pull the gimp gently so as to hide its cut end under these first few stitches.

When you have stitched around the entire buttonhole, cut the end of the gimp very close to the last stitch. The straight end of the buttonhole is finished with a small bartack, perpendicular to the buttonhole.

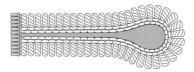

After taking the last stitch, bring your needle between the fabric and canvas, about 1" (2.5 cm) away from the buttonhole. Pull on the thread, creating a ripple in the garment fabric. Proceed to cutting the buttonhole twist very close to this ripple. As the fabric returns to its normal position, the cut end of your thread will be hidden between the layers of fabric and canvas at the jacket front.

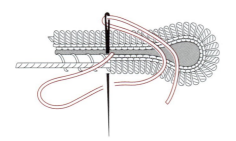

Continue working around the buttonhole, keeping the keyhole shape intact by fanning stitches out.

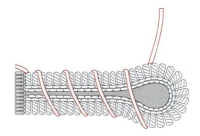

Whip-stitch the buttonhole closed until after the final pressing.

Final Pressing

Following the pressing techniques outlined on page 11, the jacket is now carefully and completely pressed. The pressing is done before the buttons have been sewn on, to permit the iron greater access. The pressing proceeds step by step, as follow:

1. The underside of one **lapel**, the underside of the collar, and the underside of the second **lapel**.

On the Inside of the Jacket

2. The **facing**, from the bottom of the **lapel** to the hem on one side of the jacket; and the lining bel ow the **waist**, first on one side of the jacket, and then on the other. Be careful to use a tailor's ham to press shaped areas of the jacket.
3. The lining in the **chest** area on both sides of the jacket.
4. Across the hem on the lining side, from one side of the jacket to the other.

On the Outside of the Jacket

5. Each front of the jacket from shoulder to hem, and the side seam.
6. The jacket back from shoulder to hem.

Sleeves

7. On the right side of the fabric, the front seam, and the undersleeve.
8. With the sleeve board inside the jacket, the topsleeve, from biceps to hem, creasing the sleeve lightly from elbow to hem.
9. The lining underarm area.

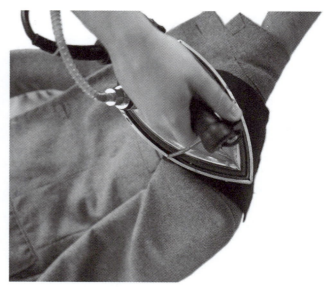

10. Holding a press mitt inside the shoulder of the jacket, press each shoulder and sleeve cap on the right side of the fabric.
11. The right side of each **lapel**.

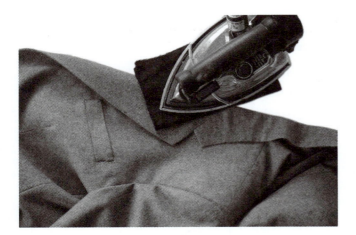

12. With the **lapel** and collar lying flat over the pressing board, press the **gorge** line, and a light crease at the neck edge of the **gorge** line.

Setting the Buttons

To mark the button placement on a single-breasted jacket, place the two fronts of the jacket together, facings touching.

Place a pin through the keyhole of the buttonhole to mark the button placement on the right side of the jacket.

Marking the button placement for a double-breasted jacket is somewhat more complicated, since there are both buttons and buttonholes on both sides of the jacket.

The buttonholes are placed on the left side of a double-breasted jacket using the same measurements as were used for the single-breasted jacket.

The placement of the buttons on the left side of the jacket is determined by measuring from the keyhole to the center front line, and applying this measurement from the center front line away from the jacket edge.

With the jacket closed, and the center front guidelines matching, place a pin through the top button mark on the left side of the jacket. This pin will indicate the placement of the one buttonhole which is needed on the right side of the jacket. It also indicates the placement of the one button which must be placed on the inside of the left side of the jacket.

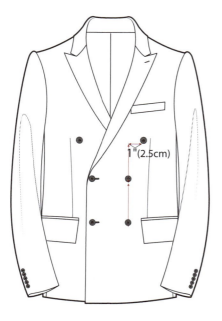

1"(2.5cm)

Once the placement of the buttons and buttonholes which fall below the **lapel** have been completed, two buttons are attached to the jacket above the bottom of the **lapel**, one on either side of the jacket. The vertical distance between all buttons remains the same, but the vertical alignment does not. The top buttons are each moved 1" (2.5 cm) horizontally, in the direction of the armhole.

After the final pressing of the jacket, the buttons are sewn to the jacket using a double strand of waxed, pressed, silk buttonhole twist thread.

Most tailors double their thread by placing two strands through the eye of the needle (as illustrated) – a challenge, indeed. This allows the needle to move to different points along the length of the thread as you sew, thus reducing the probability of the thread being weakened, by being pulled by the needle, over and over again, at the same spot.

The stitches taken on the front of the jacket to attach the button, do not go through all the layers of the fabric, and therefore, do not show through the **facing**. The needle is brought through each hole in the button twice, anchoring each side of the button with four strands of thread. A ¼" (6 mm) shank is created by holding the button away from the jacket as you stitch.

The stitches completed, the thread is wound around the shank several times. Four knots are then stitched at the base of the shank, catching the thread which comes from each of the four holes in the button. A button secured to the jacket in this way is not likely to be lost without warning.

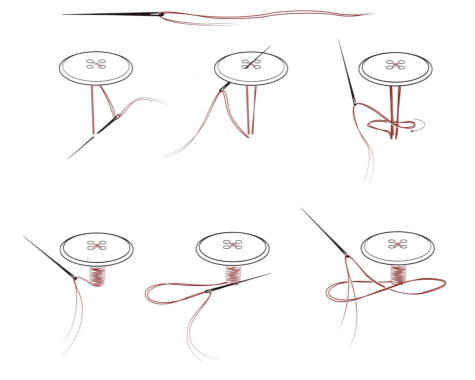

7 THE PANTS

IRONWORKING THE PANTS

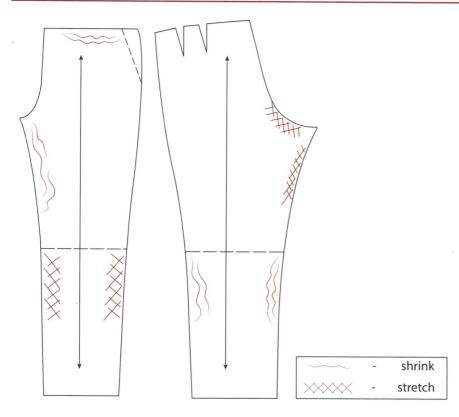

∼∼∼∼	-	shrink
✕✕✕✕✕	-	stretch

The pants can often be held in lower esteem in a suit when compared to the jacket. This may be due to the extensive amount of detail and attention placed in the jacket; however, a great suit cannot exist without pants that have been carefully constructed and shaped to fit the client.

Traditionally pants patterns position seams on the outside and inside of each leg. This is aesthetically expected, but in many ways interfering with the creation of a flattering shape to the pant leg. When viewed from the side (page 19), legs are not straight. Instead, they tend to follow a gentle S curve, forward at the thigh, and then backwards at the calf.

To achieve this shape in the finished garment, the trouser front and back panels must be ironworked, stretching and shrinking fabric in strategic places.

The front leg should be folded in half, lengthwise, matching the vertical seams from hem to **crotch**. Starting from the bottom, the calf area (below the knee notch) is stretched at the outer edge of the piece. Proceeding upwards, the thigh area is shrunk on the outer edges of the piece, using steam liberally and concentric circular motion of the iron.

Once ironworked correctly, the front leg will not lay smoothly on a flat surface, but instead show the added volume created at the front of the thigh and at the side of the calf.

The back leg is treated somewhat similarly, by folding it in half and matching the vertical seams from hem to above the knee notches.

Shaping is not particularly required above the knee, as this would reduce the room available for the customer's musculature. However, we will shrink the outer edges of the pattern below the knee, so as to create a gentle forward swoop to the lower leg below the calf.

REINFORCING THE CROTCH

The front of the **crotch** is reinforced to strengthen the bias against stretching and to protect the fabric from moisture.

The **crotch** reinforcement is a 7" (17.8 cm) square of pocketing fabric which has been folded on the diagonal and pressed to a curve along the fold.

It is basted at the **crotch** on the wrong side of both pants fronts. The folded edge of the reinforcement should be in, towards the body of the pants, and the top should extend about ½" (1.3 cm) above the fly notch.

Trim the reinforcement even with the edge of the **crotch**, and overcast the pants and reinforcement together along the outer edge.

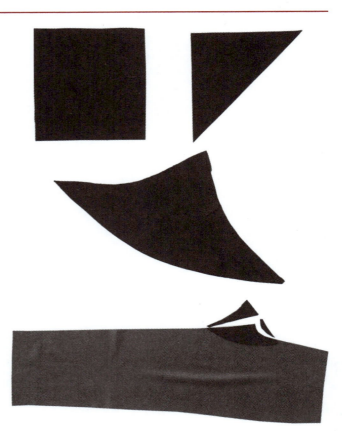

THE PANTS POCKETS

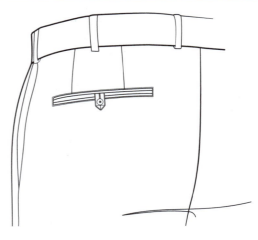

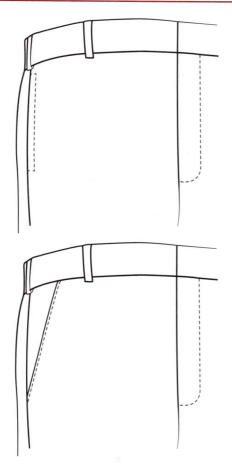

If, as suggested in Chapter 2 (page 23), you have chosen a pants pattern designed for side pockets, you will now be able to create any of the front pocket styles by following the instructions detailed here, or applying these techniques to your own design variations.

The back pocket, shown here, is a double-piping pocket, with or without a buttonhole tab.

Patterns for both pockets discussed here are found on pages 263–265.

The Slant Pocket

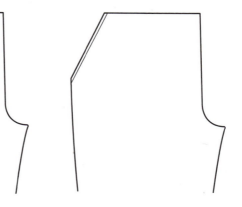

If your pattern is designed for slant pockets, the pants front patter has probably been cut on the diagonal at the top of the side seam.

If you would like to put slant pockets in trousers which have been designed for side pockets, you can adjust your pattern by using the SLANT YOKE pattern on page 264.

Place the slant yoke on the pants front fabric, at the top of the side seam. Chalkmark the notches at the **waist** and side seam, and remove the pattern. The pattern assumes a pants side seam allowance of ⅝" (1.9 cm).

Cut one piece of pocketing for each pocket, 16" (40.6 cm) wide and 12" (30.5 cm) long, on straight grain. Fold the pocketing in half and trim the bottom outer corners to a curve.

Chalkmark a line from notch to notch, and then add a second line, ¼" (6 mm) above the first as seam allowance. Trim away the fabric above the seam allowance.

Using the slant yoke pattern once more, cut from garment fabric, on straight grain, nap down, one yoke for each pocket. Press to the wrong side of the fabric ¼" (6 mm) hems at the bottom of the yoke and at the unnotched side.

Using the pattern labeled SIDE AND SLANT FACING on page 265, cut from garment fabric, on straight grain, two pieces of **facing** for each pocket. On the longest edge of each piece, press a ¼" (6 mm) hem to the wrong side.

Place one piece of pocketing on the wrong side of the pants front, extending ¼" (6 mm) above the top of the pants, and ⅝" (1.6 cm) out at the side seam. Place the **facing** right side down on the pants front, the unfolded edge of the **facing** flush with the diagonal cut at the top of the pants. Machine-stitch the **facing**, pants, and pocketing together, using a ¼" (6 mm) seam along the diagonal edge.

On the right side, topstitch along the diagonal edge about ¼" (6 mm) from the fold.

Trim away the pocketing above the **facing**.

Bring the **facing** and the **facing** seam to the wrong side of the pants, and press in place. The seam should be brought slightly to the back, so as to avoid it showing in the finished pants.

On the wrong side, topstitch along the folded edge of the **facing**, attaching the **facing** to the pocketing only. These stitches do not go through to the front of the pants.

Place the yoke, notch to notch, at the top of the pants side seam, and pin in place.

Fold the pocketing in half, matching the curved edges. Pin the yoke to the pocketing.

Open out the pocketing and topstitch the yoke to the pocketing.

Fold the pocketing once more, inside out this time, in order to begin a French seam. Begin ½" (1.3 cm) below the side notch using a ⅜" (1 cm) seam, and taper the seam to ⅛" (3 mm) at the curve and across the bottom of the pocket.

Turn the pocket right side out and press. Topstitch around the pocketing seam ¼" (6 mm) from the edge.

Just below the pocket opening, on the side of the pocketing closest to the garment fabric, slash about 1" (2.5 cm) into the pocketing and **facing**. This slash will eventually enable you to hold the pocket aside while the side seams are being sewn. The side seams will be sewn only after all pockets and the fly have been constructed.

The Side Pocket

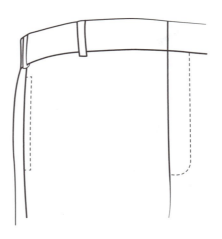

The side pocket is placed in the side seam on the front of the pants. The pocket opening is between 6" (15.2 cm) and 6½" (16.5 cm) long, and begins 2" (5 cm) down from the top edge.

Notch the top and bottom of the pocket opening. The notches should be no deeper than ⅛" (3 mm).

Using the pattern labeled SIDE AND SLANT FACING on page 265, cut from garment fabric, on straight grain, two pieces of **facing** for each pocket. On the longest straight edge of the **facing** pieces, press a ¼" (6 mm) hem towards the wrong side.

Place one piece of pocketing on the wrong side of the trouser front, allowing ⅝" (1.6 cm) pocketing to extend beyond the lower notch, and ⅜" (1 cm) at the center of the **waistline**.

Cut one piece of pocketing for each pocket, on straight grain, 13" (33 cm) long and 16" (40.6 cm) wide. Fold the pocketing in half on the width, and trim the outside bottom edges into a curve (as shown).

Place one **facing** piece face down on top of the side seam, ½" (1.3 cm) below the top. Chalkmark the notches on the **facing**. Machine-stitch from notch to notch on a slight curve. Use your pattern's seam allowance at the top and bottom of the pocket opening, tapering to a minimum of ¼" (6 mm) seam allowance at the center. The depth of the curve at the center of the pocket should not be more than ¼" (6 mm). Tack well at the top and bottom of the stitchline.

The pocketing and garment fabric are now slashed right to the stitchline at each notch. The excess fabric is trimmed away, leaving a ¼" (6 mm) seam allowance along the stitchline.

Bring the **facing** to the wrong side of the pants front. The **facing** seam should also be drawn to the edge of the wrong side, so that it is not visible from the front. On the right side, topstitch along the pocket opening, ¼" (6 mm) from the edge. Tack well at the top and bottom.

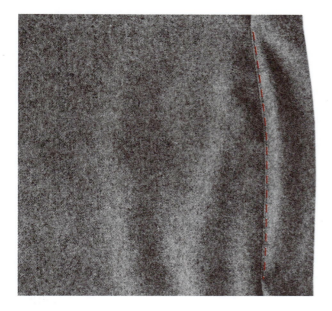

Bring the **facing** out to the side of the trousers, and topstitch the **facing** to the seam allowance, very close to the seam.

On the wrong side, the folded edge of the **facing** is topstitched to the pocketing. Catch the pocketing and **facing** only. These stitches *do not* go through to the right side of the pants.

Place the second **facing** piece, face down on top of the first, matching edges at the top and bottom. The folded edge should be facing up.

With the pocketing opened out, topstitch the second **facing** piece to the pocketing.

The pocketing is now folded over, on top of the **facing**. Make sure that the curved edges of the pocketing are even. Pin through the pocketing and catch the **facing** underneath.

The pocketing is again folded, this time inside out, in order to begin a French seam. Pull the trouser leg up and out of your way. Begin with a ³⁄₈" (1 cm) seam at the bottom of the pocket opening, and taper to ¹⁄₈" (3 mm) as you stitch around the curve and across the bottom of the pocketing.

Turn the pocketing and press. Topstitch around the bottom of the pocketing again, ¼" (6 mm) from the edge to complete the French seam.

Just below the pocket opening, on the side of the pocketing closest to the garment fabric, slash about 1" (2.5 cm) into the pocketing and the **facing**. This slash will eventually enable you to hold the pocket aside as the side seam is being sewn. The pocketing in not caught in the side seam.

The side seam will be sewn only after all the pockets and the fly have been constructed.

The Back Pocket

The back pants pocket is a double-piping pocket, with or without buttonhole tab, constructed somewhat differently from the double-piping pocket for jackets.

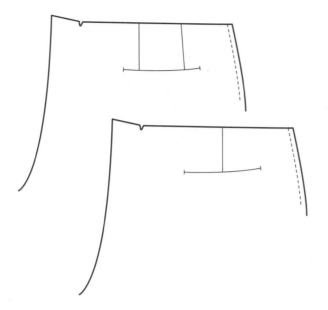

The pocket placement line, 5″ to 5½″ (12.7 to 14 cm) long, is drawn on a slight curve, the center of the line being about ⅛″ (3 mm) lower than the sides. This curve will help prevent the pocket from gaping open when not in use. The pocket placement line is drawn at the bottom of the dart, or darts, and 2″ (5 cm) from the side stitchline. Check the length of the darts. If they are longer than 3½″ (8.9 cm), the pocket will be too low, and you will end up sitting on your wallet, or whatever you keep in your back pocket. Simply shorten the darts to 3½″ (8.6 cm) to avoid the possibility of this discomfort.

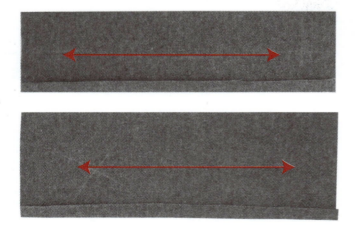

Use the pattern labeled BACK PIPING (page 263) and BACK FACING (page 266), and cut from garment fabric, crossgrain, one **piping** and one **facing** piece for each pocket.

Press one ¼″ (6 mm) lengthwise hem to the wrong side of each piece.

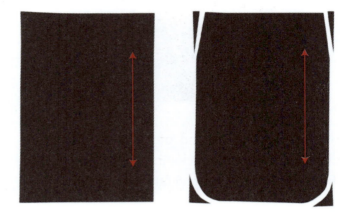

From pocketing material, cut two pieces, 10″ (25.4 cm) by 7″ (17.8 cm), straight grain. With the pocketing pieces together, trim top and bottom (as shown).

Place one piece of pocketing on the wrong side of the pants back, allowing ¼″ (6 mm) of pocketing to show above the pants at the center of the pocket.

Draw the pocket placement line on the wrong side of the **piping** and baste the **piping** to the pants along this line, catching the pocketing underneath as you baste.

Slash through the center of the stitchlines, and cut ⅜" (1 cm) prongs at either end.

Using a small machine-stitch (about sixteen stitches per inch), sew completely around the pocket placement line. Stitch ⅛" (3 mm) above and below the line, and exactly at the beginning and end of the line at either side.

Draw the **piping** to the wrong side, and baste around the pocket opening, leaving a thin edge of **piping** visible above and below. Steam press the pocket from the right side.

Machine-stitch on the right side of the trousers, very close to the sides and bottom edge of the **piping**.

On the inside of the pants, place the **facing** right side down, and center it on top of the pocket opening. The folded edge of the **facing** should be visible.

On the wrong side, machine topstitch the folded edge of the **piping** to the pocketing.

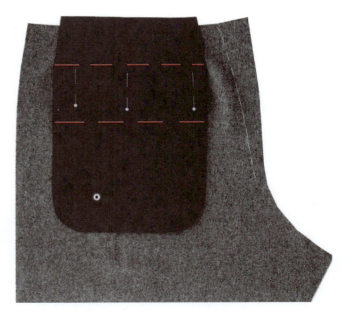

Place the second piece of pocketing on top of the first, matching the edges. Pin through the second piece of pocketing and catch the **facing**. The broken line in this photograph indicates the position of the facing under the pocketing.

The two pocketing pieces are again placed together, this time, inside out, in order to begin a French seam. The trouser leg will have to be pulled up and out of your way. Stitch around the pocket using a ⅛″ (3 mm) seam.

Now that the exact placement of the **facing** has been determined, the second piece of pocketing is removed, so that the **facing** can be machine-stitched to it. Topstitch across the bottom edge of the fabric, along the folded edge.

Turn the pocketing, and press. Stitch around the pocketing once more, this time ¼″ (6 mm) from the edge, to complete the French seam.

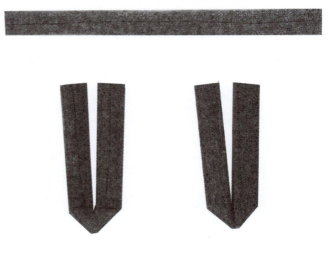

The buttonhole tab is constructed from a strip of garment fabric, straight grain, 1½″ (3.8 cm) by 4″ (10.2 cm). Stitch the strip lengthwise, using a ⅜″ (1 cm) seam, and press the seam open.

Turn the strip to the right side and press the seam to the center. The strip is now folded into an arrow shape and topstitched (as shown).

Insert the tab into the pocket opening, leaving a ⅝″ (1.6 cm) slit in the tab below the top **piping**.

To complete the back trouser pocket, sew a ½″ (1.3 cm) button just below the bottom **piping**.

Topstitch at the sides and across the top of the pocket, very close to the **piping**.

THE PANTS FLY

The pants fly is constructed after the front pockets have been completed.

The fly-front closing illustrated here is called a French fly. The back of the fly is extended to form a buttonhole tab.

You will need a pattern labeled FRENCH FLY (see page 268). Trace these patterns and cut them out.

Place the fly pattern, notch to notch, on the front of the pants to determine the length of the fly.

Leave about ¼" (6 mm) of the pattern above the top of the pants front, and trim away the rest.

Place the FRENCH TAB (see page 267), so that the top of the buttonhole on the tab is aligned with the **waist** stitchline. The button will eventually be placed at the **waist** stitchline.

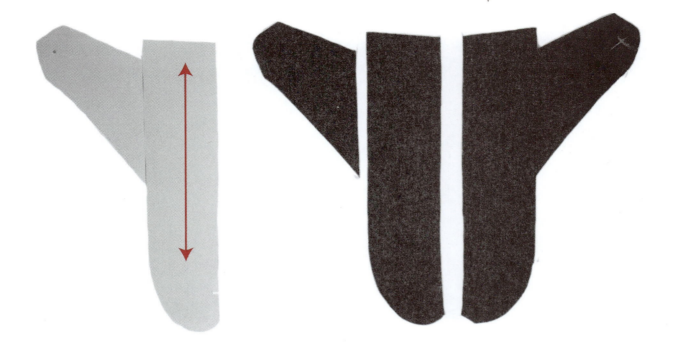

With the French tab in place on the pattern, cut two French fly pieces from garment fabric, on straight grain, and mark the top of the buttonhole. Right sides of the fabric facing up, trim the French tab from the fly on the left.

Place the French fly right side down on a bias strip of pocketing and machine-stitch along the outer edges of the fly.

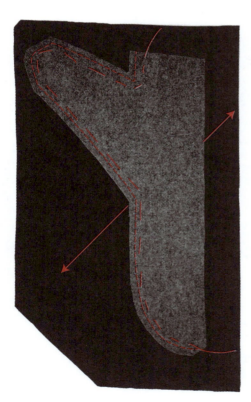

Trim the pocketing to a ¼" (6 mm) seam, and leave ¾" (1.9 cm) pocketing at the unstitched edge.

The bottom of the reinforcement should be ½″ (1.3 cm) below the pants notch.

Turn the fly to the right side and topstitch close to the outer edge. Machine-stitch a ⅝″ (1.6 cm) buttonhole on the tab.

Trim the zipper tape ¼″ (6 mm) past the metal zipper stop, and place it face down, on the right side of the pants at the center front; the metal zipper stop should be ½″ (1.3 cm) above the notch. If the zipper tape is made from synthetic yarn, gently singeing the cut ends will prevent it from fraying.

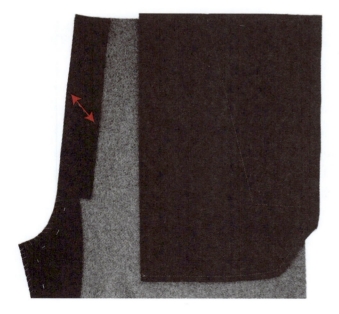

Cut a bias piece of pocketing, 1½″ (3.8 cm) wide and ½″ (1.3 cm) longer than the fly, and place it on the wrong side of the pants, at the center front.

Place the pants fly, face down, on top of the zipper, matching fly notch to pants notch. Fold back the pocketing.

Baste the fly, zipper, pants, and reinforcement together. Use a zipper foot, and stitch close to the teeth of the zipper. Stitch from **waist** to notch, tacking well at top and bottom.

Slash at the notch, right up to the stitchline.

Press the zipper and fly seam open. On the right side, topstitch at the edge of the fly seam on the pants front. Hold the fly **facing** out of the way as you stitch.

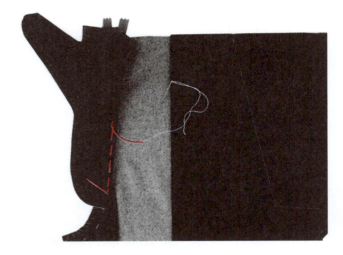

On the wrong side, the zipper seam allowance is concealed by folding first the reinforcement, and then the fly **facing** on top. The layers of pocketing are basted and then machine-stitched or slip-stitched along the edge. The garment fabric is not caught in these stitches.

Apply a bias-cut, woven fusible to the wrong side of the left fly, leaving a ¼" (6 mm) margin of fabric free along the outer edge. Overcast along the outer edge of the fly.

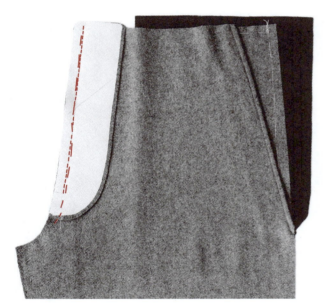

Right sides together, baste and then machine-stitch the left fly to the left pants front, **waist** to notch.

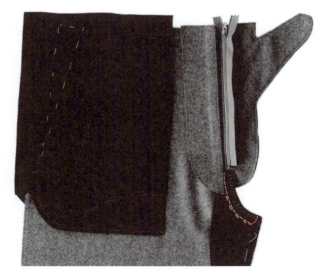

Press the seam allowance towards the fly and topstitch the fly to the seam allowance, stitching very close to the seam, **waist** to notch.

Slash the notch all the way to the stitchline. Bring the fly and the fly seam to the wrong side of the pants and press in place.

Place the two pants fronts together, right sides touching, and stitch along the **crotch** seam from the notch to 1" (2.5 cm) from the inseams. Tack well at either end.

At the **waistline**, the left front should overlap the right by ¼" (6 mm), and taper naturally to the bottom of the zipper. Baste the fly closed; basting close to the fold on the edge of the left front.

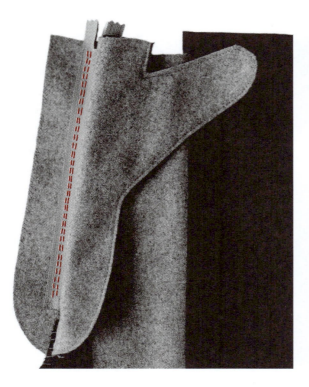

On the inside, pull the fly aside, and machine-stitch the zipper to the left fly. Only the fly and the zipper are caught in these stitches, and *not* the front of the pants. Machine stitch two rows on the zipper tape: one very close to the zipper teeth, the other at the edge of the tape.

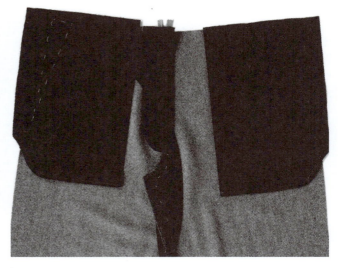

About 1¼" (3.2 cm) from center front, on the left front of the pants, chalkmark a line parallel to the folded edge of the fly, and taper the line to center front, ½" (1.3 cm) below the bottom of the zipper. Baste through the front of the pants, catching the left fly (but not the right) underneath.

Machine topstitch along the chalkline, from the **waist** around to the notch, catching only the left fly underneath. Tack well at the notch. The fly is complete.

After the waistband has been constructed, a ½" (1.3 cm) button will be attached at the **waist** stitchline for the French tab.

THE PANTS SIDE SEAMS

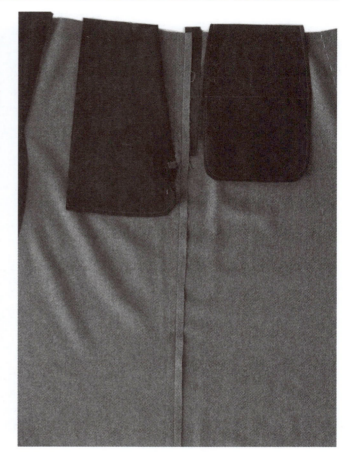

The pants side seams are sewn only after all pockets and the fly have been completed, and before beginning the construction of the waistband.

Cut a bias strip of pocketing about 8" (20.3 cm) long and 1½" (3.8 cm) wide, to be used as reinforcement for the hip area of the side seam.

Baste the reinforcement to the wrong side of the back of the pants, at the top of the side seam. Machine-stitch the pants side seams, being sure to keep the front pockets out of the way as you stitch. The reinforcement is caught in the stitchline.

Press the seam open.

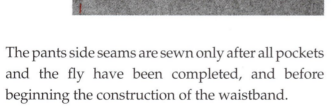

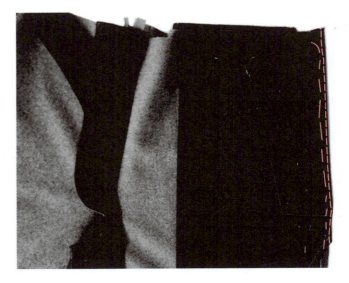

Bring the pocketing strip forward, fold it over the pants seam allowance, and press it in place.

Fold and press the edge of the front pocketing so that it reaches just to the edge of the back seam allowance.

Baste and then machine stitch along the edge of the front pocketing, catching the back seam allowance, and the reinforcement strip. *Do not catch the outside of the trousers in this stitch.*

THE PANTS WAISTBAND

The waistband is attached after the side seams have been sewn and before the **crotch** and inseams. The width of the waistband is a matter of preference, the average width being 1½" (3.8 cm).

From the inside, the waistband is covered by a strip of pocketing; just below the **waistline** a curtain of pocketing lines the top of the pants.

Measure across the top of one side of the pants from the center front to the center back stitchline. This measurement should equal one half of the **waistline** measurement. The center back seam at the **waist** is usually 1½" (3.8 cm) wide to allow for alterations.

Place the top edge of the waistband **interfacing** face down at the top edge of the wrong side of the garment fabric. The **interfacing** extends onto the waistband an amount equal to the seam allowance. The excess garment fabric is left at the center front of the waistband. Machine-stitch the **interfacing** and garment fabric together, stitching close to the edge of the garment fabric.

From garment fabric, cut on crossgrain, two waistband halves. The length should equal one half of the **waistline** measurement (including the pants center back seam allowance), plus 4" (10.2 cm). The width equals the width of the finished waistband, plus seam allowance on top and bottom. The seam allowance should be whatever you are using as seam allowance at the pants **waistline**.

The garment fabric is now pulled down, over the top of the **interfacing** and machine-basted in place. Stitch along the stiffening. The bottom of the garment fabric should now be at the bottom edge of the waistband **interfacing**.

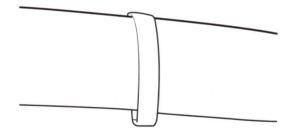

Cut two pieces of waistband **interfacing**, the length equal to one half of the pants top measurement (including center back seam allowance). The **interfacing** is, therefore, 4" (10.2 cm) shorter than the garment fabric waistband.

Measure the width of the stiffening on the waistband **interfacing**, and trim if necessary. It should be equal to the width of the finished waistband. The fabric visible below the stiffening should equal the **waistline** seam allowance.

Cut a strip of garment fabric long enough to construct seven belt loops, or carriers. The length of each loop, of course, depends on the width of the waistband, and the amount of seam allowance you are using at the **waistline**. The loops must be long enough to run from the top of the **waistline** seam allowance down to ¼" (6 mm) below the **waist** stitchline, and then extend up and over the top of the waistband by about ½" (1.3 cm). The finished loops should be about ⅜" (1 cm) wide.

Press the seam allowance open and cut the fabric strip *before* turning it to the right side. It will be very difficult to turn a strip which is equivalent to the length of four loops or more. On the right side, press the seam allowance to the center of the strip and cut the loops.

Baste the belt loops on the right side of the pants, 2½" (6.4 cm) from center front, at the side seam and at the center of the back of the pants. The seams on the loops should be facing up.

The loop for the center back seamline will be attached after the waistband is complete.

If you will be adding a watch pocket, the pocketing from the front right pocket should be pulled down and out of the way, so that it will not be caught in the **waistline** seam. This will require slashing about 1" (2.5 cm) into the pocketing and **facing** next to the pocket edge, as well as opening the top 1" (2.5 cm) of the seam attaching the pocketing to the sideseam reinforcement

If you are not adding a watch pocket, you may want to baste both front pockets and back pockets at the pants **waistline**, to gain better control of these multiple layers.

Machine-stitch the waistband and **interfacing** to the pants, stitching just next to the edge of the stiffening. The belt loops are caught as you stitch.

If you will be adding a watch pocket, the section of the seam from the fly to the pocket opening on the right front should be pressed open. If not, press the entire **waistline** seam allowance towards the waistband.

On the right side, topstitch the belt loops down ¼" (6 mm) from the seamline.

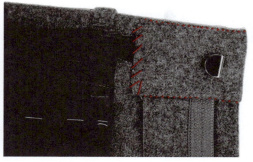

Bring the loops up and over the top of the waistband and tack them in place by hand, using a back-stitch.

Fold the extension to the wrong side of the waistband and baste in place. Using silk finishing thread, slip-stitch the folded edges and cross-stitch the cut end to the waistband **interfacing**.

Tailors' belt fasteners are made of four metal pieces which fit together. Practice attaching these using a scrap of fabric first, before attempting to set the fasteners into your pants.

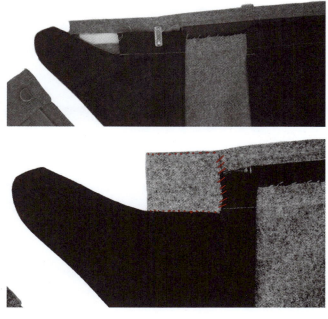

Attach the hook to the end of the left waistband, just beyond the center front. A small piece of **interfacing** is placed on the wrong side under the metal, as reinforcement for the fabric.

Attach the eye to the right waistband, using a piece of **interfacing** as reinforcement for the garment fabric. Fold and baste the extension in place. Using silk finishing thread, slip-stitch the folded edges and cross-stitch the cut end to the waistband **interfacing**.

If you choose to add a watch pocket to your pants, this should be done now, before attaching the **facing** and curtain. Instructions for the construction of the watch pocket can be found on page 235.

The waistband **facing** and the curtain below it are now constructed from pocketing. Cut two **facing** pieces on the crossgrain, 3" (7.6 cm) longer than the finished waistband half. The facing width is equal to the finished waistband, plus seam allowance at the top and bottom.

With the curtain pleat at the pants side seam, hand stitch the **facing**/curtain seam allowance into the waistband seam allowance.

The two curtain pieces are cut on the bias, 2" (5 cm) longer than the **facing**. The width is twice that of the finished waistband, plus seam allowance at the top and bottom.

Fold the curtain in half lengthwise, and at the center, press a box pleat, each side of which is ½" (1.3 cm) deep.

Bring the **facing** up to cover the back of the waistband. Fold and baste the **facing** ¼" (6 mm) from the top, and cover the raw edge of the waistband extension. Leave about 3" (7.6 cm) free at the back so that the center back seam can eventually be sewn without obstruction.

Place the curtain, pleat opening face down, on top of the **facing**, and machine-stitch them together.

Press the seam allowance up towards the **facing**.

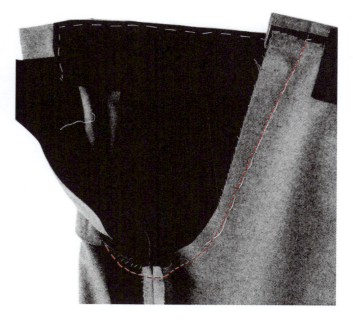

At this point, the inseams are sewn. Keep in mind that the back inseam seam allowance may be wider than the front seam allowance (page 28).

Pin the inseams together at the knee notch, and begin basting towards the top. The front inseam is about ⅜" (1 cm) longer than the back to allow for the forward stretch of the leg. Place this ⅜" (1 cm) **ease** in the upper thigh area of the front inseam. Stretch the back inseam gently as you machine stitch, so that there is only **ease**, and not tucks, in the front inseam. Press the seam open.

The center back seam is now sewn from the top of the waistband, along the **crotch**, to the fly. Press the seam open.

With the pants turned right side out, and the inseam and outseam of each leg aligned, press a crease from hem to hip level, front and back. Press first on the inseam and then on the outseam side of each leg.

If there are front pleats, the front crease meets the deeper of the two pleats at the waistline (the pleat closest to center front).

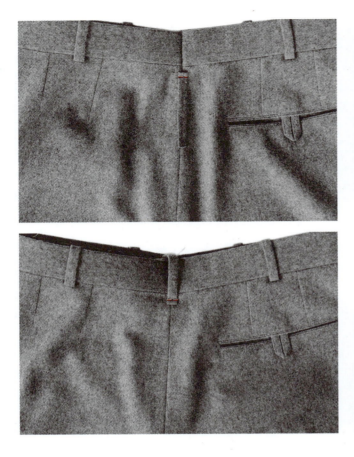

Fold the loop over the top of the waistband, and stitch it into the **interfacing**.

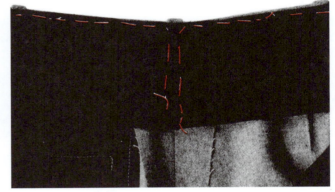

At the center back, ¼" (6 mm) below the **waistline** seam, place the raw edge of the last belt loop, seam facing upwards. Back-stitch the top edge of the loop into the pants. Bring the loop up, and back-stitch once more, just above the first stitches to hide the raw edge of the loop.

Fold the curtain and **facing** on either side of the center back seam, and baste in place. The top and ends of the **facing** and curtain are finished with a small back-stitch, using silk finishing thread.

To avoid the center back belt loop interfering with future alterations, some tailors choose to have two belt loops, one on either side of the center back seam, about 2" (5 cm) apart.

The Watch Pocket

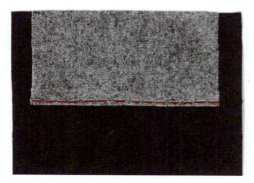

During the construction of the pants **waistline**, before attaching the **facing** and curtain, a small pocket may be placed in the **waist** seamline. This was formerly used as a watch pocket, but is today more commonly used for other small valuables – large bills, for example.

You will need a piece of pocketing, straight grain, 4" (10.2 cm) by 8" (20.3 cm) and a straight grain piece of garment fabric, 3¼" (8 cm) by 2" (5 cm), to be used as **facing**.

Fold up ¼" (6 mm) at the bottom edge of the **facing** and topstitch the **facing** and the pocketing together. Leave ⅜" (1 cm) pocketing visible at either side of the **facing**.

At the bottom edge of the pocketing, fold under ⅜" (1 cm), and press.

Bring the bottom of the pocketing up so that the folded edge is now ⅝" (1.6 cm) from the top of the unfaced side of the pocketing.

Sew a ⅜" (1 cm) French seam at each side of the pocket. These seams should finish ¼" (6 mm) before the folded edge of pocketing. Turn the pocket right side out and press.

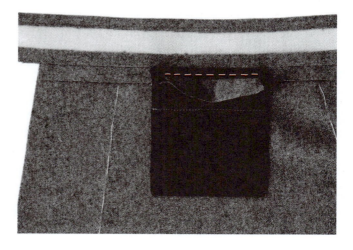

Stitch the folded edge of the pocketing to the bottom seam allowance of the waistband. Stitch through to the right side of the pants, and secure the stitches at either end.

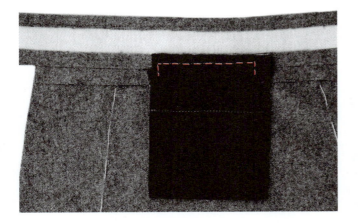

The top edge of the faced side of the pocket is now stitched through to the top seam allowance of the waistband, and the waistband itself. Each end of the stitchline is secured with a short vertical row of stitching.

On the front of the pants, the **waistline** seam is opened between the vertical stitchlines, to create access to the watch pocket.

On the inside, the side pocket is laid flat on top of the smaller pocket, and the construction of the waistband is continued.

THE PANTS HEM

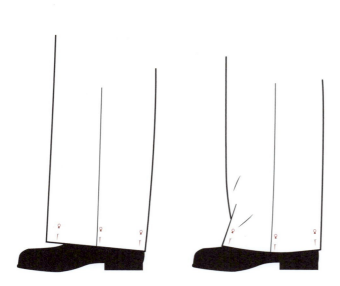

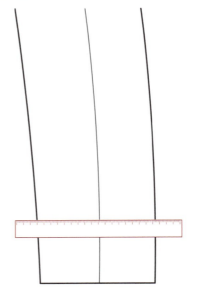

The pants hem should reach to about the middle of the back of the shoe, and cover the top of the shoe in the front. If the hem hits the front of the shoe, the pants will "*break*" at about ankle level. A slight break at the front is absolutely acceptable. The break, or lack of it, is a matter of preference. The top of the shoe, as a rule of thumb, should be covered, with the possible exception of very narrow drainpipe trousers, which can sometimes be hemmed as far up as the ankle bone, and intentionally show a glimpse of the customer's socks. Pin the bottom of the pants to the desired length.

Chalkmark the hem foldline on the right side of the fabric.

Baste the hem up, keeping the stitches about 1″ (2.5 cm) below the top of the hem. A piece of cardboard, placed in the pants leg at the hem, will facilitate the basting and prevent the stitches from catching the other side of the pants.

Fold back about ³⁄₈″ (1 cm) at the top of the hem and hem-stitch the hem into the pants, using silk finishing thread. These stitches should not be visible on the right side of the garment; nor should any puckering be visible, from having pulled the thread unnecessarily tight.

The Pants Cuff

Bottom Edge

2

1

3

If you have chosen cuffs instead of a straight hem for the bottom of the pants, you will have left quite a bit of fabric below what you determined to be the bottom edge of the pants (page 28). Now, several lines are drawn on the right side of the fabric, as guides in creating the cuff.

First, draw a line indicating that will be the bottom edge of the pants; keeping in mind that cuffed pants need to start out slightly longer than those with straight hems, as some of the length always gets lost in the folds. About ¼″ (6 mm) extra length will be sufficient.

Draw one line above the first, and two lines below it, all at a distance equal to the width of the cuff. An average cuff is about 1½" (3.8 cm) wide.

Below the last line, leave about ¾" (1.9 cm) hem, and trim away whatever fabric is left at the bottom of the pants.

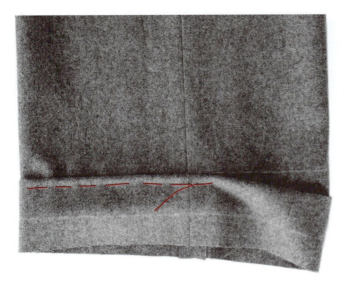

Working on the right side of the pants, fold the fabric on line #3, and bring the fold up to meet line #2. This fold will be the top of the finished cuff. Baste around the top of the cuff, attaching it to the pants.

Fold the ¾" (1.9 cm) hem to the wrong side of the pants, and baste around the bottom of the cuff, attaching the hem to the pants.

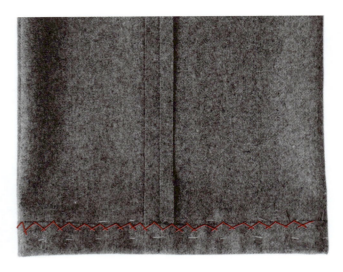

On the wrong side of the pants, cross-stitch along the top of the hem, catching the inner layer of the cuff as you stitch.

Press the cuff flat from the right side.

The Heel Stay

A strip of fabric, called the heel stay, is now applied to the hem at the back of the pants. Its purpose is to protect the hem from wear in the area that will come into contact with the back of the shoe.

Cut a strip of garment fabric, about 7" (17.8 cm) long and 3" (7.6 cm) wide, and fold (as shown).

Place the fabric just above the hem fold at the center of the back of the pants. Secure the heel stay to the hem by back-stitching along the folded edges, and cross-stitching the raw edges at either end. These stitches should catch only the hem, and not go through to the right side of the pants.

8 | THE VEST

The popularity of the vest regularly goes in and out of fashion. That said, custom tailors will traditionally uphold the timeless style of the three-piece suit as the ultimate look for any self-respecting gentleman.

While there are many variations in design, the classic tailored vest is single breasted, with two or four **welt** pockets. It is customary that only one vest button be visible above the jacket **lapel** when both vest and jacket are buttoned. If too much vest is showing, it will interfere with the line of the **lapel**. The front of the vest should be long enough to cover the belt buckle.

If the design calls for a **lapel** to be extended from a noticeably concave neckline, the **lapel** can be constructed as a separate faced piece, sewn into the vest front at the break line.

The front of the classic tailored vest is constructed of garment fabric, and is reinforced with a layer of woven fusible **interfacing**. The vest back is made of lining fabric, coordinated in color with the front fabric. Since the vest is close-fitting, and dyes from colored linings might stain the shirt, the front and back vest pieces are lined with a white-colored lining as a precaution. The vest is faced along the front edge with a strip of garment fabric which extends around to the center back at the neckline.

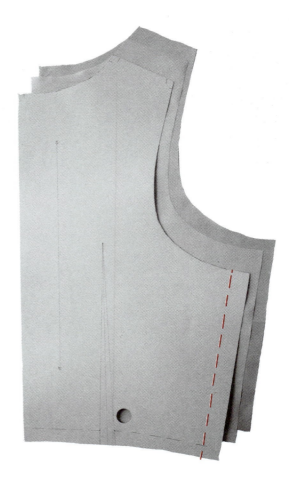

Cut the vest front from garment fabric and chalkmark the pattern information on the right side of the fabric, rather than by tailor tacking. Since we will be applying fusible to the wrong side of the vest front, the tailor tacks would become caught in the fusible, and be difficult to remove.

Slash the dart to 1" (2.5 cm) from the tip, and trim the seam allowance at the dart ends to ⅜" (1 cm) if necessary.

Cut the vest back from lining fabric, making sure that the side seam allowance is ½" (1.3 cm) wider than that on the vest front. This is done to permit future alteration of the vest (which will involve the back of the vest rather than the front).

The back dart will not be slashed as was the front, since the fabric here is less bulky.

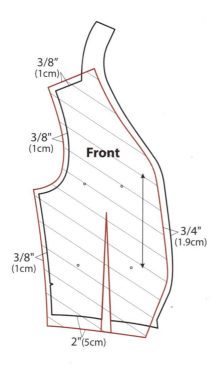

3/8" (1cm)

3/8" (1cm)

Front

3/8" (1cm)

3/4" (1.9cm)

2"(5cm)

fabric free at the front edge, the shoulder, and the armhole. The fusible does not extend into the side seam allowance, nor below the hem fold.

Cut the vest lining from a white lining fabric, using the vest pattern. The lining is cut larger than the vest at the shoulder, armhole, side seam, and hem, by the dimensions indicated in the illustration. Along the front edge, the lining is cut ¾" (1.9 cm) narrower than the pattern.

The back lining is cut identical in size to the back vest.

Using the directions for the construction of the jacket pockets, place **welt** pockets, double-**piping**, or patch pockets on the front of the vest. The placement line for the breast-level pocket is 4½" (11.4 cm) long, and 5" (12.7 cm) for the pocket at the **waist**.

It is not necessary to use reinforcement pieces for the construction of the vest pockets, since the entire front of the vest has already been reinforced with fusible.

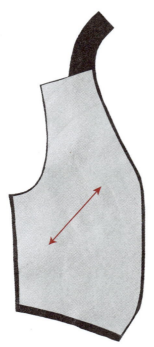

Apply bias-cut woven fusible to the wrong side of the vest front, leaving a ¼" (6 mm) margin of

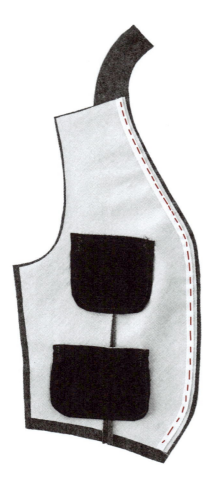
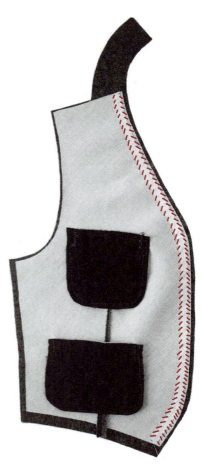

Place a ⅜″ (1 cm) wide cotton twill tape (which has been soaked in cool water and pressed) along the vest front edge, from shoulder to hem fold. The cotton tape is basted about ¹⁄₁₆″ (1.5 mm) within the seam line. At the center of the diagonal line connecting side neck and top button, the tape is pulled gently, creating tiny ripples on the fabric along the edge of the tape. This pulling the tape will assist in drawing the vest towards the body in this bias area, and prevent the vest from gaping open.

The tape is slip-stitched to the vest using silk finishing thread, on both sides of the tape. The stitches should not be visible on the right side of the fabric.

Press the tape.

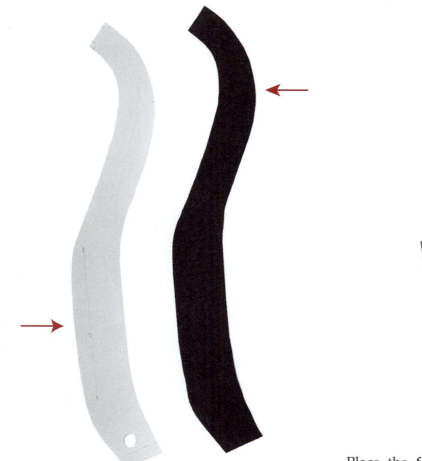

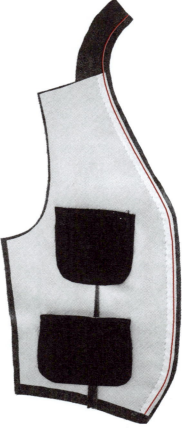

Cut the **facing** from garment fabric, straight grain, using the vest front pattern. The **facing** is about 3" (7.6 cm) wide at center front, and slightly narrower at the diagonal, and around the back neck.

Place the **facing** and vest front together, right sides touching, and machine-stitch about $\frac{1}{16}$" (1.5 mm) beyond the tape in the seam allowance, from center back neck to the bottom of the vest.

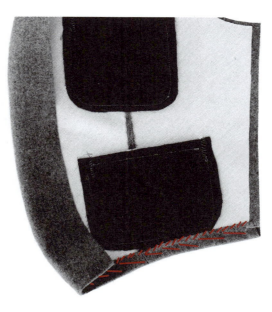

Press the seam towards the **facing**, trim if needed, and baste up the hem. The hem is secured into the fusible using silk thread, and small diagonal stitches which are not visible on the right side of the fabric. *Be careful* not to stitch through both layers of pocketing, or you will shorten the inside of the pocket considerably.

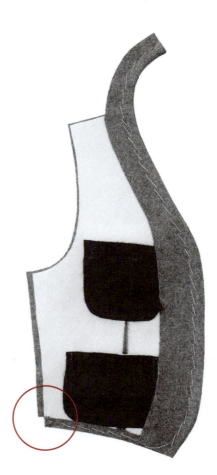

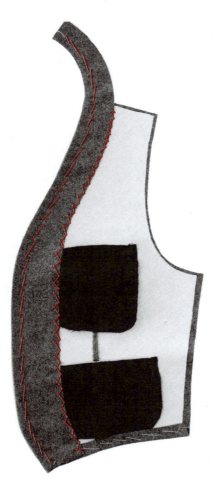

At the top of the hem, the side seam allowance is slashed to the stitch line. The seam allowance below the slash is folded, basted into the hem, and finished with a slip-stitch along the side.

The **facing** and the **facing** seam are now brought to the wrong side of the vest and basted in place along the front edge. Cross-stitch the inner edge of the **facing** into the fusible, using silk thread. Stitches should not be visible from the right side of the vest.

Press the **facing** from the wrong side.

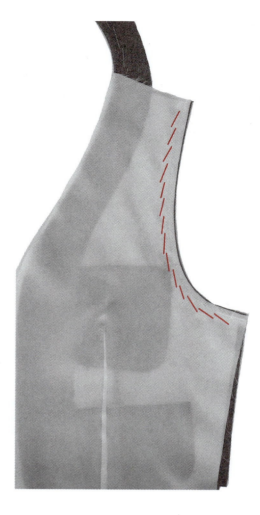

Machine-stitch the dart in the front lining, and press it towards the side seam.

With the right side of the lining touching the right side of the vest front, baste the two together along the armhole. The armhole seam is machine stitched and trimmed to ¼″ (6 mm). The curved area of the armhole is slashed close to the stitchline.

Remove the basting stitches around the armhole.

The front lining and lining seam are now brought to the wrong side of the vest and basted in place.

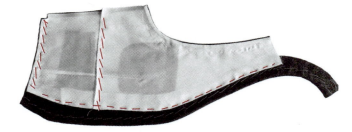

A ½" (1.3 cm) pleat is basted into the lining at about mid-dart level, for lengthwise **ease**. The lining is folded along the front edge and basted just covering the cross stitches along the inner edge of the **facing**. The bottom of the lining is folded in such a way as to leave ¼" (6 mm) of garment fabric exposed below the edge of the lining.

The lining is slashed to the stitchline above the hem, at the side seam, and if necessary where the shoulder meets the **facing**. Fold and baste in place.

Using silk finishing thread, slip-stitch the lining along the edge of the **facing** and across the hem.

The vest back and vest back lining are cut and prepared identically. Machine-stitch the darts and the center back seams. The darts are pressed towards the side, and the center back seams are pressed open.

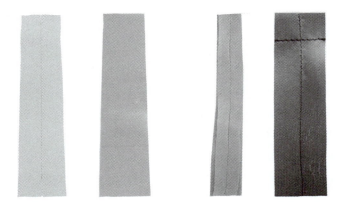

A belt is now constructed from the same fabric used on the back of the vest. Cut two belt halves, straight grain, ¾" (1.9 cm) by 1" (2.5 cm) finished width, and 1" (2.5 cm) longer, finished, than the width of the back of the vest at mid-dart level.

Stitch each piece lengthwise, and press seam open. Stitch across the narrow end of one of the belt halves, and turn both belts to the right side.

Press the seam to the center of the belt.

At the narrow end of the open belt-half, attach a vest buckle (available at tailoring supply stores), and back-stitch or topstitch the buckle in place.

If required by your design or buckle type, you may construct a loop from the back vest fabric, straight grain, twice the width of the belt by ⅜″ (1 cm) finished. Attach the loop to the belt, 1″ (2.5 cm) away from the buckle.

Close the belt, and baste it in place on the back of the vest, at about mid-dart level. Top-stitch the belt to the vest back (as illustrated).

Place the vest back on top of the back lining, right sides touching, and baste along the armhole, easing the vest armhole in from the lining edge about ⅛″ (3 mm). Trim the lining even with the vest back at the armhole, and machine-stitch the armhole. Trim the armhole seam allowance to ¼″ (6 mm).

Clip the curved area of the armhole seam allowance close to the stitchline.

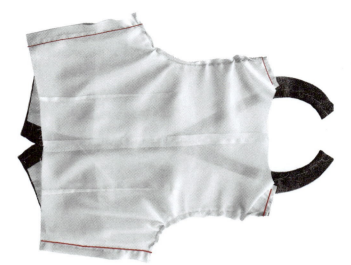

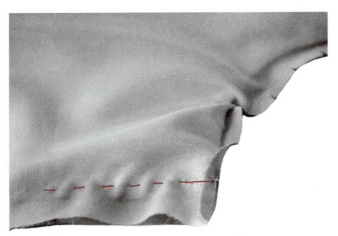

Machine-stitch the side seam, catching all layers and tacking well at the underarm.

Baste, and then machine-stitch, the shoulder seam, placing about ¼″ (6 mm) **ease** in the lining at the shoulder. *Do not* stitch all the way to the end of the lining-neck edge, as we will need room to fold this edge shortly.

Turn the vest so that the right side of the lining is visible, and stitch the center back neck-line seam. Press seam open.

Reaching through the neck, flip the vest inside-out and machine-stitch the back hemline.

Machine-stitch the side seams in a manner which will hide all seam allowances. With the wrong side of the white vest lining on top, insert the vest fronts between the two back layers. The front and back armholes should be touching. Don't forget that the side seam allowance on the back is ½″ (1.3 cm) wider than on the front). Baste the vest front and back together at the side seam. Place the back lining over them and baste at the side seam.

At the top of the side seam, bring the armhole seam allowance, and a bit of the vest back fabric onto the lining, and baste it in place. This will prevent the white lining from showing at the underarm in the finished garment.

Turn the vest right side out. On the right side and on the wrong side of the vest back, baste the lining fabric along the edge of the garment fabric at the neckline.

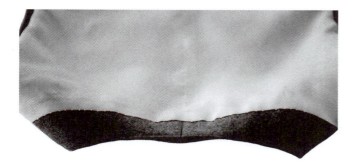

Slip-stitch these seams using silk finishing thread.

Before positioning the buttons and buttonholes, steam press the vest gently over a tailor's ham.

Buttons and buttonholes on the vest are accomplished following the instructions on pages 199–200. ½" (1.3 cm) buttons are appropriate for the vest front.

9 | ALTERATIONS

TAPERING THE JACKET LAPEL

Because of constant changes in fashion, a frequent tailoring alteration is the tapering of jacket lapels.

Transfer onto the canvas a chalkline indicating the new finished edge of the **lapel**.

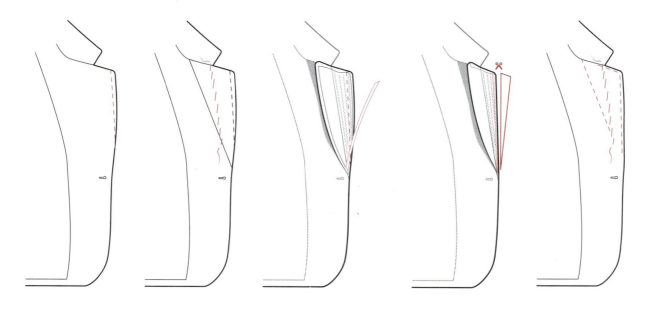

The first step in this alteration is to chalkmark, on the front of the **lapel**, a line indicating the desired change in width.

Baste through the **lapel**, just beyond the jacket roll line, to control the layers of fabric while you work.

Open the **facing** seam from collar notch to the bottom of the roll line, and remove the tape from the outer edge of the **lapel**. It is not necessary to remove the tape which lies across the top of the **lapel**, unless you are also changing this line.

Trim the canvas (but not the garment fabric) along the chalkline, and baste ⅜″ (1 cm) cotton twill tape (which has been soaked in cool water and pressed) along the length of the **lapel**. Allow the tape to extend into the seam allowance, beyond the canvas, by about ¹⁄₁₆″ (1.5 mm), to give the **lapel** a thinner edge.

Slip-stitch along both edges of the tape, using silk thread. The stitches should go through to the underside of the **lapel**, but should be small enough to be all but imperceptible.

Trim the garment fabric seam allowance to ⅜" (1 cm) beyond the tape, and trim slightly closer at the tip of the **lapel**.

The **lapel** seam allowance is now folded up onto the tape, and finished according to the instructions beginning on page 146.

If the **lapel** adjustment has been of a significant amount, it may be necessary to modify the collar, to maintain a pleasing balance between collar and **lapel**. The collar can be tapered in the same manner as was the **lapel**, or, if you wish, a new collar can be drafted (page 170) and applied (page 173) using a new undercollar and (if necessary) the garment fabric from the old topcollar.

ADJUSTING THE SLEEVE LENGTH

The jacket alteration done most often is probably the adjustment of the sleeve length. The length of the sleeve is primarily a matter of preference, and of comfort. The jacket sleeve may be as short as ½" (1.3 cm) above the bottom of the shirt cuff, or as long as is comfortable to your client.

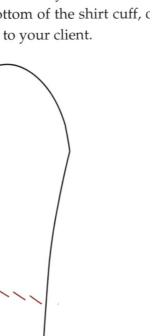
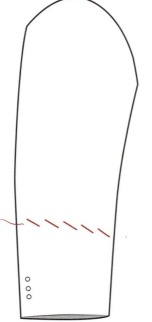

Because of the layers of fabric at the sleeve vent, the cuff is too bulky to be folded up and pinned accurately to determine the correct length. Chalkmark on the cuff the amount to be shortened, or make note of the amount to be lengthened.

Baste around the sleeve about 8" (20.3 cm) above the hem, to control the lining while you work.

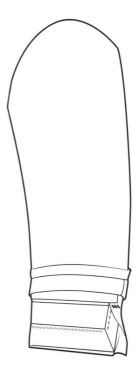

Remove the cuff buttons, and, with the sleeve inside out, loosen the lining at the hem and along the vent. Bring the lining up out of your work area.

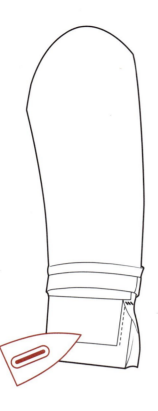

Remove the hem stitches and press out the original hem foldline. Use a sleeve board for this pressing, or insert a press mitt into the bottom of the sleeve.

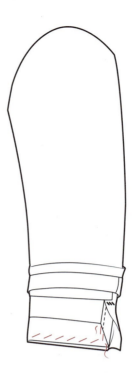

Diagonal-stitch the hem into the reinforcement and slip-stitch the ends of the vent closed.

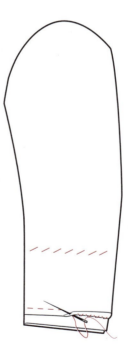

Fold and press the new hemline and press a miter at the bottom of the topvent (page 190).

Baste the lining in place along the vent (page 192), and place the lining hem fold about ¾" (1.9 cm) above the sleeve hem. Keep the hem basting about 1" (2.5 cm) above the lining hem fold.

Fold back the lining hem and hem-stitch one layer of lining into one layer of garment fabric.

Replace the sleeve buttons (page 203) and press the sleeve (page 201).

RELINING THE JACKET

To re-line a jacket for which the pattern is not available, remove the old lining carefully. Separate the lining pieces into front, back, side, and sleeves; and press each well.

The old lining is now used as a pattern for the new one.

If there is reason to believe that the lining's poor condition is due to its being too small for the jacket, add an extra ⅛″ (3 mm) to all vertical seams, and leave enough fabric at center back to create a controlled pleat (page 158).

The body of the jacket is lined first, in a slightly different manner than during the jacket's original construction.

If there is a Barcelona lining pocket (page 151) in the old lining, the pocket can be removed whole, and sewn into the new lining.

Sew the front and back of the lining together at the side seams, and anchor this lining shell into the jacket at the **waistline** notches.

With the lining and jacket seams aligned, baste down the center back seam and around the edges of the lining (page 161). The use of a mannequin, or even a hanger, will make this job easier.

The front of the lining is basted and then attached into the **facing** using a slip-stitch. The lining is back-stitched into the armhole seam allowance, as it was done during the original construction (page 195), and the hem is closed using a hem-stitch (page 194).

Once the body lining is complete, the jacket and lining sleeves are turned inside out so that the seam allowances of jacket and lining sleeves can be basted together.

The top of the sleeve lining is folded and basted to the jacket lining around the armhole, and finished with a slip-stitch.

ALTERING THE JACKET WIDTH

A jacket which is too wide in the body should be pinned to fit, tapering gradually into the seamline. If the jacket is too tight, do not open the seams in order to decide how much of the seam allowance to let out. You have more control over the alterations if you remove old stitches only after the new ones are in.

If the alteration cannot possibly avoid the underarm, open the armhole seam, just in the underarm area.

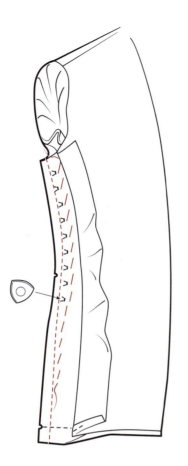

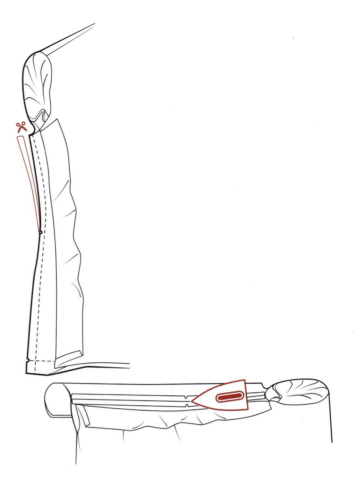

Open the lining at the side seam, and baste the front and back of the jacket together, just beyond the pins.

Transfer the pin marks to chalkmarks, and press the seam flat.

Machine-stitch along the chalk guideline.

Remove the old stitches, and trim the seam allowance. Press the seam open.

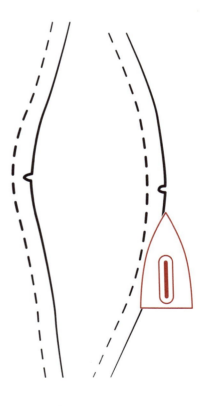

If there is a significant shaping in the seam, there may now be puckering at the **waistline** caused by pulling from the seam allowance. Steam-press the seam allowance at the **waistline**, stretching it into a reverse curve. This will lengthen the seam allowance in the shaped area and relieve the puckering.

If the alteration has involved less than 1" (2.5 cm), it may be possible to ease the sleeve back into the armhole without adjusting the sleeve.

If, however, despite valiant effort, you find it impossible to gracefully fit the sleeve into the now smaller armhole, reduce the **ease** by tapering the sleeve underarm seam. Do not taper the back seam. This would distort the shape of the sleeve.

With the armhole finished, replace the jacket lining (page 162) and the sleeve lining (page 191).

ADJUSTING THE PANTS WAISTLINE

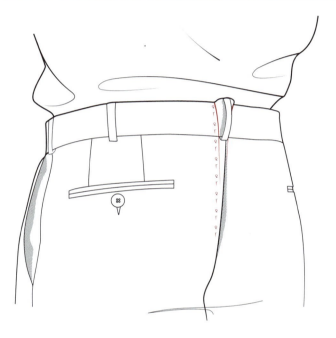

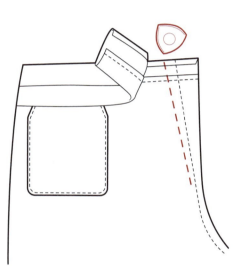

If the pants are too loose at the **waistline**, pin them to fit (as illustrated), without opening the center back seam. If the pants are too tight, the seam must be opened first, and then pinned.

Remove the center back belt loop, and on the inside, pull the waistband **facing** and curtain away from the center back seam. Transfer the pin marks to chalkmarks, and press the center back seam allowance flat.

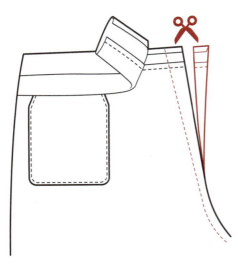

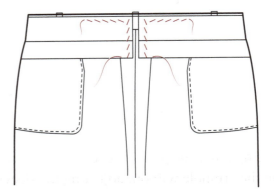

Attach the center back belt loop (page 234) and, on the inside, baste the waistband **facing** and curtain in place. Back-stitch along the basted edges, using silk finishing thread.

Machine-stitch the new seam, beginning at the top of the waistband, and tapering gradually into the **crotch**. Remove the old seamline, and trim the seam allowance. If you have the fabric, leave as much as 1½″ (3.8 cm) seam allowance at the top of the center back seam to allow for future alterations. Press the seam open.

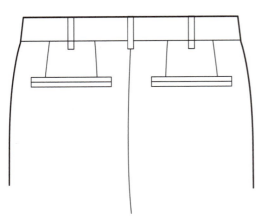

ALTERING THE PANTS FOR MUSCULAR INNER THIGHS

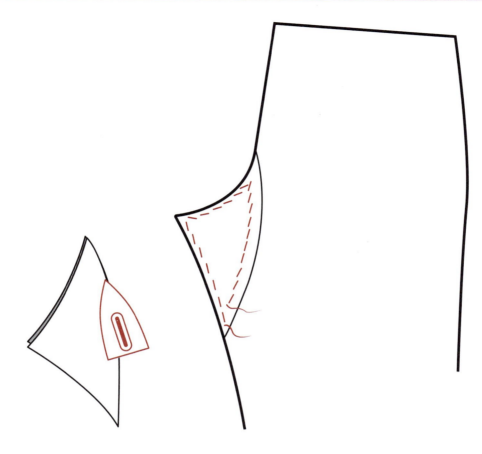

Men with muscular inner thighs may need to have a patch of lining sewn into the back of the pants from the **crotch** down about one-third of the distance between the knee and the top of the inseam. The lining patch is needed if the fabric in this area shows signs of wear, caused by the constant friction of the inner thighs rubbing together. The lining patch can help by assisting the pants fabric in sliding more smoothly over the skin in this area. The friction still occurs, but since the fabric moves more easily now, it occurs with less force, and not always at the same point on the pants fabric.

Cut the lining patch about 9" (22.9 cm) square, on the straight grain. Fold it on the diagonal, and press the fold into a curve.

Baste, and then overcast the patch into the seam allowance at the **crotch** and upper inseam on the back of the pants.

TAPERING THE PANTS LEG

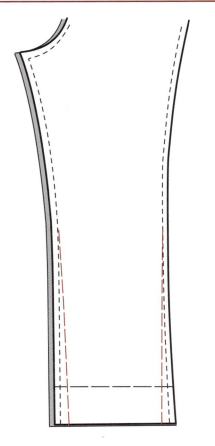

Pants with legs that are too wide below the knee can be altered to a straight or tapering leg design quite simply.

With the pants inside out, and the hem down, press the seam allowances flat. Starting at the knee, at both the inseam and outseam, draw chalklines to the bottom of the pants, narrowing the leg the same amount at the inseam and outseam. Machine-stitch along the chalklines and trim away the excess seam allowance.

You will note that the inseam seam allowance may be wider at the back of the pants than at the front (page 28). Retain this unequal seam allowance as you trim the excess fabric. Press the seam open and hem the pants.

ADJUSTING THE PANTS LENGTH

The adjustment of the pants length is done following the directions on page 236. Before beginning, let down the old hem and press well.

PATTERNS

Back pocket piping

Slant yoke

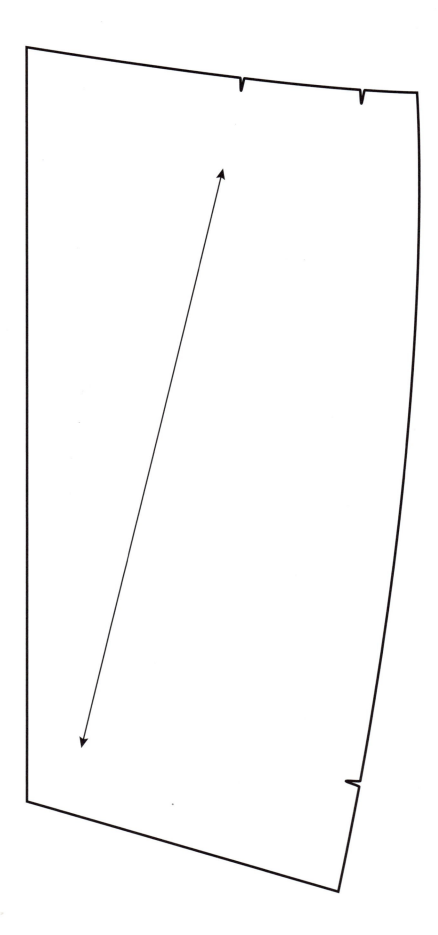

Side and slant pocket facing

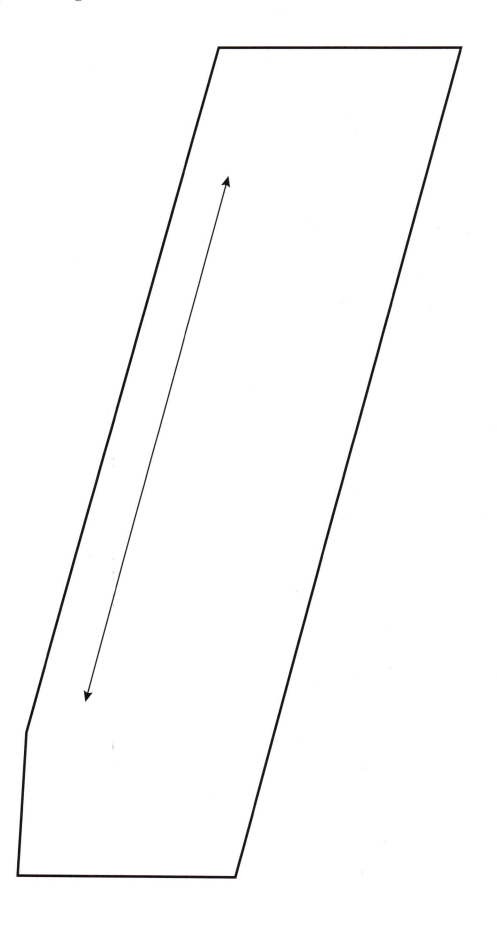

Back pocket facing

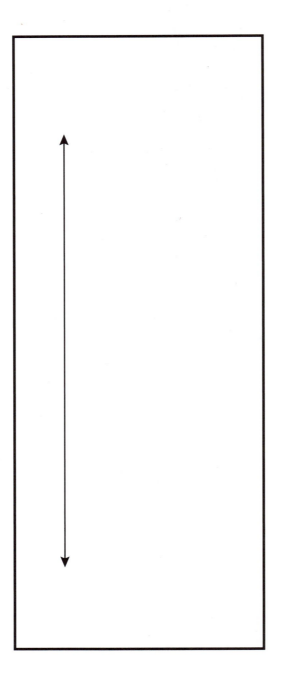

French tab

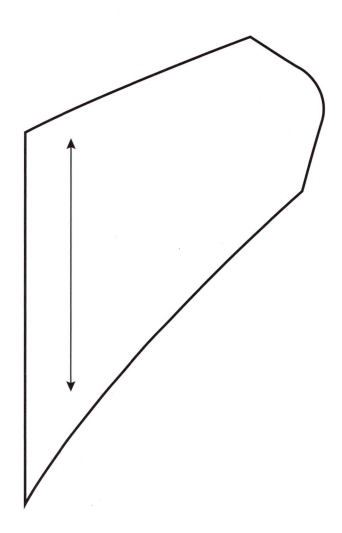

French fly

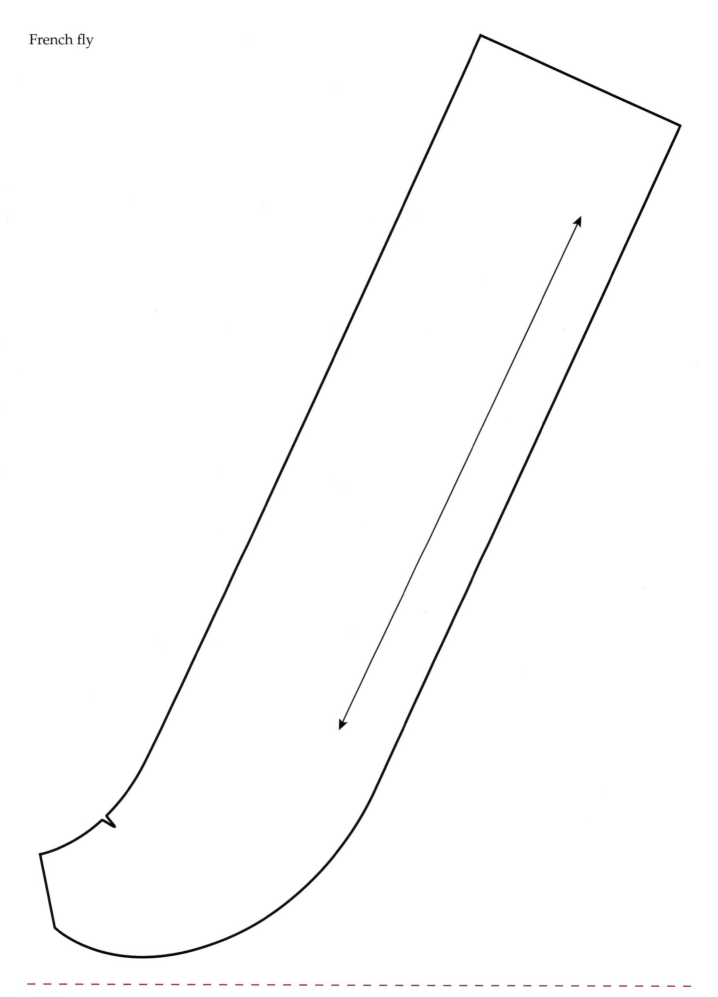

Shoulder pad

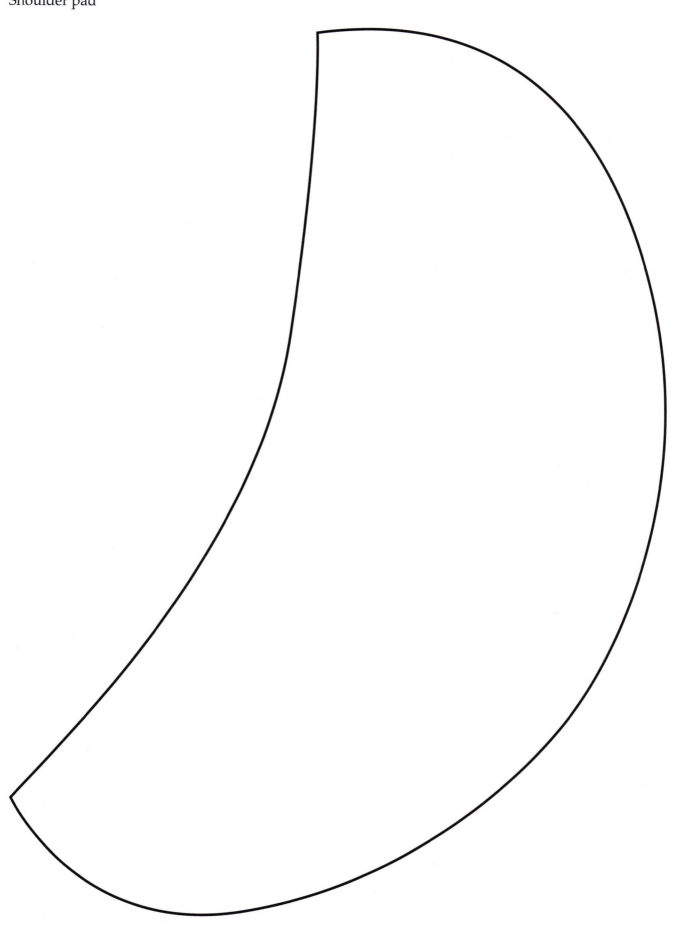

TAILORING SUPPLY SOURCES

UNITED KINGDOM

MacCulloch & Wallis
25–26 Dering Street
London, W1S 1AT
Tel: (+44) 020 7629 0311
www.macculloch-wallis.co.uk

USA

WAWAK
1059 Powers Road
Conklin, NY 13748
Phone: (+1) 800 654 2235
www.wawak.com

B. Black & Sons
548 South Los Angeles Street
Los Angeles, CA 90013
Phone: (+1) 213 624 9451
www.bblackandsons.com

Bergen Tailors & Cleaners Supply Corp.
9021 Old River Road
North Bergen, NJ 07047
Phone: (+1) 800 932 4128
http://bergentailorsupply.com

AUSTRALIA

M. Recht Accessories
53–57 Cambridge Street
Collingwood, Victoria 3066
Phone: (+61) 1300 941 941
http://mrecht.com.au/

ITALY

F.lli Caccioppoli s.n.c.
Via Antonio Ciccone, 8
80133 Naples, Italy
Phone: (+39) 081 281 452
www.caccioppolinapoli.it

Ditta Piero Zamboni
Via Bellaria, 16/B
40139 Bologna, Italy
Phone: (+39) 051 392 980
www.foderezamboni1948.com/

USEFUL BIBLIOGRAPHY

Aldrich, W. 2006. *Metric Pattern Cutting for Menswear*. Fourth Edition. Blackwell Publishing. Oxford, United Kingdom.

Bridgland, A. S. 2010a. *The Modern Tailor, Outfitter and Clothier – Volume I*. Obscure Press. Lavergne, Tennessee.

Bridgland, A. S. 2010b. *The Modern Tailor, Outfitter and Clothier – Volume II*. Obscure Press. Lavergne, Tennessee.

Bridgland, A. S. 2010c. *The Modern Tailor, Outfitter and Clothier – Volume III*. Obscure Press. Lavergne, Tennessee.

Cabrera, R. 1984. *Classic Tailoring Techniques: A Construction Guide for Women's Wear*. Fairchild Books. New York.

Di Lorenzo, M. F. 2010. *Tailoring Techniques for Fashion*. Fairchild Books. New York.

Doyle, R. 2005. *The Art of the Tailor: With a Needle, a Thimble and 10,000 Stitches*. Sartorial Press. Stratford, Canada.

Editors of Creative Publishing. 2011. *Tailoring: The Classic Guide to Sewing the Perfect Jacket*. Creative Publishing International. Minneapolis, Minnesota.

Editors of Time-Life Books. 1974. *The Art of Sewing: Basic Tailoring*. Time-Life Books. New York.

Hostek, S. 1970. *Men's Custom Tailored Coats*. Tailor-Craft. Seattle, Washington.

Ledbetter, N. M. and Thiel Lansing, L. 1981. *Tailoring: Traditional and contemporary techniques*. Reston Publishing. Reston, Virginia.

Maclochlainn, J. 2011. *The Victorian Tailor: An Introduction to Period Tailoring*. St. Martin's Griffin. New York.

Mauck, F. F. 1947. *Modern Tailoring for Women*. MacMillan. New York.

Powell, P. 2011. *Tailored Fashion Design*. Fairchild Books. New York.

Reader's Digest. 2011. *New Complete Guide to Sewing: Updated Edition*. Reader's Digest. New York.

Schaeffer, C. B. 2013. *Couture Sewing: Tailoring Techniques*. Taunton Press. Newtown, Connecticut.

von Nordheim, T. 2012. *Vintage Couture Tailoring*. Crowood Press. Ramsbury, United Kingdom.

ONLINE RESOURCES

The Cutter and Tailor
www.cutterandtailor.com/forum/

Made by Hand – the Great Sartorial Debate
tuttofattoamano.blogspot.com

Parisian Gentleman
http://parisiangentleman.co.uk/

GLOSSARY

Chest

Measurement taken horizontally around the torso, just below the armpit. When measuring the chest, be sure to position the tape measure on the apex of the pectoral musculature at the front, and on the apex of the shoulder blades at the back.

Chest line

A reference guideline on all pattern pieces placed horizontally at chest level. This is used during fittings to ensure the balance of the garment is correct.

Crotch

The curved seam line from center front waistband to center back waistband, between the legs.

Ease

Correct fitting of garments requires specific amounts of volume, beyond the exact body measurements of the customer, so that apparel items are comfortable to wear. This is called "wearing ease," and is somewhat a matter of preference. Finely tailored apparel will traditionally include less wearing ease when compared to ready-to-wear clothing and casualwear. When used as a verb, "easing" refers to the act of creating additional volume in certain areas of the garment by selectively shrinking the fabric. This can be achieved in certain seams, such as the jacket armhole and the pants inseam. The roll line of the lapel is also eased in, using a twill tape, so as to create additional volume and avoid gaping at the chest.

Facing

A facing is a section of fabric cut specifically to finish an edge or an opening in the garment. Facings are present in several places in a tailored suit, including pockets, vest and jacket front and pants waistband. When the term "facing" is used by itself, it most commonly refers to the jacket front facing, which is visible on the lapel.

Fitting line

The fitting line is the line inside the cut edge of the garment piece, which will become the stitchline.

Flap

A lined section of fabric, roughly rectangular in shape, inserted in certain styles of pocket constructions. In addition to its aesthetic value, the flap serves the purpose of preventing dirt, dust and other unwanted things to inadvertently fall inside the pocket.

Gorge

The gorge line is the line (curved or angled) at which the front part of the collar meets the lapel. This line extends from the side neck point to the tip of the lapel. The position of the gorge line is somewhat a matter of style, with higher gorge placements usually seen in British and Italian tailoring, while a lower, more slanted gorge is associated with the boxier American silhouette.

Interfacing

Generic term used to identify any of the multitude of fabrics used to provide structure and support to garments. Interfacings can be floating (or sewn in) or fusible. Hymo, chest canvas, French linen canvas, horsehair, flannel and pocketing are all used as interfacings in the construction of tailored jackets. Fusible interfacings include woven, non-woven, weft and knits.

Lapel

On the forepart of the jacket, the lapel is the area that is folded back onto the chest. Lapel shape is entirely a matter of design preference.

Melton

Melton is a dense, smooth, boiled wool cloth, commonly used for overcoats and hunting outerwear. In tailored jacket construction, melton is used to construct the undercollar. The finishing of this particular cloth makes it highly resistant to fraying, allowing it to be used without seam allowances, which in turn avoids unnecessary bulk in the collar area.

Pant inseam

The vertical seam line on the inner part of the pant leg, from crotch to ankle.

Pant outseam

The vertical seam line on the outer side of the pant leg, from waistband to ankle. Trouser pockets are commonly inserted at the upper part of pant outseams.

Pant/Trouser waist

Measurement taken around the lower abdomen, at the exact level at which the customer wears his trousers.

Piping

A thin strip of fabric, folded and sewn to finish the open edges of certain styles of pockets. In the United Kingdom, these are often referred to as jets (i.e. double-jetted pocket).

Pitch

The word "pitch" refers to the vertical alignment of the garment, or of a part of the garment. The overall balance or pitch of the jacket is a great concern during early fittings. A very precisely adjusted sleeve pitch is a clear indicator of a finely tailored garment. The "front pitch" and "back pitch" are specific points (notches) marked on the armhole and the sleeve. These are used to position the sleeve so as to achieve the exact pitch required by the client.

Rise

The vertical height of the crotch, from the waistband to the top of the inseam. This is not the actual curved edge of the trouser front. Often calculated as the lengthwise difference between outseam and inseam.

Scye

Tailors and cutters refer to certain circular or elliptical seams by using the term "scye." Most commonly the term is used to identify the armhole, onto which the sleeve is sewn. "Scye depth" is the vertical distance from top to bottom of the armhole, measured from the completed armhole.

Seat

Horizontal measurement taken at the widest part of the buttocks. Often referred to as "hip."

Waist/natural waist

The narrowest part of the torso, at the same level as the belly button.

Waistline

A reference guideline on all pattern pieces placed horizontally at waist level. This is used during fittings to ensure the balance of the garment is correct.

Welt

The term "welt" refers to a strip of fabric (usually wider than ½" or 1.2 cm) used to finish garment and pocket openings. The breast welt is a rhomboid-shaped piece of fabric which traditionally makes the visible component of the pocket on the left chest of jackets.

IMAGE CREDITS

INDEX